SLAVES AND HOUSEHOLDS
IN THE NEAR EAST

SLAVES AND HOUSEHOLDS
IN THE NEAR EAST

edited by

LAURA CULBERTSON

with contributions by

Indrani Chatterjee, Laura Culbertson, Matthew S. Gordon, Kristin Kleber,
F. Rachel Magdalene, Hans Neumann, Andrea Seri, Jonathan S. Tenney,
Ehud R. Toledano, and Cornelia Wunsch

Papers from the Oriental Institute Seminar

Slaves and Households in the Near East

Held at the Oriental Institute of the University of Chicago
5–6 March 2010

THE ORIENTAL INSTITUTE OF THE UNIVERSITY OF CHICAGO
ORIENTAL INSTITUTE SEMINARS • NUMBER 7
CHICAGO • ILLINOIS

Library of Congress Control Number: 2011924051
ISBN-13: 978-1-885923-83-7
ISBN-10: 1-885923-83-X
ISSN: 1559-2944

The Oriental Institute, Chicago

THE UNIVERSITY OF CHICAGO

ORIENTAL INSTITUTE SEMINARS • NUMBER 7

Series Editors

Leslie Schramer

and

Thomas G. Urban

with the assistance of

Rebecca Cain and Natalie Whiting

Publication of this volume was made possible through generous funding
from the Arthur and Lee Herbst Research and Education Fund

Cover Illustration: Fragment of the so-called Nasiriya Stela showing bound captives.
Alabaster. Mesopotamia, Akkadian, ca. 2220–2159 BC.
Courtesy of the Iraq National Museum, Baghdad, IM 59205

Printed by Edwards Brothers, Ann Arbor, Michigan

TABLE OF CONTENTS

PREFACE v

INTRODUCTION

   1. Slaves and Households in the Near East 1
       Laura Culbertson, University of Chicago

SECTION ONE: EARLY MESOPOTAMIA

   2. Slavery in Private Households toward the End of the Third Millennium B.C. 21
       Hans Neumann, Westfälische Wilhelms-Universität, Münster

   3. A Life-Course Approach to Household Slaves in the Late Third Millennium B.C. . . . 33
       Laura Culbertson, University of Chicago

   4. Domestic Female Slaves during the Old Babylonian Period 49
       Andrea Seri, University of Chicago

SECTION TWO: THE ISLAMIC NEAR EAST

   5. Preliminary Remarks on Slaves and Slave Labor in the Third/Ninth Century
       ʿAbbāsid Empire 71
       Matthew S. Gordon, Miami University

   6. An Empire of Many Households: The Case of Ottoman Enslavement 85
       Ehud R. Toledano, Tel Aviv University

SECTION THREE: SECOND AND FIRST MILLENNIUM EMPIRES

   7. Neither Slave nor Truly Free: The Status of the Dependents of Babylonian
       Temple Households 101
       Kristin Kleber, Freie Universität Berlin

   8. Slavery between Judah and Babylon: The Exilic Experience 113
       F. Rachel Magdalene, Universität Leipzig; and *Cornelia Wunsch,*
       University of London

   9. Household Structure and Population Dynamics in the Middle Babylonian
       Provincial "Slave" Population 135
       Jonathan S. Tenney, Loyola University New Orleans and University of
       Copenhagen

SECTION FOUR: RESPONSE

  10. Slaves and Households in the Near East: A Response 149
       Indrani Chatterjee, Rutgers University

PREFACE

This volume contains papers presented at the sixth annual Oriental Institute Seminar, entitled Slaves and Households in the Near East, on March 5–6, 2010. Twelve scholars assembled to present contributions to the topic of slavery, and built a discussion of the topic that has culminated in the chapters of this volume. The seminar would not have been possible without the enthusiasm and expertise of Mariana Perlinac, Assistant to the Director, and Meghan Winston, Special Events Coordinator. I thank Fred Donner, Matthew Stolper, and Chris Woods for serving as chairs at the seminar and engaging the topics. The volume also reflects the enthusiasm, patience, and hard work of many people, especially of series editors Tom Urban and Leslie Schramer of the Oriental Institute Publications Office, as well as Rebecca Cain and Natalie Whiting. I am also indebted to the inspired progenitor of the Seminar Series and Director of the Oriental Institute, Gil Stein, for creating this series and giving me this remarkable chance to learn more about a fascinating topic. Above all, I would like to thank the participants of the seminar and contributors to this volume for sharing their expertise and submitting interesting ideas. Kathryn Babayan, Robert Englund, and Martha Roth have published elsewhere, but their insights from the seminar can be seen throughout the volume.

Laura Culbertson

Seminar participants, from left to right: Back row: Christopher Woods, Ehud R. Toledano, Hans Neumann, Matthew S. Gordon; middle row: Jonathan S. Tenney, Robert Englund, Martha Roth, Kristin Kleber, Laura Culbertson; Front row: Fred Donner, Andrea Seri, Indrani Chatterjee, Kathryn Babayan, and F. Rachel Magdalene. Photo by Anna Ressman

1

SLAVES AND HOUSEHOLDS
IN THE NEAR EAST

LAURA CULBERTSON

INTRODUCTION

Slavery, in innumerable permutations, is recognizable to historians of any period of human history. Yet scarcely any other social group is less accessible in historical sources than the enslaved. The biases of written records account for many impediments to developing an understanding of slavery, along with significant differences in sociocultural, legal, and economic systems across time and place. The problems of understanding slavery as a historical phenomenon also result from the various theoretical traditions, scholarly approaches, and discursive strategies employed in different fields and subfields. Consequently, a common framework for the study of slavery is elusive even if often expected. The study of Near Eastern slaveries, the focus of this volume, has reached an optimal point for exploring new ideas and source approaches after the preceding decades witnessed production of a variety of comparative studies, revisions to old paradigms, introduction of valuable case studies, and critical examinations of slavery in various historical contexts. The increasing recognition of slavery's negligible role in labor spheres of Near Eastern societies also prompts new questions about the place, purpose, and experience of slavery in specific Near Eastern contexts.

The present volume is a compilation of proceedings from a two-day seminar held at the Oriental Institute on March 5–6, 2010. The purpose of this collaboration of scholars was to greet recent imperatives to develop new approaches and to reassess the very presence of enslaved people in old and new source materials. Respondents to the seminar invitation included an unusual assortment of specialists, with combined expertise spanning four millennia of Near Eastern history. The seminar provided a venue for comparison of sources, methodologies, and problems associated with the study of non-Western and pre- or early-modern slavery. The Oriental Institute itself was an interesting location for such an occasion, having already produced a venerable legacy of scholarship on Near Eastern slavery, including the ever-provocative works of the Assyriologist I. J. Gelb.

APPROACHING SLAVERY THROUGH HOUSEHOLDS

At the outset of the seminar, the participants agreed that no essential form of "Near Eastern" or "Oriental" slavery exists, nor any such universal definition capable of unifying the disparate and gradational realities of enslaved people in Near Eastern societies. Nevertheless, a common analytical fulcrum was incorporated into discussions to promote focused discussions and delimit an immense and expansive topic. This focal point was the household or enslavement-household nexus (Toledano, this volume). Scholars of medieval and early modern Near Eastern societies have already explored household approaches, building new paradigms and perspectives of use to other fields (Babaie et al. 2004; Gordon, 1999, 2000; see

1

Toledano, this volume for full citations; see also Gross 2001). The notion of household in the pre-modern world — whether understood as an idea, a physical space, an economic unit, a legal institution, or social or biological group — is of course an enormous subject in its own right that has earned considerable treatment elsewhere. For the purposes of the Oriental Institute seminar, the concept of household allowed the participants to maintain a more focused discourse than would otherwise have been possible, centering discussions on the dynamics of enslaved people in their immediate contexts. Households, as domestic units, temple and state institutions, or legal and symbolic entities, are the sites through which a historian can most meaningfully understand the experiences, roles, labors, and realities of the enslaved. The household encompasses the heterogeneous community in which slavery and non-slavery coexisted. The papers presented herein employed this notion directly or indirectly to varying degrees, depending on the conditions of data, need for groundwork, or specific problems of the context under investigation.

Other benefits resulted from using the household as a prism through which to view the dynamics associated with slavery. First, the approach released the participants of the obligation to create overarching, general definitions of slavery when much ground work remains to be done. Regardless of how one defines it, the concept of slavery is in some way tied to asymmetrical relationships, whether the asymmetry is economic, political, or symbolic. A study that isolates slaves for treatment, positing a uniform definition for "slave" while simultaneously neglecting the relationships around them, risks assuming that slavery is an inherent condition that takes a similar shape across time and place without regard for context. Slavery is not in fact definable without reference to relationships within the broader social, economic, and legal concepts that surround it. Using a household approach, scholars may implicate many of the constituents whose relationships make up the phenomenon of slavery. By considering relationships of slaves in households, the participants created opportunities to view the dynamics of the relationships established or transformed by the concept of slavery.

The household emphasis also encouraged the contributors to complicate the law- and economy-centered approaches to slavery that have dominated study in Near Eastern contexts, inviting new social and cultural dimensions to the topic. Approaches that privilege the legal standing and economic functions of enslaved persons often isolate narrow aspects of the experience of slavery or view the enslaved as simple functions of larger, reified systems. The diversity of experiences and realities of enslaved people across time and place, as well as the evidence that enslaved persons could and did exercise certain behaviors that would today be described as "freedoms," resist inflexible legal or economic definitions. Economic treatises and legal codes presented slaves as chattel, while documents pertaining to daily life contradict this image and offer a more complex picture of slavery in Near Eastern societies. Already in 1946, Mendelsohn (1949: 88) claimed that the presentation of slaves as mere chattel was a fiction. Starr (1958: 18) later noted that scholars often assume that there was a "tremendous cultural cleft" between slaves and non-slave populations, another generalization that is increasingly compromised by ever-improving access to non-royal data. Reading legal and economic documents through legal and economic paradigms only provides one side of the story.

Finally, the approaches try to relate to the nature of documentation from the respective societies under investigation. Few of the historical settings examined in this volume yielded self-consciously penetrating sources about slavery. The sources, largely legal, economic, and administrative records, must be combed for information about enslaved people, who are usually mentioned in the context of family, household, or institutional matters. Indeed, slavery cannot be examined in isolation from the contemporary institutions and events (Engerman

2000: 480). Taking a household approach means that the scholar is not extracting tidbits about slaves without regard to their setting or the context in which they are implicated. Rather, the scholars can critically assess slavery on the terms of the sources.

Concerning the sources from the ancient Near East, it must be emphasized that the documentation at present is not capable of supporting some of the theoretical studies undertaken in other fields. The classical, European, and New World slave traditions benefit from a comparatively wider variety of documentation, mediating access to slavery through languages more continuously engaged or long deciphered and accessible to scholars than those of the Near East. By comparison, the documents from the earliest Near Eastern societies pertaining to slavery are short and unevenly recovered to a severe degree, even if rigorous efforts to catalog and publish are mitigating these problems daily. Further, the languages used and cultural traditions reflected in these documents are vaguely understood in key areas; specialists continue to debate terminology of slavery on both paleographic and linguistic grounds (see Englund 2009). This comparison is not admitted to the discussion to imply that classical or New World sources are without complications,[1] but merely to alert the non-specialist to the unique difficulties of the present content. As Seri suggests (this volume), the state of the data often disqualifies some early Mesopotamian societies from systematic inclusion in comparative studies of current theoretical investigations such as revolt, rebellion, or philosophical queries about the nature of agency and oppression.

SCOPE, SOURCES, AND TRADITIONS

The concentration on slavery in historical societies across different periods of Near Eastern history means that both the seminar and resulting volume are comparative longitudinally rather than cross-culturally in the traditional sense. The longitudinal organization of topics was intended to sever cultural and temporal boundaries of scholarly inquiry.[2] This convening of scholars of ancient, medieval, and early modern Near Eastern periods resulted in an exchange of theoretical and source problems and an invigoration of new questions. The exchange also introduced scholars of the ancient Near East to some of the innovations presently emerging from medieval and early modern scholarship, allowing contemplation of approaches beyond the traditional reliance on classical works.

Slavery in the ancient Near East was long regarded as an economic and legal topic, an inevitable reduction resulting in part from the nature of the sources. In Mesopotamian studies, the Assyriologists I. J. Gelb and Igor Diakonoff conducted the foundational systematic studies of slavery in ancient Mesopotamia, infusing their work with theoretical questions and paradigms adopted from economic philosophies. These and subsequent studies on the economic function of slaves examined issues of value, sale, labor, and the degree to which slaves reinforce state structures. Starting in the 1950s, some anthropologists denounced the economy-centered approaches as materialist, functionalist, or positivist, arguing that the extraction of slaves from social hierarchies impedes understanding of slavery (e.g., Siegel 1945, 1947; see

---

[1] See Walter Johnson's (2001: 11–13) consideration of sources in *Soul by Soul*, a discussion of slavery in nineteenth-century New Orleans that relies on letters and court records.

[2] Cross-cultural studies of slavery in different periods of Near Eastern history have been undertaken elsewhere (e.g., Marmon 1999; Miura and Philips 2000), along with definition-based studies of specific forms of slavery across time (e.g., Amitai 2006).

also Patterson 1977; Kopytoff 1982; and Dandamaev 1984). Meanwhile, prolific legal studies on Mesopotamian and biblical records have produced a useful corpus on slavery in legal
constructions and the terminology of function, status, sale, and theoretical rights of slaves
in Mesopotamia and Levantine legal-literary traditions (e.g., Mendelsohn 1949; Chirichigno
1993; Westbrook 1995a, 1998). These studies also entail limitations for the study of slavery,
however, because legal constructions do not always or usually overlap with discursive and
practical realms of daily life.

During a century of scholarship on the medieval Islamicate empires, legal studies generally entertained the topic of slavery, with emphasis on juridical schools that produced the
majority of documents useful for discussions of slavery. It was long noted, however, that
slavery in Islamicate societies was as much a cultural phenomenon (see Patterson 1977:
421). Recently, studies in medieval and early modern slavery in the Near East have fruitfully
undertaken comparative studies and introduced new approaches to the topic, including considerations of household dynamics at royal, military, or elite levels (e.g., Babaei et al. 2004;
Gordon 1999, 2000; Marmon 1999; Toledano 2007). The approaches include sociocultural
and religious investigations, as well as in-depth considerations of race and ethnicity in connection to slavery (e.g., Lewis 1990).

The longitudinal collaboration not only enabled conversation about the intellectual legacies undergirding our current work, but also provided opportunity for critical examination of
sources and how we should approach them when investigating slavery. The most frustrating
aspect of any attempt to study slavery in any remote context involves the nature of the sources,
in which the voices of slaves may be the least accessible and most manipulated. In the pre-
modern world, few people, let alone slaves, possessed the means or entitlement to produce
written documents. Scholars of the ancient Near East rely upon administrative, economic,
and legal documents, which use administrative and legal fictions and abstracted, formulaic
language to condense time and events into abbreviated records. Interpretation of such documents beyond their basic nuts and bolts is often difficult. In general, scholars of medieval
Near Eastern societies contend with different source limitations, lacking legal, economic,
and administrative records indicating much about the daily mechanics of slave trade. Thus,
there are different challenges in the retrieval of voices and data about enslaved people that
collaboration could only assist.

In addition, scholars of all fields contend with the tensions between documents of daily
life and the religious, political, or literary treatises that hold authoritative positions in their
respective communities. Even if monuments such as the Law Codes of Mesopotamia, for
example, prescribe courses of action for mundane affairs, scholars must determine whether
such treatises indeed played a decisive role in daily life practices by evaluating whether the
documents of daily life resist or conform to such prescriptions. A similar tension between
textual dogma and evidence of daily practice can be noted in studies of slavery in Islamicate
contexts, and, as we now see, between records of Judean slave-holding practices and the slaves
laws enumerated in the Hebrew Bible as described by Magdalene and Wunsch in this volume.

Even though this project involved a broad temporal scope, most of the contributors adopted a microhistorical or particularist approach. These studies treat temporally and geographically limited data sets and social contexts, situating the topic in historical and social
contingencies. Arguments supporting such approaches already emerged in a number of fields
(see Toledano 2002) because the microhistorical perspective avoids universalizing slave experiences or neglecting key aspects of a particular context. The combination of a longitudinal
collaboration and microhistorical research method allowed the contributors to consider the

survival rate and longevity of slave systems and the practices related to slavery. Consensus emerged that most of the situations under examination were short-lived, contingent upon specific historical, social, and economic conditions, and constantly in fluctuation.

Another purpose of the longitudinal assemblage of topics was to sever some of the reliance of slavery studies on classical and New World paradigms, the salient works of which are too numerous to cite in this introduction. Although studies from classical antiquity and New World history, archaeology, and anthropology continue to serve as invaluable models for inquiry and rich resources for scholars of less crystallized areas of scholarship to consult, the gross exporting of slavery paradigms across time and place is dangerous and unwarranted.

THE SEMINAR

To engage the above-outlined matters, the seminar included twelve scholars specializing in different periods of Near Eastern history. In the opening session of the seminar, Robert Englund, Hans Neumann, Laura Culbertson, and Andrea Seri focused on slavery in the earliest states of ancient Mesopotamia. Englund overviewed the earliest Near Eastern notational systems for slaves, which pertained to "corporate" or institutional slaves, that is, groups of enslaved humans dependent on large household units, who had no rights of possession, performed labor, and were listed in economic rosters alongside animals and inanimate objects. The limitations of these lists are substantial, inasmuch as they present slaves as human herds that would be indistinguishable from animals were it not for the inclusion of personal names. Based on this, the designation "chattel" seems applicable to these corporate slaves, but Englund noted the difficulties of accessing more about them, including linguistic or ethnographic background of such persons (Englund 2009).

Shifting to another dimension of slavery in early states, Neumann, Culbertson, and Seri examined slavery in the context of private households in Mesopotamia at the end of the third and first half of the second millennium B.C. These papers relied heavily on legal documents pertaining to the affairs of private households instead of the contemporary Law Codes of early Mesopotamian kings (e.g., those of Ur-Namma, Lipit-Ishtar, and Hammurapi), and thus shifted discussion from the ideals and abstractions of slavery in Mesopotamia to the lived reality of slaves in household contexts. Noting that household composition was not standardized (see Roth's 1987 investigation), these studies also attempt to conduct groundwork for examining how household characteristics affect household slaves and vice versa.

In the second session, Matthew Gordon, Kathryn Babayan, and Ehud Toledano discussed slaves and households in the Abbasid, Safavid, and Ottoman contexts respectively. Engaging issues of mobility and the various social courses traveled by Abbasid-era slaves, Gordon innovatively compared two separate groups of slaves associated with the imperial household: singers and soldiers. Gordon examined the integration of these two groups into the upper echelons of the imperial networks, as either military commanders, or as the intimates of rulers (and potentially mothers of heirs), and their ability to consolidate these positions into their own wealthy, if fragile, households. Babayan's seminar paper provided an examination of documents called *majmu'a*s from Safavid-era Isfahan in Iran. *Majmu'a*s are anthologies or collections of written entries, owned by elites, which can be thought of as archives of daily life. These documents provide information about slavery that tells of practices beyond the courtly and legal spheres, introducing other discursive realms. For example, among the entries included in these anthologies are formulas of manumission, and Babayan discussed how these declarations of freedom implicate the body parts of the slaves in the manumission process, while invoking an interesting mixture of sexuality and piety. Toledano's contribution illuminated relationships of slaves and household dynamics in the seventeenth- and eighteenth-century Ottoman empire, and contextualized shifts in the dynamics within larger political developments. Toledano discussed the complicated issues of attachment, the bond between slave and household, within the context of an empire of many households. Enslavement was discussed as an alternative to clientage and a means by which people could incorporate themselves into politically, socially, and economically fluid households.

A third session included Jonathan Tenney's presentation on data from the late second millennium B.C., and F. Rachel Magdalene and Kristin Kleber's discussions of the imperial context of the first millennium B.C. Tenney's paper focused on fragile conjugal families who worked as institutional slaves, which he examined through historical demography. Using administrative documents from fourteenth-century B.C. Nippur, Tenney reconstructed family composition and noted similarities to laboring slave families in cross-cultural examples. Kleber discussed the controversial terminology associated with temple personnel from Neo-Babylonian times called *širku*s and engaged debates about whether or not people who bore the designation *širku* should be considered slaves. She argued that the role and position of these individuals is best understood by reconstructing the social dynamics among *širku*s and other types of people with similar designations. Tenney and Kleber's approaches differ in one key respect. The population under investigation in Tenney's data is never anywhere designated with terminology of slavery in the ancient sources, yet he takes them to certainly be slaves given the quality of their lives, cross-cultural evidence, and the fact that one would be hard-pressed to insist that this population was in fact "free." Kleber, on the other hand, identifies a native term, which is akin to but not synonymous with "slave" based on the role and social place of *širku*s in the temple household. The contrast is of significance to the definitional issues discussed below. Magdalene's paper (here co-authored with Cornelia Wunsch) introduced hitherto unknown Neo-Babylonian legal documents from which four generations of Judeans in exile can be reconstructed. Living in southern Babylonia, these Judeans participated in Babylonian society even to the extent of conducting local business and owning slaves. A comparison of their slave-holding practices with slave laws of the Hebrew Bible showed that the Judeans did not adhere to the biblical prescriptions for slave dealings, conforming rather to known local Babylonian customs.

To draw out salient themes and questions, Martha Roth and Indrani Chatterjee, a Mesopotamianist and South Asianist respectively, provided responses to these papers and critically articulated some of the problems and possible future directions of the study of slavery.

Several intriguing problems emerged from this collaboration that warrant summarization. First, the author acknowledges that the sampling of case materials from the ancient Near East slanted heavily toward Mesopotamia and the cuneiform world, even though evidence for slavery is indeed far more widespread. Ancient Egypt, for example, certainly presents an interesting context for the study of slavery, but such has been much neglected and complicated by the lack of sources comparable to those of cuneiform cultures, as well as by the lack of a recognizable institution that may be definitively called slavery — as opposed to forms of servitude, clientage, or conscription. The cuneiform record, even in its vastness and increasing accessibility, bears some limitations of its own, including the above-mentioned constraints of scope and administrative language.

While gender has become a routine consideration in slave studies and factors into the chapters presented in this volume, race and ethnicity remain patently difficult elements to consider. The matter is confounded by the fact that slaves originated in both native and foreign populations in the Near Eastern societies under discussion, and that, in ancient societies especially, the construct of race usually cannot be demonstrably correlated to social classes and labor divisions, if it is a reality of social discourse at all (Bahrani 2006). Issues of foreignness, city affiliation, and household affiliation are more prevalent and identifiable indicators of social standing, but even these markers can be transformed. Herein Magdalene and Wunsch highlight one aspect of this problem in their discussion of slaves who bore confusingly composite personal names, in one case including elements of the Akkadian, West Semitic, and Egyptian languages. Of course, determining the nuances of slave onomastics can be tricky, especially because patterns of slave names and slave naming may not be sustained over generations, as is also noticed among Turkish military slaves in the Abbasid era.

The exclusion of archaeology or other forms of evidence poses another limitation to this study. Even though archaeology gives insight and representation to the parts of society that are not prominent in the written record, this field has generally contributed little to studies of slavery in the Near East at present. This is no doubt because, as the following chapters demonstrate, enslaved people were integrated into households and not necessarily distinguishable from non-slave household members with whom they interacted on a daily basis. The fogginess imposed on the boundary between slave and non-slave household members precludes easy identification of "slave spaces" or "slave materials" such as New World plantation excavations may allow. As a result, our reliance on written documentation remains strong.[3]

Another problem concerns our approaches. In fact, this collaboration has not resulted in the production of a common methodology for studying slavery in Near Eastern societies. Aside from the choice of a common focal point, the household, participants otherwise selected methodologies best suited to their data and historical context. The approaches thus found at the seminar and in this volume are many and varied, including: socioeconomic (Neumann), tracing life-courses of slaves (Culbertson, Gordon), tracing gender (Babayan, Seri), historical demography (Tenney), comparison of contemporary forms of slavery (Gordon, Kleber), comparison of contemporary legal sources on slavery (Magdalene and Wunsch), sociopolitical (Toledano), and legal (Culbertson, Kleber). The following is an overview of some key themes to emerge at the Oriental Institute seminar that also appear throughout this volume.

DEFINING SLAVERY

The papers in this volume confirm the long-standing supposition that slavery in the Near East was never a substantial factor in production spheres of the economy, nor the primary means of labor organization. If slavery in most Near Eastern societies was not predicated on labor, then what is it? It is impossible to cite every occasion at which a scholar lamented the troubles associated with defining slavery. As has already been noted, "it is difficult to create a definition of slavery comprehensive enough to cover all social institutions generally classified as slavery yet sufficiently clear to distinguish it from other forms of dependence" (Karras 1988: 5). Engerman (2000: 480) added that "any specific definition of slavery has legal, cultural, political, and economic aspects, and it is often hard to know exactly where to draw the line among labor institutions as well as between legal slavery and the use of slavery as a metaphor for any form of human poverty and domination." Neither definitions nor legal

---

[3] For illuminating examples of the issues associated with slavery and archaeology, see the contribution of Andrews and Fenton (2007) in Timothy Insoll's *The Archaeology of Identity,* and Thompson 2002.

and economic paradigms are portable. Terminologies from legal sources often provide the basis for defining the parameters of slavery and articulate the differences between people bearing a designation we translate as "slave" and people who do not bear this designation. The discordance between legal source and reality has been noted for a variety of ancient contexts, however, including classical Athens. Vlassopoulos (2009), for example, noted a "bifurcation between law and reality" concerning slavery in this context. In Near Eastern contexts, historians and linguists debate about the differences between servitude, bondage, slavery, and other expressions of oppression, subjugation, or unfreedom, even if these terms do not have exact correspondences in in native terminologies. Many unfree conditions are evident in the historical records that do not bear the designation "slavery," yet cannot sufficiently be defined by another term to the mind of the scholar (see Tenney, this volume). This definitional problem persists in modern discourses about slavery, some scholars having postulated a category of "practices like slavery" to cover situations in which the term "slave" is not applied by the practitioners but the behavior is difficult to characterize by another word (e.g., van de Glind and Kooijmans 2008). The issue of semantics is not purely semantic; as Chatterjee argues at the conclusion of this volume, terms come with histories that must be critically understood before erroneous assumptions creep into discussions without justification.

Studies of slavery in the ancient world are indebted to the works of the classical historian Moses I. Finley (especially 1964, 1968, and 1973). Finley articulated the spectra of social statuses and treated slavery as inextricable from historical and sociopolitical developments. Regarding slavery as a social function, Finley moved the understanding of slavery beyond description and economic function and in the direction of practice and status dynamics. The place of slavery in social and political organizations is of interest to the contributors of this volume, who also aim to view slavery as a variegated phenomenon to be understood in the context of non-slavery and specific historical contexts. Many of Finley's discussions of slavery consist of distilled generalizations based on seemingly boundless knowledge of ancient sources and comparative studies in ancient societies, and thus his arguments and "schematic models" (1964) are both illuminating and limited in application to specific contexts.

The application of Finley's holistic paradigms to Near Eastern contexts is especially problematic. Even if many of Finley's insights inform Near Eastern studies, he regarded the ancient Near East as a world fundamentally different from the Greco-Roman one, stating that analytical integration of the two worlds is impossible "without resorting to disconnected sections, employing different concepts and models" (1973: 28). Moreover, Finley characterized Near Eastern economies as institutionally embedded systems, dominated by temples and palaces that "monopolized anything than can be called 'industrial production' ... and organized the economic, military, political, and religious life of the society through a single complicated, bureaucratic, record-keeping operation" (ibid.). This despotic, embedded-economy model has run its own course within Mesopotamian studies, with dwindling proponents over the decades as evidence for private economic activity received increasing treatment (van Driel 2000), or as scholars reinvestigated the theoretical validity of the institution-versus-private economy dichotomy (Steinkeller 2004).[4] Thus, even if aspects of Finley's approach to slavery inform the present undertaking, his generalizing definitions of slavery must be applied with extreme caution.[5]

---

[4] A full discussion of ancient economies and the intellectual legacies or philosophical underpinnings of twentieth-century scholarship on this topic is reserved for the sake of space. See Stol 2004: 904ff. for an

overview of the debates about the structure of ancient Mesopotamian economies.

[5] For a discussion of how archaeology has exploded many of Finley's paradigms, see Green 2000.

Orlando Patterson's (1982: 5, 13) concept of "social death" is perhaps the most famous and widely engaged definition of slavery to emerge from recent decades. According to Patterson, slavery is "the permanent, violent domination of natally alienated and generally dishonored persons" who have been stripped of heritage and past. Even though this summary is often regarded as a description of the lived experience of slavery, it is more accurately characterized as a conceptualization or ideology of slavery (Brown 2009: 1248). Patterson extracted this conceptualization from comparative studies of New World slavery, but it has proven helpful for scholars of any historical context because it releases the topic from the constraints of legal language, thus promising transportability among contexts including to those instances for which no clear lexicon of slavery is available. The social death ideology also unhinges the definition of slavery from labor and economic matters, an especially important benefit for the Near East where the evidence will not allow reduction of slavery to the exploitation of human subsistence labor. Most importantly, perhaps, Patterson specifies that slavery is "not a static entity but ... a complex interactional process, one laden with tension and contradiction in the dynamics of each of its constituent elements" (1982: 13).

The concept of social death is not without criticism, however, much of which rejects the totalizing, abstract, or generalizing nature of the concept or notes the unsustainability of this definition when affixed to specific historical or political contexts, including those of the New World. As the ensuing chapters in this volume demonstrate, enslaved people in Near Eastern contexts could engage in social maneuvering and hierarchical ascension even within the confines of slavery and cannot be considered socially dead or dispossessed. Moreover, slave status could be terminated or transformed through a variety of mechanisms (e.g., payments, court proceeding, religious conversion), meaning that the formerly enslaved could return to their homes and families, not permanently displaced from their original social networks or birth entitlements as a result of becoming a slave.

Despite the snares of seeking definitions, the staking of some provisional boundaries and descriptive features is necessary for a productive discussion. For this reason, some common strands are here enumerated to establish a basis for discussion. These items do not culminate in a "definition of Near Eastern slavery," but serve as a connected series of correlative themes and problems that manifest differently according to case study.

1. The terms translated as "slave" generically refer to the lesser constituent in an asymmetrical relationship, where lesser may be hyphenated with some kind of social, symbolic, or even cosmic ranking. Of course, not all asymmetrical relationships are slavery, but slavery is always expressed in terms of hierarchy, obligation, and often domination. This relationship archetype is contemporaneously evoked in different discursive and textual spheres within any society, as suggested by the preceding comments about monolithic or dogmatic texts versus records of daily life. Each of these domains may describe slavery in different terms even if using the same native term. Ideological and religious conceptualizations of slavery often describe a hierarchical relationship. Kings are slaves of gods, and subjects are slaves of kings (Westbrook 1995b: 149). The Sumerian term arad is applied to enslaved men, but can also express the lesser ranking of any man relative to higher rank. Such is evident in personal names, such as that of the vizier Arad-Nanna, whose name is literally "slave of the god Nanna." In the Islamic world, naming conventions using the Arabic term *'abd* ("slave"), followed by one of the names of God, are ubiquitous, as in the oft-attested names Abdullah or Abdurrahman. But slavery is also a lived experience and legal status in most of the places under investigation, beyond a general description

of relative rungs of sociopolitical organization. In these cases, slavery, even if subsumed under a single term, is described as subordination, dependence, bondage, debt, clientage, or subservience. In short, slave relationships are invoked in both general ideological contexts and specific legally supported daily relationships. The latter situation is the subject of the subsequent points and contributions in the volume.

2. A polarity of slavery and freedom is untenable in the case studies, as many studies have already agreed (e.g., Adams 2010; Baker 2001). The concept of freedom — "which had no meaning and no existence for most of human history" (Finley 1964: 237) — is particularly anachronistic in light of the hierarchical conceptions mentioned in the previous point, which indicate that all people were enslaved to another rung. Moreover, regardless of whether legal terms label such statuses or whether the discursive systems contain designations, in practice there were numerous in-between places between slavery and non-slavery, most notably demonstrated in the contributions of Magdalene and Wunsch and Kleber in this volume. Finley (1964) already famously explored this in-between phenomenon in Athenian history, noting the spectrum and degrees of enslavement that may exist in one context.

3. Even if the terms we translate as "slave" vary widely according to context, in general the people bearing such a designation had diminished legal rights and entitlements in comparison to the non-slave persons with whom they interacted. This does not mean that enslaved people had no rights, because social, religious, ideological, or cultural practices could ensure the protection of slaves. Rather, the relative diminution of entitlements means that the slave had to socially operate within confines and parameters that would not be posed in non-slavery. Institutionalized social and legal systems such as courts reinforced the imbalance of rights and compelled enslaved people to fulfill their obligations during the period of enslavement. In many contexts, the diminished rights over slaves included bodily ownership of a slave, such as sexual rights or ability to brand or mark the slave. Regardless of how slavery was indicated or represented in legal formulations, slavery was a recognizable social identity in all the contexts under discussion. This is not necessarily due to race, as many slaves originated within the indigenous population, but could be the result of different kinds of physical marking.

4. Aside from specific historical phenomena (e.g., the military slavery documented in the ninth to nineteenth centuries; see Gordon and Toledano, this volume), slavery did not encompass broad self-sustaining classes and populations of people, even in many cases of institutional slavery. The experience of slavery varied according to individual or family, resulting in numerous attested paths into and out of slavery in any single time or place. The terms and conditions of enslavement could vary among individual slaves even within the same household, according to the specific circumstances and contingencies surrounding the enslavement of the individual. This accounts for the inability of any contributor to this volume to describe slavery in single comprehensive definition.

5. Slavery was not always a permanent condition, and the terms and conditions of enslavement were specific to the circumstances under which enslavement was established. Aside from birth, slavery often originated out of predicament, to adopt a term from Brown (2009: 1246). Financial crisis, criminal behavior (see Neumann, this volume), family disintegration, capture in wartime, or other crises often resulted in the creation of enslavement. Slavery could be as much a remedy to certain predicaments as a set-back, by

offering outsiders or disenfranchised persons a protected legal status and acknowledged social bond (see below). Voluntary slavery, an issue notoriously difficult for modern thinkers to comprehend (Engerman 2000: 482), is attested across Near Eastern history and beyond.

6. Related, enslaved persons were also not without power to participate in political dynamics at the immediate level of the household to which they were attached. Within the specific confines of enslavement, slaves could act to preserve or transform their quality of life. That is, many of the enslaved people discussed in this volume exercised a considerable degree of what we might call "freedoms" or even "creativity under constraint" (after Mahoney 2008). Slavery was thus not a unilaterally downward social death sentence, with many slaves rising along with their owners (see Kopytoff 1982), or forging new social networks (Gordon, this volume).

The following sections elaborate on some of the most important areas to emerge from the present collaboration, with attention to areas that warrant future exploration and comparison.

SLAVES IN HOUSEHOLDS

Viewing enslaved people in the context of households proved an interesting and fruitful approach. Abandoning the notion that slaves constituted uniform social groups allowed the contributors to note the vagaries of specific histories and circumstances. This allows us to view slaves across social dimensions, looking at slaves at both the top (e.g., Gordon) and bottom (e.g., Tenney) of society. As members of households, slaves were afforded certain statuses akin to, but certainly not equal to, free members of the household. The household affiliation itself could be equivalent to protection and secure legal status (Culbertson, Toledano), rather than a social death. There remains some debate about the nature of attachment between slave and household, which can be based on contract, coercion (Tenney), birth (Kleber), or some intricate combination thereof. In some contexts, slaves possessed the ability to forge bonds for themselves in order to achieve a favorable household affiliation (Toledano). Administrative records, laconic and one-sided, are perhaps insufficient resources for understanding the complex nature of slave-household bonds, and it must again be noted that the idea of slave agency is not without criticism of being anachronistic (Johnson 2003: 115).

Several case studies show that household affiliation was not always permanent and inflexible. Consideration of slaves in household context allows many of the authors to trace the movement of slaves into and throughout the society in question. Households, in fact, acted as portals through which foreigners (Magdalene and Wunsch, Toledano), social outsiders, and even criminals (Neumann) could be (re)integrated into society and set on new directions. Or, by way of gaining a household affiliation, disaffected or lowly persons could gain a legally protected status (Culbertson, Seri), skill set or specialization (Neumann), or entitlement to transfer into other social categories (Kleber). In some cases, slaves could use their household affiliations to pursue the creation of their own households (Culbertson, Gordon). Magdalene and Wunsch discuss a situation in which non-slave families of outsiders could also modify or adapt slave-owning practices to integrate into a new realm.

Slavery was also a component of the administrative or institutional aspect of a state. The relationship between slaves and states was once cast as one of oppression, labor exploitation, or management of foreign captives, but even as early as the 1950s at least a few Near Eastern scholars abandoned the notion that ancient states were built on the backs of slave labor and war prisoners (Starr 1958; Degler 1959). It is now recognized that institutional and imperial slaves had a variety of purposes beyond menial labor and the relationship between slaves and administrative or imperial households showed the same complexity as relationships within private households. Babaie and colleagues (2004), for example, already discussed how slaves became members of the royal household of Safavid Iran and were capable of gaining access to spaces and individuals forbidden even to free royal household members, thus creating new political dimensions in the royal center. In other cases, one enslaved person could bear many designations associated with enslavement, serving both a private household and, through bequeathal, donation, or pledge, an institution. Thus slaves could act as connections between state and private households that both slaves and masters could manipulate (Kleber, Seri). If households, both elite or institutional, were "building blocks" of society, to use Toledano's terminology, slavery cannot be mapped out without mapping the sociopolitical organizations and developments of households. Whether elite associations could mitigate the experience of slavery is not easily determined from our sources.

MOBILITY, ENTRY, AND EXIT

The mobility of slaves and the mutability of slave status emerged as another important theme; indeed the authors face difficulty concretizing the conditions associated with slave status, even while adhering to microhistorical perspectives. Several types of mobility were noted, including the above-mentioned integration of foreigners and social outsiders. Gordon (1999, 2000) has elsewhere shown that Turkish slave soldiers in ninth-century Samarra ascended in rank to create their own institutional power structures, and their own households, complicating networks of imperial elites. Informed by these findings, Seri, Culbertson, and Kleber have here attempted to show the movement of slaves through imperial and elite networks. Tenney's data, by contrast, show an example in which an institution adopted measures that prevented slave mobility, sealed slaves into closed communities, diminished the stability of slave families, and ultimately left death or escape as the only means by which one could exit his or her plight. Other attested strategies for altering status and bonds included use of a court system or the exploitation of social networks.

The manumission of slaves is an equally complex situation. The freeing of slaves in non-Western, pre-modern contexts is mischaracterized if described as the liberating deliverance of a slave into a "free" realm where he or she had rights and entitlements equal and comparable to most non-slave people. However, it has been demonstrated in a variety of contexts that manumitted slaves are rarely on equal footing with their masters, and a web of strings and conditions could come attached to the manumission (Baker 2001; Kleber, this volume).

ABANDONING THE PARADIGM OF SLAVE VERSUS FREE

Often underlying the problems of defining slavery are appeals to the dichotomy of slavery versus freedom. Historians of Near Eastern history have repeatedly pointed out the inapplicability of this polarity, and noted that the idea of complete individual freedom was in fact unknown in the pre-modern world (Adams 2010; Englund 2009; Finley 1964; Toledano 2002). Moreover, as Roth already noted, "although discussions of social and legal categories tend to focus on polar or binary pairs ... relational statuses are more nuanced in the daily operations of social interactions" (Roth 1998: 174). Therefore, in order to understand slavery, or any social group, in the pre-modern world, it is important to place it within a context which reflects these nuanced social interactions, as well as the various in-between forms of unfreedom. The construction of societies into households and institutions suggests that most persons, not only slaves, were woven into hierarchies and subject to other entities, ranking vertically up to the king or emperor, who themselves were subject to divine authority. Enslaved people, as Kopytoff (1982) noted before, are dispersed throughout this system by way of their household attachments, affiliations, bonds, and dependencies. As Toledano elsewhere remarked, slavery is "a phenomenon we identify with the end of social existence. Scholars are used to dealing with slavery in the context of marginality, not as part of elite history" (2002: 57). He proposed the notion of an "integrated continuum" (ibid., p. 58), in contrast to a slave-free dichotomy, "with varying degrees of servitude and honor for each type of slaves." It follows that slavery itself is a sliding scale, as Englund called it at the seminar.

Thus one result of the Oriental Institute seminar is a consensus that scholars should dispense with the slave-free dichotomy; perhaps if there is any meaningful dichotomy to society it involves household affiliation versus no household affiliation. While many non-slave persons could lack a household attachment, slaves are one social group that was always, and by definition, attached to a household or institution. By those means, slaves were one group that was guaranteed a social status that was not completely or necessarily at the bottom of society.

BEYOND ECONOMY

The non-financial value of slaves also emerges as a theme that warrants further exploration. In ancient Near Eastern studies, questions about the non-economic value of slaves have received little treatment, while economic and legal approaches have dominated due to the administrative and economic nature of most of the textual sources. In medieval Islamic studies, however, social and cultural approaches to slavery have flourished, and in this regard, a fruitful dialogue results from our collaboration and new observations about the value of slaves are put forth.

While there are cases in which slaves could be kept as an exploited labor resource (Tenney), the values of slaves to households could be multifaceted. As in Rome, slaves contributed to the social status of the household and their value was composed of many intersecting factors: economic contribution, social prestige, and political networks. Slaves, female (Seri) and male (Babayan 2010), also served the household as sexual and reproductive resources. Neumann's discussion of the prices of slaves in the late third millennium B.C. finds that the sale price of certain slaves exceeded average amounts, and he hypothesizes that these more costly slaves possessed specialized skills. It can further be surmised that the cost of slaves with specialized skills may fluctuate with the individual slave's mastery of these skills, with more highly skilled slaves not only adding to the household economy but also to the prestige of the household as reputable craftsmen. Masters gained prestige, political prowess, and religious benefits by donating slaves to religious institutions (Kleber, Seri) or by performing piety through an act of manumission (Babayan 2010), and thus slaves offered value even in their release.

CONTEXTS, CONTINGENCIES, AND CONDITIONS

As already discussed, generalizing approaches to slavery are useful for understanding the topic and especially for charting discourses, promoting cross-cultural comparison, or mapping historical trajectories and transformations. Conducting groundwork is important as well, however, rooting discussions in data and fostering ongoing dialogues among historians who take different approaches. In this study, microhistorical approaches allowed us to explore the contingencies of enslavements in different contexts. The experiences of slavery varied according to the status of the household to which a slave is attached, the position of the household vis-à-vis the status of those households around it, and according to political and historical circumstances. Even within the course of a single life-span or over a generation, circumstances shifted. This is noted in particular with the death of a household head (Culbertson, Kleber, Tenney) or political transformation (Toledano).

In more contexts than not, slavery is an ephemeral designation with many permutations and many possible entry and exit paths, as discussed above. Interestingly, in some cases it appears that slaves themselves may have no better idea about the nature, duration, or conditions of their enslavement (Culbertson, Kleber), while sometimes slaves and masters dispute the nature of enslavement.

Related to this is the question of the durability, sustainability, or fragility of slave traditions and systems. At the seminar, our temporally broad set of cases allowed us to note that none of the traditions or systems examined were able to sustain themselves beyond a few generations, if that, at least not without major renovation. The transcendence of legal and social terminologies[6] and written culture disguises the fragility of practices and institutions of slavery. This includes institutional practices such as the *naditu*s of Seri's paper, the exploited, closed system of slaves that Tenney examines, and the *mamluk*s of Gordon's study; Toledano's contribution traces transformations in slave-household dynamics over the course of two centuries.

FINAL REMARKS

This examination has regarded slavery as a social, cultural, and political phenomenon as much as an economic one. As society, culture, and politics are in constant flux, so changes the way slavery is done.

Many questions and directions for future research are opened up by this investigation, and several methodological questions remain to be addressed. However, one advantage of the household approach to slaves is clear: by situating slavery within the context of household — whether household is understood as a domestic estate, state institution, or temple — we view slaves more directly in history. As members of households, slaves were not at the margins of history and society, but belong to historical and social processes. Even though slavery was never the dominant source of labor in the Near East, it was always a complex of social apparatuses that managed relationships of economic or social obligation and debt, integrated outsiders into social establishments such as households, and shifted trajectories of upward and downward mobility for those who endured the predicament of enslavement.

---

[6] Consider, for example, the survival of the Akkadian term *wardu* over two millennia and its consistent presence in legal documents; or the frequent appearance of *mamluk* institutions across temporally and geographically varied Islamicate societies.

BIBLIOGRAPHY

Adams, Robert McC.
2010   "Slavery and Freedom in the Third Dynasty of Ur: Implications of the Garshana Archives." *Cuneiform Digital Library Journal* 2010: 2.

Amitai, Reuven
2006   "The Mamluk Institution, or One Thousand Years of Military Slavery in the Islamic World." In *Arming Slaves: From Classical Times to the Modern Age*, edited by C. L. Brown and P. D. Morgan, pp. 40–78. Gilder Lehrman Center for the Study of Slavery, Resistance, and Abolition. New Haven: Yale University Press.

Andrews, Susan C. and James P. Fenton
2007   "Archaeology and the Invisible Man: The Role of Slavery in the Production of Wealth and Social Class in the Bluegrass Region of Kentucky, 1820–1970." In *The Archaeology of Identities: A Reader,* edited by T. S. Insoll, pp. 230–49. New York: Routledge.

Babaie, Sussan; Kathryn Babayan; Ina Baghdiantz-McCabe; and Massumeh Farhad
2004   *Slaves of the Shah: New Elites of Safavid Iran.* Library of Middle East History 3. New York: I.B. Taurus.

Babayan, Kathryn
2010   "On Manumission and Declarations of Freedom in 17th Century Iran." Paper presented at the Oriental Institute Seminar Series 7, March 5th, 2010.

Bahrani, Zainab
2006   "Race and Ethnicity in Mesopotamian Antiquity." *World Archaeology* 38/1: 48–59

Baker, Heather D.
2001   "Degrees of Freedom: Slavery in Mid-First Millennium B.C. Babylonia." *World Archaeology* 33/1: 18–26.

Brown, Vincent
2009   "Social Death and Political Life in the Study of Slavery." *American Historical Review* 114/5: 1231–49.

Chirichigno, Gregory C.
1993   *Debt-Slavery in Israel and the Ancient Near East.* Journal for the Study of the Old Testament Supplement Series 141. London: Sheffield Academic Press.

Dandamaev, Muhammad A.
1984   *Slavery in Babylonia: From Nabopolassar to Alexander the Great (626–331 B.C.).* Revised edition. Edited by M. A. Powell and D. B. Weisberg, translated by V. A. Powell. DeKalb: Northern Illinois University Press.

Degler, Carl N.
1959   "Starr on Slavery." *Journal of Economic History* 19/2: 271–77.

Engerman, Stanley
2000   "Slavery at Different Times and Places." *American Historical Review* 105/2: 480–85.

Englund, Robert K.
2009   "The Smell of the Cage." *Cuneiform Digital Library Journal* 2009: 4.

Finley, Moses I.
1964   "Between Slavery and Freedom." *Comparative Studies in Society and History* 6/3: 233–49.
1968   "Slavery." *International Encyclopedia of the Social Sciences*, edited by David L. Sills and Robert King Merton. New York: Macmillan.

1973 *The Ancient Economy*. Sather Classical Lectures 43. Berkeley: University of California Press.

Gordon, Matthew S.

1999 "Turkish Officers of Samarra: Revenue and the Exercise of Authority." *Journal of Economic and Social History of the Orient* 42/4: 466–93.

2000 "The Commanders of the Samarran Turksih Military: The Shaping of a Third/Ninth-Century Imperial Elite." In *A Medieval Islamic City Reconsidered: An Interdisciplinary Approach to Samarra*, edited by C. F. Robinson, pp. 119–40. Oxford Studies in Islamic Art 14. Oxford: Oxford University Press.

Green, Kevin

2000 "Technological Innovation and Economic Progress in the Ancient World: M. I. Finley Re-Considered." *The Economic History Review*, n.s., 53/1: 29–59.

Gross, Ariela

2001 "Essay: Beyond Black and White: Cultural Approaches to Race and Slavery." *Columbia Law Review* 101/3: 640–90.

Johnson, Walter

2001 *Soul by Soul: Life Inside the Antebellum Slave Market*. Cambridge: Harvard University Press

2003 "On Agency." *Journal of Social History* 37/1: 113–24.

Karras, Ruth Mazo

1988 *Slavery and Society in Medieval Scandinavia*. Yale historical publications 135. New Haven: Yale University Press.

Kopytoff, I.

1982 "Slavery." *Annual Review of Anthropology* 11: 207–30.

Lewis, Bernard

1990 *Race and Slavery in the Middle East: An Historical Enquiry*. Oxford: Oxford University Press.

Mahoney, Mary Ann

2008 "Creativity Under Constraint: Enslaved Afro-Brazilian Families in Brazil's Cacao Area, 1870–1890." *Journal of Social History* 41/3: 633–66.

Marmon, Shaun E., editor

1999 *Slavery in the Islamic Middle East*. Princeton: Markus Wiener.

Mendelsohn, Isaac

1949 *Slavery in the Ancient Near East: A Comparative Study of Slavery in Babylonia, Assyria, Syria, and Palestine, from the Middle of the Third Millennium to the End of the First Millennium*. Oxford: Oxford University Press.

Miura, Toru, and John Edward Philips, editors

2000 *Slave Elites in the Middle East and Africa: A Comparative Study*. London and New York: Kegan Paul International.

Patterson, Orlando

1977 "Slavery." *Annual Review of Sociology* 3: 407–49.

1982 *Slavery and Social Death: A Comparative Study*. Cambridge: Harvard University Press.

Roth, Martha T.

1987 "Age at Marriage and the Household; A Study of Neo-Babylonian and Neo-Assyrian Forms." *Comparative Studies in Society and History* 29/4: 715–47.

1998 "Gender and Law: A Case Study from Ancient Mesopotamia." In *Gender and Law in the Hebrew Bible and Ancient Near East*, edited by V. H. Matthews, B. M. Levinson,

T. S. Frymer-Kensky, pp. 173–84. Journal for the Study of the Old Testament, Supplement Series 262. Sheffield: Sheffield Academic Press.

Siegel, Bernard J.

1945   "Some Methodological Considerations for a Comparative Study of Slavery." *American Anthropology* 47: 357–92.

1947   *Slavery during the Third Dynasty of Ur*. American Anthropological Association, Memoirs 66. Chicago: University of Chicago.

Starr, Chester G.

1958   "An Overdose of Slavery." *Journal of Economic History* 18/1: 17–32.

Steinkeller, Piotr

2004   "Toward a Definition of Private Economic Activity in Third Millennium Babylonia." In *Commerce and Monetary Systems in the Ancient World: Means of Transmission and Cultural Interaction* (Proceedings of the Fifth Annual Symposium of the Assyrian and Babylonian Intellectual Heritage Project, Held in Innsbruck, Austria, October 3rd–8th 2002), edited by R. Rollinger and C. Ulf, with the collaboration of K. Schnegg, pp. 91–111. Oriens et Occidens 6. Stuttgart: Franz Steiner.

Stol, Martin

2004   *Mesopotamien: Die altbabylonische Zeit*. Orbis Biblicus et Orientalis 160/4. Göttingen: Vandenhoeck & Ruprecht.

Thompson, F. Hugh

2002   *The Archaeology of Greek and Roman Slavery*. London: Duckworth.

Toledano, Ehud R.

2002   "Representing the Slave's Body in Ottoman Society." In *Representing the Body of the Slave*, edited by T. E. J. Wiedeman and J. F. Gardner. Studies in Slave and Post-Slave Societies and Cultures. London: Frank Cass.

2007   *As if Silent and Absent: Bonds of Enslavement in the Islamic Middle East*. New Haven: Yale University Press.

van de Glind, Hans, and Joost Kooijmans

2008   "Modern-Day Child Slavery." *Children and Society* 22/3: 150–66.

van Driel, G.

2000   "Institutional Versus Non-Institutional Economy in Ancient Mesopotamia." In *Interdependency of Institutions and Private Entrepreneurs (MOS Studies 2)* (Proceedings of the Second MOS Symposium, Leiden 1998), edited by A. C. V. M. Bongenaar, pp. 5–24. Publications de l'Institut historique-archéologique néerlandais de Stamboul 87. Leiden: Nederlands Historisch-Archaeologisch Instituut te Istanbul.

Vlassopoulos, Kostas

2009   "Slavery, Freedom and Citizenship in Classical Athens: Beyond a Legalistic Approach." *European Review of History* 16/3: 347–63.

Westbrook, Raymond

1995a   "Slave and Master in Ancient Near Eastern Law." *Chicago-Kent Law Review* 70. 1631–76.

1995b   "Social Justice in the Ancient Near East." In *Social Justice in the Ancient World*, edited by K. D. Irani and M. Silver, pp. 149–63. Westport: Greenwood Press.

1998   "The Female Slave." In *Gender and Law in the Hebrew Bible and the Ancient Near East*, edited by V. H. Matthews, B. M. Levinson, and T. S. Frymer-Kensky, pp. 214–38. Journal for the Study of the Old Testament, Supplement Series 262. Sheffield: Sheffield Academic Press.

SECTION ONE:
EARLY MESOPOTAMIA

2

SLAVERY IN PRIVATE HOUSEHOLDS TOWARD THE END OF THE THIRD MILLENNIUM B.C.

HANS NEUMANN, WESTFÄLISCHE WILHELMS-UNIVERSITÄT, MÜNSTER

The time of the Third Dynasty of Ur (twenty-first century B.C.) is one of the best documented periods of Mesopotamian history. Presently, some 75,000 published cuneiform texts of the Ur III period are available. The overwhelming majority of the documents come from archives of the state economy and administration, while on the other hand, only 2,000 texts (in particular private legal documents) come from the areas outside of the state administration (i.e., the private households). Most of the Ur III documents come from the southern Mesopotamian places Girsu, Umma, Ur, Puzriš-Dagan, Nippur, and recently Garšana. Taking into account the specific situation of the tradition and also the uneven geographical and archival distribution of the Ur III sources, it can be stated that the present number and the nature of sources — supplemented by a law code (Codex Ur-Namma), court documents, royal and private inscriptions, and literary texts in part going back to an Ur III tradition — encourage studies on socioeconomic problems of ancient Mesopotamia.

At the outset of this study, it must be emphasized that slavery never played a dominant role in the production spheres of ancient Near Eastern cultures. On the basis of the studies published by Siegel (1947), Mendelsohn (1949), Falkenstein (1956–57, vol. 1: 82–95), Diakonoff (1974),[1] Gelb (1976 and 1979),[2] Cardellini (1981), Dandamaev (1984),[3] Oelsner (1977), Steinkeller (1989), Stolper (1989), Neumann (1989), Westbrook (1995), Weiler (2003), and Wilcke (2007a: 53–58) we know that nowhere in the ancient Near East did slaves form the main class of workers. This is also true for the Neo- and Late Babylonian societies in the first millennium B.C., when slavery was more significant than in earlier periods of ancient Near Eastern history. In general, it should also be emphasized that the labor of slaves took place mainly in private households rather than in the economic spheres of the palace or temple institutions, but in this connection we must also consider the structural differences between the respective state sectors of economy throughout the history of the ancient Near Eastern societies, which vary according to specific regional conditions.[4] The state of documentation about slavery must also be taken into consideration, because relevant documentation is often missing or non-existant to begin with.[5]

---

[1] In this connection, see also Stucevskij 1988.

[2] See Gelb 1982 regarding the terminology for slaves and other dependent persons in the social context; see also Krecher 1987.

[3] This is the revised English version of Dandamaev 1974; see also Oelsner 1988.

[4] In relation to property issues, see, for example, Komoróczy 1978 (with citations) and the contributions in Brentjes 1988; also Renger 1995. In relation to the continuities and differences in economic structures, see, for example, Renger 2002 and the relevant comments to this article in Marzahn 2002 and Neumann 2002.

[5] See also the comments in Neumann 1989: 221 n. 4.

Despite these general remarks, the question of the extent and significance of slavery in private domestic households remains interesting, especially for the period of the Third Dynasty of Ur, or Ur III period, in Mesopotamia (which corresponds to the twenty-first century B.C.). To this day scholars express an assumption that the Ur III kingdom is best characterized as a patrimonial state, whose economic institutions strictly controlled all essential economic means, including the spheres of agriculture, cattle-breeding, trade, and craft. As such, it is said that the space and possibility for private property, and private economic initiative or activity, did not and could not exist in the Ur III period. The ensuing debates about the existence and nature of Ur III private economy are also based on theoretical presuppositions, which I have discussed elsewhere.[6] Approaching the matter from different points of view, Steinkeller (2004) and Wilcke (2007b)[7] have most recently fleshed out the problem of private economic activity and highlighted the question of the existence or nonexistence of markets in Mesopotamia under the kings of Ur. In this respect, the following remarks are to be understood as a specific source-related contribution to discussions about the social and economic structures of the Neo-Sumerian society under the Ur III kings.

If we speak about slavery in private households in the Ur III period, it should be understood that we are speaking about conditions only at the level of the middle and upper classes. These people lived and worked within the urban milieu and were therefore also associated in different ways with the economic structures of the royal provincial administration (palaces and temples). The cuneiform sources corresponding to this activity include tens of thousands of economic and legal records, which may be investigated for references to private slavery and the conditions and circumstances thereof.

According to the available data, it is still difficult to correctly judge the actual number of slaves in private ownership. As a rule, a wealthy family in Ur III Babylonia owned at least one or two slaves. Of course, the concrete number of slaves in private ownership depended not only upon the wealth of the slave owner, but also upon the precise kind of activities the master wanted the slaves to do. This is why the number of slaves can differ widely from family to family.[8] Using the Ur III court records, Falkenstein (1956–57, vol. 1: 87 n. 5) determined that the highest number of slaves attested in a private household is six. According to sale contracts that originate from northern Babylonia, we find that a certain high-ranking man named SI.A-a, a chief shepherd (na-gada) who was actively engaged in the local economy for twenty-nine years,[9] owned at least three male slaves at the value of 7 to 9 shekels of silver and four female slaves at the value of 1/2 to 3 1/3 shekels of silver, or more than 7 shekels of silver.[10]

According to the court record *NATN* 302 from the city of Nippur,[11] in which there is an inheritance dispute between the brother and the widow of the famous merchant Ur-DUN,[12] the contested estate included — aside from fields "outside the city" (iri-bar-ra), household utensils, property in the city (iri-ša$_3$-ga) — seventeen male slaves and ten female slaves. The

---

[6] See the criticism of this in Neumann 2002.

[7] See also Wilcke 2008.

[8] In this connection, see Mendelsohn 1949: 119.

[9] For the SI.A-a archive, see most recently Garfinkle 2003.

[10] Male slaves: TIM 9 103 = FAOS 17 116 (7 gin$_2$), PIOL 19 384 = FAOS 17 113 (8? 1/3 gin$_2$ + 1 u$_8$-bar-ğal$_2$-la), MVN 8 151 = FAOS 17 66 (9 gin$_2$); female slaves: PIOL 19 359 = FAOS 17 112 (1/2 gin$_2$), TIM 5 12 = FAOS 17 114 (1 1/2 gin$_2$), PIOL 19 376 = FAOS 17 115 (3 1/3 gin$_2$), ZA 93 6 (1 ab$_2$ mu-3 + 1.1.0 še gur; at a price of 6 1/2 shekels for the cow [see Falkenstein 1956–57, vol. 2: 296 to lines 13–14], and about one shekel of silver for the barley [see Steinkeller 1989: 134]; this represents a value of more than 7 shekels of silver).

[11] See Neumann 2004: 5–6 no. 1.5 (with citations).

[12] For details, see Owen 1980.

substantial number of slaves alone makes it clear that Ur-DUN, the former owner, must have been a very wealthy merchant.[13] Given that, at that time, the average price of a man was about 10 shekels of silver, and that the prices of women were around 5 to 6 shekels,[14] we may assume that the slaves altogether had a value of around 3 to 4 minas of silver, and this factored into the overall value of the family's estate. Perhaps the value of the slaves was even higher than this, if we consider a sale document from Nippur (*NRVN* 1 215 = FAOS 17 30). Here, the document mentions Ur-DUN's brother Alala as the buyer of a slave woman. The same woman, Šaganzu, appears in *NATN* 302, and her price was upward of 12 shekels of silver.[15] This is more than twice as much as the average price of a woman in the Ur III period.

As a rule, the majority of attested slaves in private Ur III households in Babylonia consisted of indigenous people with Sumerian, Akkadian, and Hurrian names.[16] A free man or a free woman and their entire family could be enslaved as the result of court proceedings. In this context, the enslavement could be considered a kind of criminal punishment,[17] but this was not the main source of slavery in private households. House-born slaves and people who became slaves because of debts were of much greater importance and number than enslaved criminals. Such slave sales are attested by more than eighty sale documents of different origin[18] as well as by court records that deal with the confirmation of slave status after disputes in which slave men and women contested their enslavement.[19]

Regarding enslavement that arose *ex delicto*, the attested catalysts for this consequence included theft, damage to immovable property, as well as robbery and homicide. As already briefly mentioned, an entire family could be enslaved after the culprit's death or flight. According to the court record ITT 2[1] 2789 (= *NG* 2 41)[20] from the city Girsu, the enslavement of a wife and her daughters resulted from the fact that her husband committed a murder. Because the culprit himself was already killed under some unknown circumstances (or perhaps already executed according to Codex Ur-Namma §1),[21] his property and his family were handed over to the sons of the victim. After the flight and the recapture of the culprit's wife and daughters, they tried to contest their enslavement in court. In spite of repeated attempts to plead their case, they were unsuccessful and their status as slaves was confirmed by the judges.

The sale of people whose enslavement arose *ex delicto* is also attested even in the earlier Sargonic period (twenty-fourth to twenty-third centuries B.C.). According to the sale document MVN 3 102 from the Diyala region, a father and his son received certain amounts of silver as the price for the daughter.[22] The listed witnesses to this sale are designated as *šībūt kiššātim* "witnesses of *kiššātum*." As Westbrook (1995: 1638) made clear, the term *kiššātum* "refers to a non-consensual form of servitude," which "arose *ex delicto*. It appears to have been the penalty for certain minor offenses, such as petty theft." Most likely, this document refers to a seller's obligation arisen *ex delicto*, addressed by the sale of slaves, even if we have no idea which offense stood behind this situation.[23]

---

[13] See note 38 below.

[14] See Steinkeller 1989: 138; see also Falkenstein 1956–57, vol. 1: 88–90.

[15] See Steinkeller 1989: 203.

[16] See Wilcke 1976–80: 503.

[17] See Falkenstein 1956–57, vol. 1: 84.

[18] See Steinkeller 1989: 4 and 128–33; see also Falkenstein 1956–57, vol. 1: 88 (slave purchase

according to court documents). In this connection, see now also Molina 2008.

[19] For this problem, see, for example, Falkenstein 1956–57, vol. 1: 86; Neumann 1989: 225 with n. 29.

[20] See Neumann 2004: 12 no. 1.14 (with citations); Westbrook 1995: 1645.

[21] For this problem, see Neumann 2004: 12 n. 22.

[22] See Neumann 2004: 18–19 no. 2.1 (with citations).

[23] In this context, see also Westbrook 1996.

In cases in which debt was the catalyst for enslavement, persons direly in debt are attested as having sold themselves into slavery to work off what they owed.[24] However, it was a much more common practice for parents to sell or pledge their children for debts instead of themselves.[25] The latter instance can be seen in the loan document L 11053 (= *ZA* 53 22) from Girsu, which concerns a loan of 8 shekels of silver. Here, the debtor swore an oath by the king, promising that in the case of insolvency he would hand his son over to the creditor to be a slave. As far as we presently know, this practice is unattested before the Ur III period.[26] In the most common situation, however, debtors pledged their slaves for loans and debts.[27] A court record from Umma (BM 106470), just recently presented by Sallaberger (2008: 167–68), concerns the sale of a debtor's son to repay a debt. The creditor confirmed here under oath that 10 shekels of silver — half of the debt of 20 shekels of silver — are repaid by the human's sale.

As a rule, the prices mentioned in slave sale contracts are indicated as amounts of silver, and it can be assumed that these purchase prices were in fact paid in silver. Paying in kind — that is, with wool, barley, cattle — is also attested, but much less frequently.[28] In fact, a court record from Girsu (BM 22858 = HSAO 9 182 no. 1 obv. ii 3′–9′) shows that in some cases paying in kind was not exactly popular with the seller. This case tells us that a dispute over the payment for a slave girl came to court when the seller of the girl was not paid with silver, but rather with wool and barley. Unfortunately, the conclusion of the case is broken.[29]

It is still difficult to determine where and in what ways slaves were employed in the private households during the Ur III period because the cuneiform sources of this time contain few, if any, indications about this kind of daily activity. We can be certain that the majority of slaves were unskilled, unspecialized workers who, for the most part, performed some nonspecific services for their masters. Female slaves are known to have also served as wet nurses and nannies, and in some instances as singers or dancers.[30]

Aside from these examples, it can be shown that some slaves served as assistant workers or qualified employees even in the production spheres of the private households. In some cases we know the professions or occupations of slaves. These were, for instance, "barber" (šu-i), male or female "cupbearer" (sagi), "malster" (munu₄-mu₂), and "farmer" (engar).[31] This means that privately owned slaves were employed in spheres such as personal hygiene and medicine and could be involved in beer production and agriculture. The latter instance is attested already in the Sargonic period, from which time we find a letter-order from Girsu (ITT 1 1119 = FAOS 19 Gir 21) showing the following situation: the sender of the letter asked the addressee for a field, and he said in this connection "my slaves have to cultivate it" (lines 7–8: urdu₂-ĝu₁₀-ne / [ḫ]e₂-uru₄-n[e]).[32] Slaves undoubtedly also served as gardeners in private households. In a document from Nippur concerning the sale of an ox (*NRVN* 1 219 = FAOS 17 52), the buyer is characterized as a slave of somebody who was a chief builder (urdu₂-PN-šidim-gal). This could mean that the slave, here acting as a buyer, was engaged in

---

[24] See Neumann 1989: 223 with n. 19; Steinkeller 1989: 132.

[25] See Neumann 1989: 223 with n. 20; Steinkeller 1989: 132.

[26] See Çığ, Kızılyay, and Falkenstein 1959: 85.

[27] See Neumann 1989: 224 with n. 23.

[28] See Falkenstein 1956–57, vol. 1: 88–90; Steinkeller 1989: 133 and 135–38.

[29] See Molina 2004: 175–76.

[30] See Neumann 1989: 222 with n. 12.

[31] See Falkenstein 1956–57, vol. 1: 88 n. 5; Neumann 1989: 223 n. 14.

[32] See Kienast and Volk 1995: 96–97.

construction work and could conduct relevant business on behalf of his owner. According to a court record from Umma (BM 110379), just recently published by Molina (2008: no. 4), a slave was connected with the so-called ĝiš-gid₂-da, or lancer service (line 13). According to Englund (1990: 75 with n. 247) the ĝiš-gid₂-da work is mentioned in connection with fishing, suggesting the possibility that the slave was a fisherman, perhaps conscripted here for military purposes.[33]

The slave sale contracts of the already mentioned chief shepherd (na-gada) SI.A-a, who started his career as an ordinary shepherd (sipa),[34] point out that at least some of the slaves SI.A-a bought were connected with the breeding of livestock. This can also be demonstrated by the Umma document *SNAT* 373. According to this text, the slave Īzib-šināt was in the service of a shepherd called Namrilum. Īzib-šināt was apparently implicated in some kind of crime involving his responsibilities vis-à-vis the livestock (probably theft), but we unfortuantely are not told enough about the background of this situation to assess what occurred.[35]

Looking at the occupations of the buyers mentioned in the Ur III slave sale contracts, it is easy to note that merchants (dam-gar₃) acted as purchasers of slaves on several occasions.[36] This is not surprising, given that the main creditors in this society were in fact merchants, who could cause their debtors to sell them members of their families in cases of insolvency.[37] The sale of family members to merchants could either discharge the debt to the merchants/ creditors, or could achieve the debtor's liquidity in general, discharging the debt to a third party. At the same time, the purchase of slaves was a merchants' investment in living capital that could be resold or be employed.

Regarding the employment of slaves in a merchant's house, the aforementioned court record *NATN* 302 from Nippur may be of interest. The document concerns an inheritance dispute between the brother and the widow of the famous merchant Ur-DUN, namely Alala and Geme-Su'ena respectively. Among other things (enumerated above), the contested estate included male and female slaves. Ur-DUN, their former owner, was a wealthy merchant whose activity probably spanned over twenty years, and he was particularly connected with the royal house. We also know that Ur-DUN personally undertook commercial journeys.[38] This could suggest to us that at least some of the male slaves mentioned in the court record *NATN* 302 were connected with the commercial activities of Ur-DUN and his family, including his brother Alala, who was also a very active businessman in Nippur.[39]

In terms of social and economic history, the employment of skilled slaves in workshops owned by craftsmen is of special significance. Documentation shows that craftsmen could privately own slaves in the Ur III period. This speaks well for the possibility that at least in some cases the slaves worked as more-or-less qualified, specialized employees in the workshops of craftsmen. In the court record ITT 2¹ 2775 (= *NG* 2 196), lines 12–22, a slave was awarded to a goldsmith (ku₃-dim₂) by judges. Another goldsmith acted as a witness to this settlement, and the son of a third goldsmith swore a declaratory oath to solidify the new

---

[33] See the discussion in Molina 2008: 132.

[34] See Garfinkle 2003: 164 n. 11.

[35] See Wilcke 1991.

[36] See, for example, the list of the buyers in the sale documents in Steinkeller 1989: 119–20.

[37] For this, see Neumann 1979: 51–53; 1992b: 169–76; 2007: 293–94. In this connection, see also Garfinkle 2004; for Nippur, see Wu Yuhong 2003.

[38] For the dam-gar₃ Ur-DUN, see Neumann 1992a: 86–89; 1999: 51–52.

[39] For Alala, see Neumann 1992b: 168–69.

conditions.[40] We don't know anything about the legal background of the judgement, but it can perhaps be assumed that the slave worked as a skilled craftsman or as an assistant worker in a goldsmith's workshop. A similar case is most likely attested in the court record *DAS* 332 bis, which concerns the production of textiles. The text could possibly refer to the purchase of a female weaver (geme₂-uš-bar); an overseer of the weavers (ugula-uš-bar) acted as a witness.[41]

In this connection, another court record from Girsu (ITT 2[1] 923 = *NG* 2 207) is of special significance. Lines 2–14 of this document refer to a dispute involving a community of smiths (simug), well known from other Girsu texts:[42] "They (= the judges) have denied Lugal-kuzu, the smith, the rights regarding Niĝir-ennu (= slave), who has been awarded to Niĝir-šakuš, the smith. That Lugal-kuzu had paid 16 shekels of silver for the slave, Nabasa (= smith) (and) Ur-Niĝizzida (= smith) have sworn. The silver was awarded to Lugal-kuzu, it was chargeable to Niĝir-šakuš. Ur-tur (was) the court officer."[43] The amount of silver cited here is very interesting because 16 shekels is a high amount for the price for a male slave. Falkenstein (1956–57, vol. 1: 88) had previously assumed that Niĝir-ennu himself was a skilled smith, given that several other smiths are involved in various aspects of the lawsuit. This implies that the cited craftsmen owned slaves who were skilled employees working in the craftsmens' workshops.[44]

It is admittedly difficult to judge what it means for a male slave's price to reach higher than 10 shekels. It can be assumed that such amounts — 15, 16, 17, or even 55 shekels of silver — indicate special abilities and skills of the purchased slaves beyond the ability to perform menial labor. The same suggestion could be applicable to female slaves whose purchase prices were higher than 10 shekels. In some cases it has to be taken into consideration that high slaves' prices also could be dependent on general rises in prices caused by economic crises, such as the one suggested by evidence from Ur dating to the rule of the period's final king, Ibbi-Sîn.[45]

There was also another method of enlisting a slave's services and this involved the hire of slaves. In addition to some indirect evidence in the court records, already dealt with by Falkenstein (1956–57, vol. 1: 91), the private hire of a slave woman is attested in the Nippur document *NRVN* 1 226. According to this badly written cuneiform text, the hired slave woman, Ālānītum, swore in the presence of witnesses not to run away.[46]

Patterns in the hiring of slaves for work in private households were completely dependent on seasonal and specific needs. In exchange for the slave's service, the lessor recieved rent at the rate of five to seven liters of barley daily.[47] About further costs we have no information, at least for the circumstances of this practice during the Ur III period.

To conclude, it can be said that the employment of slaves in private households, especially in the production spheres, can be demonstrated only to a small extent. But, if we take into account the information embedded within the otherwise well-known private business and legal records, it can be assumed that the work of privately owned slaves was definitely a social and economic factor in the Ur III period. There was indeed space and possibility for private property and private economic initiative and activity respectively, and this was a natural and

---

[40] For this text and on the problem of craftsmen's ownership of slaves, see Neumann 1993: 155.

[41] See Lafont 1985: 92–93.

[42] For the smiths in Girsu, see Lafont 1991; Neumann 1993: 97–106 and 202–03; Neumann 2000.

[43] See also Lafont 2000: 67.

[44] See Neumann 2000: 129–30.

[45] See Falkenstein 1956–57, vol. 1: 89 with n. 3; in this connection, see also Neumann 1993: 85 with n. 452.

[46] For this text, see Wilcke 2000: 46 with n. 109.

[47] See, for example, Waetzoldt 1980: 137; Neumann 1993: 154 with n. 879.

essential part of the Ur III economy as a whole, which was otherwise dominated by the "big households" of the palace and temple.

ABBREVIATIONS

BM	Signature of the British Museum, London
DAS	Lafont 1985
FAOS 17	Steinkeller 1989
FAOS 19	Kienast and Volk 1995
HSAO 9	Molina 2004
ITT 1	Thureau-Dangin 1910
ITT 2[1]	Genouillac 1910
MVN 3	Owen 1975
MVN 8	Calvot 1979
NATN	Owen 1982
NG	Falkenstein 1956–57
NRVN 1	Çiğ and Kızılyay 1965
PIOL 19	Sauren 1978
SNAT	Gomi and Sato 1990
TIM 5	van Dijk 1968
TIM 9	van Dijk 1976
ZA 53	Çiğ, Kızılyay, and Falkenstein 1959
ZA 93	Garfinkle 2003

BIBLIOGRAPHY

Brentjes, Burchard, editor
>1988   *Das Grundeigentum in Mesopotamien.* Jahrbuch für Wirtschaftsgeschichte, Sonderband 1987. Berlin: Akademie Verlag.

Calvot, D.
>1979   *Textes économiques de Şelluš-Dagan du Musée du Louvre et du Collège de France.* Materiali per il vocabulario neosumerico 8. Rome: Multigraphica Editrice.

Cardellini, Innocenzo
>1981   *Die biblischen "Sklaven"-Gesetze im Lichte des keilschriftlichen Sklavenrechts: Ein Beitrag zur Tradition, Überlieferung und Redaktion der alttestamentlichen Rechtstexte.* Bonner biblische Beiträge 55. Königstein: Hanstein.

Çiğ, Muazzez; Hatice Kızılyay; and Adam Falkenstein
>1959   "Neue Rechts- und Gerichtsurkunden der Ur III-Zeit aus Lagaš aus den Sammlungen der Istanbuler Archäologischen Museen." *Zeitschrift für Assyriologie und Vorderasiatische Archäologie* 53: 51–92.

Çiğ, Muazzez, and Hatice Kızılyay
>1965   *Neusumerische Rechts- und Verwaltungsurkunden aus Nippur,* Volume 1. Türk Tarih Kurumu Yayinlarindan 6/7. Ankara: Türk Tarih Kurumu Basımevi.

Dandamaev, Muhammad A.
>1974   *Rabstvo v Vavilonii VII-IV vv. do n. e. (626–331 gg.).* Moscow: Isdatel'stvo "Nauka."

1984   *Slavery in Babylonia: From Nabopolassar to Alexander the Great (626–331 B.C.).*
                Revised edition. Edited by M. A. Powell and D. B. Weisberg, translated by V. A.
                Powell. DeKalb: Northern Illinois University Press.

Diakonoff, Igor M.
1974   "Slaves, Helots and Serfs in Early Antiquity." In *Acta Antiqua Academiae Scientiarum
                Hungaricae* 22: 45–78.

Englund, Robert K.
1990   *Organisation und Verwaltung der Ur III-Fischerei.* Berliner Beiträge zum Vorderen
                Orient 10. Berlin: Dietrich Reimer.

Falkenstein, Adam
1956–57   *Die neusumerischen Gerichtsurkunden.* 3 volumes. Bayerische Akademie der
                Wissenschaften, Philosophisch-Historische Klasse. Abhandlungen, n.F., 39, 40, and
                44. Munich: Verlag der Bayerischen Akademie der Wissenschaften.

Garfinkle, Steven
2003   "SI.A-a and His Family: The Archive of 21st Century (B.C.) Entrepreneur."
                Zeitschrift für Assyriologie und Vorderasiatische Archäologie 93: 161–98.

2004   "Shepherds, Merchants, and Credit: Some Observations on Lending Practices in Ur III
                Mesopotamia." *Journal of the Economic and Social History of the Orient* 47: 1–30.

Gelb, Ignace J.
1976   "Quantitative Evaluation of Slavery and Serfdom." In *Kramer Anniversary Volume:
                Cuneiform Studies in Honor of Samuel Noah Kramer*, edited by B. L. Eichler, pp.
                195–207. Alter Orient und Altes Testament 25. Kevelaer: Butzon & Bercker.

1979   "Definition and Discussion of Slavery and Serfdom." *Ugarit-Forschungen* 11:
                283–97.

1982   "Terms for Slaves in Ancient Mesopotamia." In *Societies and Languages of the
                Ancient Near East: Studies in Honour of I. M. Diakonoff*, edited by M. A. Dandamaev,
                I. Gershevitch, H. Klengel, G. Komoróczy, M. T. Larsen, and J. N. Postgate, pp.
                81–98. Warminster: Aris & Phillips.

Genouillac, Henri de
1910   *Textes de l'époque d'Agadé et de l'époque d'Ur.* Inventaire des tablettes de Tello
                conservées au Musée Imperial Ottoman 2, Part 1. Paris: E. Leroux.

Gomi, Tohru, and Susumu Sato
1990   *Selected Neo-Sumerian Administrative Texts from the British Museum.* Abiko: The
                Research Institute Chuo-Gakuin University.

Kienast, Burkhard, and Konrad Volk
1995   *Die sumerischen und akkadischen Briefe des III. Jahrtausends aus der Zeit vor der
                III. Dynastie von Ur.* Freiburger Altorientalische Studien 19. Stuttgart: Franz Steiner.

Komoróczy, Géza
1978   "Landed Property in Ancient Mesopotamia and the Theory of the So-Called Asiatic
                Mode of Production." *Oikumene* 2: 9–26.

Krecher, Joachim
1987   "/ur/ 'Mann', /eme/ 'Frau' und die sumerische Herkunft des Wortes urdu(-d)
                'Sklave.'" *Welt des Orients* 18: 7–19.

Lafont, Bertrand
1985   *Documents administratifs sumériens provenant du site de Tello et conservé au Musée
                du Louvre.* Éditions Recherche sur les Grandes Civilisations, Mémoire 61. Paris:
                Éditions Recherches sur les Civilisations.

1991   "Les forgerons Sumériens de la ville de Girsu." In *De Anatolia Antiqua. Eski Anadolu
                I. Travaux et recherches de l'Institut Français d'Études Anatoliennes*, edited by J. des

Courtils, J.-Ch. Moretti, and F. Planet, pp. 119–29. Paris: Institut Français d'Études Anatoliennes.

2000   "Les textes judiciaires sumériens." In *Rendre la justice en Mésopotamie: Archives judiciaires du Proche-Orient Ancien (IIIe–Ier millénaires avant J.-C.)*, edited by F. Joannès, pp. 35–68. Saint-Denis: Presses Universitaires de Vincennes.

Marzahn, Joachim

2002   "'Oikos' und 'Tributwirtschaft' – Wirtschaftsmodelle des Alten Orients in der Kritik." In *Material Culture and Mental Spheres: Rezeption archäologischer Denkrichtungen in der Vorderasiatischen Altertumskunde* (Internationales Symposium für Hans J. Nissen, Berlin, 23.–24. Juni 2000), edited by A. Hausleiter, S. Kerner, and B. Müller-Neuhof, pp. 267–71. Alter Orient und Altes Testament 293. Münster: Ugarit-Verlag.

Mendelsohn, Isaac

1949   *Slavery in the Ancient Near East: A Comparative Study of Slavery in Babylonia, Assyria, Syria, and Palestine, from the Middle of the Third Millennium to the End of the First Millennium.* Oxford: Oxford University Press.

Molina, Manuel

2004   "Some Neo-Sumerian Legal Texts in the British Museum." In *Von Sumer nach Ebla und zurück: Festschrift Giovanni Pettinato zum 27. September 1999, gewidmet von Freunden, Kollegen und Schülern*, edited by H. Waetzoldt, pp. 175–84. Heidelberger Studien zum Alten Orient 9. Heidelberg: Heidelberger Orientverlag.

2008   "New Ur III Court Records Concerning Slavery." In *On the Third Dynasty of Ur: Studies in Honor of Marcel Sigrist*, edited by P. Michalowski, pp. 125–43. Journal of Cuneiform Studies Supplement Series 1. Boston: American Schools of Oriental Research.

Neumann, Hans

1979   "Handel und Händler in der Zeit der III. Dynastie von Ur." *Altorientalische Forschungen* 6: 15–67.

1989   "Bemerkungen zur Freilassung von Sklaven im alten Mesopotamien gegen Ende des 3. Jahrtausends v.u.Z." *Altorientalische Forschungen* 16: 220–33.

1992a   "Nochmals zum Kaufmann in neusumerischer Zeit: die Geschäfte des Ur-DUN und anderer Kauflaute aus Nippur." In *La circulation des biens, des personnes et des idées dans le Proche-Orient ancien* (Actes de la 38e Rencontre Assyriologique Internationale, Paris, 8–10 juillet 1991), edited by D. Charpin and F. Joannès, pp. 83–94. Paris: Éditions Recherche sur les Civilisations.

1992b   "Zur privaten Geschäftstätigkeit in Nippur in der Ur III Zeit." In *Nippur at the Centennial* (Papers Read at the 35e Rencontre Assyriologique Internationale, Philadelphia, 1988), edited by M. deJ. Ellis, pp. 161–76. Occasional Publications of the Samuel Noah Kramer Fund 14. Philadelphia: University Museum.

1993   *Handwerk in Mesopotamien: Untersuchungen zu seiner Organisation in der Zeit der III. Dynastie von Ur.* 2nd edition. Berlin: Akademie-Verlag

1999   "Ur-Dumuzida and Ur-DUN: Reflections on the Relationship between State-initiated Foreign Trade and Private Economic Activity in Mesopotamia towards the End of the Third Millennium B.C." In *Trade and Finance in Ancient Mesopotamia (MOS Studies 1)* (Proceedings of the First MOS Symposium, Leiden 1997), edited by J. G. Dercksen, pp. 43–53. Publications de l'Institut historique-archéologique néerlandais de Stamboul 84. Leiden: Nederlands Historisch-Archaeologisch Instituut te Istanbul.

2000   "Staatliche Verwaltung und privates Handwerk in der Ur III-Zeit: Die Auftragstätigkeit der Schmiede von Girsu." In *Interdependency of Institutions and Private Entrepreneurs (MOS Studies 2)* (Proceedings of the Second MOS Symposium, Leiden 1998), edited by A. C. V. M. Bongenaar, pp. 119–33. Publications de l'Institut historique-archéologique néerlandais de Stamboul 87. Leiden: Nederlands Historisch-Archaeologisch Instituut te Istanbul.

2002   "Die sogenannte *Oikos*-Ökonomie und das Problem der Privatwirtschaft im aus-
            gehenden 3. Jahrtausend v. Chr. in Mesopotamien: Bemerkungen zu J. Renger;
            Wirtschaftsgeschichte des alten Mesopotamien. Versuch einer Standortbestimmung."
            In *Material Culture and Mental Spheres. Rezeption archäologischer Denkrichtungen
            in der Vorderasiatischen Altertumskunde* (Internationales Symposium für Hans J.
            Nissen, Berlin, 23.–24. Juni 2000), edited by A. Hausleiter, S. Kerner, and B. Müller-
            Neuhof, pp. 273–81. Alter Orient und Altes Testament 293. Münster: Ugarit-Verlag.

2004   "Sumerische und akkadische Texte des 3. Jt. v. Chr." In *Texte zum Rechts- und
            Wirtschaftsleben*, edited by B. Janowski and G. Wilhelm, pp. 1–24. Texte aus der
            Umwelt des Alten Testaments, n.F., 1. Gütersloh: Gütersloher Verlagshaus.

2007   "'Gib mir mein Geld zurück!' Zur rechts- und wirtschaftsgeschichtlichen Bedeutung
            keilschriftlicher Privatarchive des 3. Jahrtausends v. Chr." In *Das geistige Erfassen
            der Welt im Alten Orient: Beiträge zu Sprache, Religion, Kultur und Gesellschaft*,
            edited by C. Wilcke, pp. 281–99. Wiesbaden: Harrassowitz.

Oelsner, Joachim

1977   "Zur Sklaverei in Babylonien in der chaldäischen, achämenidischen und hellenisti-
            schen Zeit." *Altorientalische Forschungen* 5: 71–80.

1988   Review of *Slavery in Babylonia: From Nabopolassar to Alexander the Great (626–
            331 B.C.)*, by A. M. Dandamaev. *Zeitschrift für Assyriologie und Vorderasiatische
            Archäologie* 78: 305–09.

Owen, David I.

1975   *The John Frederick Lewis Collection*. Materiali per il vocabulario neosumerico 3.
            Rome: Multigraphica Editrice.

1980   "Widows' Rights in Ur III Sumer." *Zeitschrift für Assyriologie und Vorderasiatische
            Archäologie* 70: 170–84.

1982   *Neo-Sumerian Archival Texts Primarily from Nippur in the University Museum, the
            Oriental Institute and the Iraq Museum*. Winona Lake: Eisenbrauns.

Renger, Johannes

1995   "Institutional, Communal, and Individual Ownership or Possession of Arable Land in
            Ancient Mesopotamia from the End of the Fourth to the End of the First Millennium
            B.C." *Chicago-Kent Law Review* 71: 269–319.

2002   "Wirtschaftsgeschichte des Alten Mesopotamien: Versuch einer Standortbestimmung."
            In *Material Culture and Mental Spheres. Rezeption archäologischer Denkrichtungen
            in der Vorderasiatischen Altertumskunde* (Internationales Symposium für Hans J.
            Nissen, Berlin, 23.–24. Juni 2000), edited by A. Hausleiter, S. Kerner, and B. Müller-
            Neuhof, pp. 241–65. Alter Orient und Altes Testament 293. Münster: Ugarit-Verlag.

Sallaberger, Walther

2008   "Der Eid im Gerichtsverfahren im neusumerischen Umma." In *On the Third Dynasty
            of Ur: Studies in Honor of Marcel Sigrist*, edited by P. Michalowski, pp. 159–76.
            Journal of Cuneiform Studies Supplement Series 1. Boston: American Schools of
            Oriental Research.

Sauren, Herbert

1978   *Les tablettes cunéiformes de l'époque d'Ur des collections de la New York Public
            Library*. Publications de l'Institute Orientaliste de Louvain 19. Louvain: Institut
            Orientaliste.

Siegel, Bernard J.

1947   *Slavery during the Third Dynasty of Ur*. American Anthropological Association,
            Memoirs 66. Chicago: University of Chicago.

Steinkeller, Piotr

1989   *Sale Documents of the Ur-III-Period*. Freiburger altorientalische Studien 17. Stuttgart:
            Franz Steiner.

2004   "Toward a Definition of Private Economic Activity in Third Millennium Babylonia."
                In *Commerce and Monetary Systems in the Ancient World: Means of Transmission
                and Cultural Interaction* (Proceedings of the Fifth Annual Symposium of the
                Assyrian and Babylonian Intellectual Heritage Project, Held in Innsbruck, Austria,
                October 3rd–8th 2002), edited by R. Rollinger and C. Ulf, with the collaboration of
                K. Schnegg, pp. 91–111. Oriens et Occidens 6. Stuttgart: Franz Steiner.

Stolper, Matthew W.
1989   "Registration and Taxation of Slave Sales in Achaemenid Babylonia." *Zeitschrift für
                Assyriologie und Vorderasiatische Archäologie* 79: 80–101.

Stučevskij, I. A.
1988   "Problema rabstva i, tak nazyvaemoj, 'ilotii.'" *Kavkazsko-Bližnevostočnyj Sbornik*
                8: 76–83.

Thureau-Dangin, François
1910   *Textes de l'époque d'Agadé.* Inventaire des Tablettes de Tello 1. Paris: E. Leroux.

van Dijk, J. J. A.
1968   *Cuneiform Texts: Old Babylonian Contracts and Related Material.* Texts in the Iraq
                Museum 5. Baghdad: Directorate General of Antiquities.

1976   *Cuneiform Texts: Texts of Varying Content.* Texts in the Iraq Museum 9. Leiden:
                Brill.

Waetzoldt, Hartmut
1980   Review of *Wirtschaft und Gesellschaft im Alten Vorderasien*, edited by J. Harmatta
                and G. Komoróczy. Budapest 1976: Akadémiai Kiadó. *Welt des Orients* 11: 136–42.

Weiler, Ingomar
2003   *Die Beendigung des Sklavenstatus im Altertum: Ein Beitrag zur vergleichenden
                Sozialgeschichte.* Forschungen zur antiken Sklaverei 36. Stuttgart: Franz Steiner.

Westbrook, Raymond
1995   "Slave and Master in Ancient Near Eastern Law." *Chicago-Kent Law Review* 70:
                1631–76.

1996   "zíz.da / *kiššātum*." *Wiener Zeitschrift für die Kunde des Morgenlandes* 86: 449–59.

Wilcke, Claus
1976–80   "Kauf A. II. Nach Kaufurkunden der Zeit der III. Dynastie von Ur." *Reallexikon der
                Assyriologie und Vorderasiatischen Archäologie* 5: 498–512.

1991   "Die Lesung von ÁŠ-da = *kiššātum*." *Nouvelles Asyriologiques Brèves et Utilitaires*
                1991: 16.

2000   *Wer las und schrieb in Babylonien und Assyrien: Überlegungen zur Literalität im
                alten Zweistromland.* Bayerische Akademie der Wissenschaften. Philosophisch-
                historische Klasse. Sitzungsberichte. Jahrgang 2000, Heft 6. Munich: Verlag der
                Bayerischen Akademie der Wissenschaften.

2007a   *Early Ancient Near Eastern Law: A History of Its Beginnings; The Early Dynastic
                and Sargonic Periods.* Winona Lake: Eisenbrauns.

2007b   "Markt und Arbeit im Alten Orient am Ende des 3. Jahrtausend v. Chr." In
                Menschen und Märkte: Studien zur historischen Wirtschaftsanthropologie, edi-
                ted by W. Reinhard and J. Stagl, pp. 71–132. Veröffentlichungen des Instituts für
                Historische Anthropologie e.V. 9. Wien – Köln – Weimar: Böhlau.

2008   "Der Kauf von Gütern durch den 'staatlichen' Haushalt der Provinz Umma zur Zeit
                der III. Dynastie von Ur: Ein Beitrag zu 'Markt und Arbeit im Alten Orient am
                Ende des 3. Jahrtausends vor Christus.'" In *On the Third Dynasty of Ur: Studies in
                Honor of Marcel Sigrist*, edited by P. Michalowski, pp. 261–85. Journal of Cuneiform
                Studies Supplement Series 1. Boston: American Schools of Oriental Research.

Wu Yuhong
    2003   "The Nippur Bankers' Archives during the Ur III Period." *Journal of Ancient Civilizations* 18: 23–52.

3
A LIFE-COURSE APPROACH TO HOUSEHOLD SLAVES IN THE LATE THIRD MILLENNIUM B.C.

LAURA CULBERTSON*

Despite the frozen social and legal taxonomies of the cuneiform record, slavery in Mesopotamian societies was not an absolute category. Rather, it was "a more diffuse and malleable, less crisply decisive act" (Adams 2010: 2.6; see also Diakonoff 1987). Because of the fixity of terminology, however, learning about slavery beyond the level of linguistics, paleography, and legal language is difficult if not prohibitive in many contexts. The impressive temporal and regional consistency of Sumerian terms such as arad and geme, words we translate as male and female slave respectively, suggests that slavery was a well-defined practice, standardized, and a permanent social category. But society changes regardless of the persistence of writing conventions, requiring historians to question static or inflexible characterizations and definitions of slavery while seeking methods of recovering the dynamics of enslaved people in context. In this chapter I examine the complexities of enslavement trajectories during a short, half-century window of documentation by adopting a life-course approach to household slavery.

Sumerian legal, administrative, and economic documents from the twenty-first century B.C. in Mesopotamia, more specifically from the period known as the Third Dynasty of Ur (henceforth Ur III), constitute a prodigious body of textual sources that reference facets of daily economic life, making reference to slaves. The historical setting from which our sources originate is a century of rapid political change. In southern Mesopotamia, the twenty-first century B.C. witnessed a unification of city-states by the kings of Ur, Ur-Namma and his son Šulgi. The degree to which this centralization affected local politics and society is debatable, complicated by the uneven coverage of written evidence. The nature of the ensuing, short-lived polity consequently also remains the subject of debate. This polity was organized into provinces with capital cities. At the core of the state, the provincial cities housed networks of wealthy households of elites who held important institutional titles and affiliations. Specialists suspect that the kings of Ur did implement some unifying administrative practices and economic patterns, at least affecting local record-keeping practices in different provinces. Midway through the forty-eight-year reign of Shulgi, about halfway through this political experiment, an explosion of cuneiform documentation occurred in the provincial cities of the Ur III heartland. Most of the documentation selected for this study originated during the reigns of Šulgi's sons and successors, the kings Amar-Sin and Šu-Sin, dating to a roughly twenty-year window. Textual production declined in the early years of their successor, the final king

* This paper is modified from the original version presented at the seminar entitled, "Un-free Children of Elite Households in Early Mesopotamia." I wish to thank Andrea Seri, Kathryn Babayan, Martha Roth, and JoAnn Scurlock for their comments about this paper at the seminar and in various phases of its progress. I also thank Gil Stein for encouraging the "life-course" idea and giving the paper a new angle.

Ibbi-Sin, shortly before the poorly understood and unevenly documented disintegration of the state at the end of the century.

These historical, political, and administrative circumstances result in a uniquely high volume of documents covering a short period of several decades, barely one generation, presenting an opportunity for microscopic examination of slavery during a restricted moment in history. The cuneiform documents used for this study primarily concern economic and administrative activities of the affairs of elite, private citizens with institutional affiliations and titles. In the provincial capital cities of Umma and Lagash, for example, documents show that the urban elites, including members of the households of governors, participated in local systems of dispute resolution, negotiating professional and household investments and entitlements. Because the results of resolution proceedings affected networks of relationships, these resolution systems can be considered local political orders, reflecting the ever-shifting distribution of power among the urban community (Culbertson 2009). Even though most elites engaged in a range of activities and businesses during this period, the administrative and legal language of documents condenses information, collapsing many aspects of social life and interactions into succinct reports. The documents are abbreviated, formulaic records of brief flashes of events, largely reflecting the interests and objectives of urban elites and their household assets. For this reason, social and political dynamics during this period, such as those between slaves and households, are difficult to reconstruct.

One traditional method of studying slavery using legal sources from the cuneiform world, which we may call the synthetic approach (VerSteeg 2000), involves identifying attestations of the terminology associated with slavery in the documents and compiling the attestations into surveys. Syntheses of these data may be organized according to a legal question (e.g., sale, manumission, marriage), a type of source (e.g., Law Code entry, receipt, letter, court record), or chronology.[1] Scholars, linguists, and historians can use the synthesis of data and attestations to make inferences about the terminology or legal question under investigation, or locate analytical problems by noting gaps, inconsistencies, and idiosyncrasies. Importantly, information compiled in a synthetic approach can be distilled into definitions or descriptions about the legal and economic context of enslaved people, allowing scholars to overview the possible range of attested activities associated with slaves in particular contexts. This approach is additionally invaluable for tracing the longevity and expanse of written traditions across time and place.

Despite the profitable findings of synthetic studies of slavery, a danger of flattening persists. Even if administrative and legal terminology retain a common standardization across time or across a politically or culturally unified region, society and the personal relationships operating within it cannot be standardized to such an extent. Words such as arad and geme last for centuries but meanings and contexts change, and the ascription of a legal designation (e.g., "slave") to a person in an economic or legal record may thus have little reflection of daily interactions. As Adams has recently put it, "the inclusion of an individual in the formal slave category might or might not establish that individual's breadth of prescribed activities, treatment, or even social position" (2010: 2.3). The synthetic approach can focus on individuals only in the moment reported by a single document or legal problem and cannot explore variations and idiosyncrasies in matters such as how people entered or exited enslavement. As

---

[1] Invaluable examples containing this approach can be found in VerSteeg 2000; Westbrook 1995 and 1998; and Wilcke 2007: 53–58.

a result, slavery is condensed to one social category, generalized from terminology and from the empirical observation that slaves are listed in the records in connection with an owner or overseer, and therefore slavery must be a generally downward experience.

To further understand what household slavery looked like in the Ur III period, how this status, predicament, or transition was established or transmuted, and how the wider context of private household politics and dynamics figured into the process, I propose to experiment with a life-course approach to household slavery. A life-course approach (taking inspiration from Manning 1990: 113) focuses on the transitional moments in a person's life and involves compiling series of transitions into larger chronologies. Using the approach, we can highlight the varieties of slavery, leaving a bit more room to notice the mutable aspects as well as the permanent. The life-course approach looks at events in people's lives using multiple kinds of documents to map out the range of possible courses intersecting with the key moments captured by the written records. These include the creation of enslavement through sale, transfer, manumission, and any other inferred or mentioned events occurring before, between, or after these phases. To gain a meaningful perspective on these events in the lives of the enslaved, we can align life-courses with the events and transitional moments of households, finding pivotal correspondences between the two. In short, instead of defining slavery by the use of legal terminology and reconstructing information about slavery from single terms or formulae, the life-course approach allows consideration of slavery as "an interactional process," to use one aspect of Orlando Patterson's definition (1982: 13). As is already known, people enslaved in elite Ur III households were often not born into slavery, nor did persons who were born into household enslavement necessarily remain slaves for the duration of their lives, nor did all slaves of private households die in slavery. Collecting a range of life-courses will help us better understand these variables.

The life-course approach first involves a reassessment of how to look for slavery in the documentation given its limitations and problems. Ideally, we would have numerous forms of documentation detailing the vagaries of every life trajectory, but such comprehensive documentation is lacking for any person who lived during the twenty-first century B.C., let alone any enslaved person. Access to life details about household slaves, outside of the parts of their lives spent in slavery, are generally non-existent and must be inferred or reconstructed from sources if pertinent information is provided. Not all documents mentioning slaves can fruitfully be included in this approach if they do not provide contextual information about the enslaved person or people in question. Prosopographical research allows the tracing of individual people across multiple texts in a few instances, but enslaved people are rarely identified by name in more than one document. We are thus woefully reliant on textual synthesis, survey, and description, but the comparison of multiple categories of documentation, telling about multiple stages of enslavement, opens up different views and allows us to approach slavery as a process.

For the sake of manageability in this short contribution, the discussion is restricted to instances of children or unmarried young adults who were sold into slavery by their parents or family members. This is the form of enslavement creation for which we have the most evidence, with multiple types of documentation referencing the events surrounding the sale and enslavement, providing a longer picture. These principal sources are sale documents and court records, both of which bring limitations and benefits. Importantly, both types of documents deal with transitional moments for both slaves and households. Sale documents record the moment of a person's enslavement and his or her transfer between households, reported in the context of an economic transaction between two parties. A sale itself may represent the fragmentation of the household from which the enslaved child came. The persons sold, exchanged, or enslaved via these transactions were often children or unmarried young adults. Extraction of generalizations about the nature of slavery from these documents alone has been justifiably avoided for two reasons. First, the moment of sale or exchange constitutes only one moment out of the term of enslavement, and second, we can safely assume that the newly enslaved children and young adults grew up and experienced other things beyond the single moment of sale.

Slaves are also mentioned in court records, the second type of documentation consulted for this study. Court records are reports about the dispute resolution proceedings of urban elites. Household turmoil and transition were often the catalyst for such disputes. At these occasions, enslaved household members could exploit status ambiguities and household fractures to argue for release, sometimes changing the course of their enslavement. Because the court records make reference to past events and time, we can deduce the length of enslavement for certain people or infer the origins of their enslavement.

It is often said that Ur III society was rigidly hierarchical, offering few opportunities for mobility, even among free persons. A life-course examination of sale documents and court records, however, shows that slaves did travel through different social contexts over the course of their lives, for better or worse, and by tracing these paths we find that the very sale and enslavement of children and adults could send them in a variety of directions. While some slaves spent the duration of their enslavement, and possibly lives, protesting their status, there is evidence that others remained in their owner's household. In either case, household slaves enjoyed social privileges and affiliations not accessible to most members Ur III society, including access to court.

As Neumann has overviewed (this volume), the households of Ur III elites were multifaceted and complex.[2] In addition to the household family, which could consist of a household head, his wife, their children from one or multiple marriages, and sometimes their siblings, each household could also host a combination of house-born slaves and their offspring, purchased male and female slave children, and other kinds of tenants, employees, laborers, and subordinates. The mixed make-up of these environments meant potential for interactions between persons of different statuses and backgrounds on a daily basis, and suggests that the experience of slavery in a household was conditioned by a variety of variables, contingencies, and relationships, even if we know little about the degree of harmony or discord among household members. This preliminary application of the life-course approach will show that the lives of slaves in households followed no single trajectory and a variety of conditions, circumstances, and contingencies must have factored into these situations.

SALE DOCUMENTS: CHILDREN INTO SLAVES

We start with the issue of how people entered into elite households as slaves, either by birth to enslaved parents or by sale from their parents. It should be noted before embarking on this topic that "child slavery" is not a viable concept for studies of early Mesopotamian societies. The study of "child slaves" in specific societies is a productive branch of slave studies, warranting specific theoretical examination of children in slavery after other groups (e.g., women) have been isolated for study, reducing the emphasis of slave studies away

---

[2] I refrain from offering a composite or archetype
household structure model to avoid generalization.

from the long-standing focus on adult men (Campbell, Miers, and Miller 2009: 1–18). While many societies and historical contexts offer suitable justification for positing a phenomenon of slavery specific to children,[3] a study of "Ur III child slavery" does not qualify because children in this period were neither a legal category nor a specific segment of the labor force that could be isolated into a single category. These points are only worth mentioning to preface the argument that the courses traveled by enslaved children in Ur III households were predicated upon the events, decisions, and circumstances of their families and the households to which they belonged, and were not predetermined by rigidly demarcated economic or legal classifications based on concepts of child or minority status.

Enslaved and low-ranking non-slave children in Ur III sources were a substantial part of the manual workforce. It is well known, for example, that women and children comprised the backbone of the textile industry (Waetzoldt 1972). Many thousands of children are mentioned in labor rosters and ration records of institutions, listed as recipients of subsistence rations disbursed to laborers. These children, often identifiable as children because of the reduced quantities of subsistence rations they received relative to adults, were listed in ration records alongside their parents or as groups of siblings. Children could also be listed without mention of having families, or as groups of nameless, orphaned boys who were seized and forced to work for a temple institution.[4] However, non-slave children appear in these administrative records in the same fashion, receiving remunerations for menial labor performed alongside their parents or other adults. Determining whether administrative rosters are dealing with slaves or dependent but essentially "free" laborers is difficult.[5] In either case, most of the administrative sources from the third millennium B.C. do not unambiguously demarcate a labor force specific to children, indicating rather that free and un-free families performed the same unskilled jobs for comparable rates, side by side (Studevent-Hickman 2006: 137, 161ff.).

Legal sources from Ur III society also did not postulate a formal category for children, nor do they suggest a category akin to the concept of minority. In practice, children were the property of their parents, whose socioeconomic status they typically inherited. The rights parents held over their children are evidenced by the reality that both poor and wealthy parents were entitled to sell their offspring in a financial crisis. Within the households, children of household slaves were considered the property of the household owner, his wife, or his heirs, inheriting the status of their parents. Given all these issues, I use the term "child" to indicate an unmarried dependent who lived with his or her parent(s).

Children entered household slavery by birth or sale. Ur III sources make a terminological distinction between house-born and purchased slaves, but usually not in the context of court records or sale documents. Children born to household slaves were legally considered the property of the household head, who theoretically retained rights to sell or free them. This right was often challenged at certain phases of the child's life or the household's history, as is discussed in the following section.

In the context of insurmountable financial crisis, debt, or obligation, enslavement could be established to address the situation. In some instances people sold themselves into slavery to mitigate their debts (e.g., *NG* 38), but most enslavement-sales involve children. Cases of child sale highlight the dynamics between household and families because they concern the

---

[3] See the arguments about the existence or non-existence of "child slavery" in Roman society offered in Laes 2006.

[4] For example, on the dumu-dab$_5$-ba "seized children," see Gelb 1979 or Heimpel 2009.

[5] See Tenney's discussion of this problem in this volume.

physical and legal transfer of a child from his or her blood family to a new household. Other than marriage, this was another means in Ur III society by which a person was separated from blood relatives and attached to a new family. As indicated above, enslaved families in institutional slavery were more often kept together,[6] while children without families, having been abandoned or orphaned, worked in labor gangs under the authority of institutional overseers and officials.

The records of sale-enslavements, including contracts and receipts, provide only the most basic of information about these transactions and leave aside the matters of circumstances, motivations, and the respective assumptions of buyers and sellers. The records are written with the interests of the buyers in mind, and, despite any illusion of their formulaic, legal character, they cannot be approached as neutral compositions equally representing the interests of all parties. Steinkeller (1989: 8ff.) has already outlined the formulary of Ur III sale documents and discussed the problems of identifying patterns in their construction, but a brief summary is useful here. Sale documents regarding household slaves always provide (1) an identification of the slave by name and blood parentage, the name of the buyer, and the name of the seller; (2) the price of the slave; (3) an indication of the status of the payment; (4) the names of witnesses to the sale and authorizing officials, if present; and (5) the date. The documents may additionally provide some combination of the following information: (6) a no-contest clause, in which either the seller promises not to deny or contest the sale at a later date or both buyer and seller reciprocally promise not to overturn the sale; (7) a record of any oaths taken to bolster such clauses or cement the sale; (8) a legal clause referring to symbolic or ritual acts performed at the time of the sale; (9) highly abbreviated summaries of any terms and conditions about the sale or the duration of enslavement; and (10) the name of a guarantor who was present for the sale. Thus the bulk of information on these tablets concerns names of participants and clauses protecting the buyer's investment, while little or no information concerning the characteristics or condition of the slave or specific circumstances leading to their sale are provided. Consistent with the general nature of Ur III sale records, records of slave sales presuppose that the sale was a completed, irreversible transaction.

Despite the limitations of these documents, we can reconstruct a preliminary picture of the events surrounding the sale of children, the context in which this occurred, the creation of enslavement, and transference to a new household. According to records of non-institutional slave transactions, parents pledged or sold members of the family when faced with financial emergency, and they most often selected their unmarried, especially female, children. Loan contracts show that parents pledged specific children as collateral for advances; court records indicate that creditors could and did lay claim to pledged children, taking them into their own households, when the conditions of a contract were breached.[7] In other situations, indebted men and women made contractual agreements with their creditors to temporarily loan children to work off the debt over a fixed amount of time (e.g., Molina 2008: no. 2). Some documents explicitly state that the child was purchased to perform domestic tasks for his or her owners (e.g., UET 3 51). In a presumably more permanent transaction, a parent could sell members

---

[6] On the evidence of laborers as families, see Studevent-Hickman 2006: 137, 161ff. See also, for examples of sources, *Iraq* 41 125 2 (record of various marsh workers employed by a temple, listing groups of up to three sisters, organized by the siblings' patronymic) or the document MVN 6 538.

[7] Examples of these lawsuits are found in the documents *NG* 35, in which the disputant is a girl sold by her mother, *NG* 37, in which a litigant is a girl sold by her father, and *NG* 204, concerning a father who sold his daughter.

of the family outright and collect payment in exchange. In general, the sale of children into slavery is largely associated with financial upheaval adversely affecting a household and requiring parents to implicate their children in resolving the obligation or debt. Thus two asymmetrically linked households were involved in these transactions in some manner.

Both mothers and fathers sold their children in the Ur III period. In the cases of mothers, there is too little evidence to determine if these sellers were widowed or perhaps forced into hardship after abandonment, but the possibility exists.[8] According to one court record (*NG* 44), a woman disputed the enslavement of her whole family, husband included, suggesting that women played a decisive role in matters of slavery, even if married (Siegel 1947: 13). Siblings and grandparents are also attested as having sold female children; one document (*NG* 55) reports that a grandmother participated in the sale of her female grandchild. We may surmise that the father is deceased or absent in these cases, but the circumstances are regrettably unclear (see Siegel 1947: 23).

Even though sale records report the name of parents and sellers, few of these people are identifiable through prosopographical investigation, further obstructing an understanding of the circumstances and contexts of child sales. Several documents contain seal impressions of the mother or father (e.g., FAOS 17 23, 46, 49, and 78) suggesting that the sellers in these instances had socially recognized institutional affiliations and titles, even if their names are untraceable to us now. This indicates that not all families who sold children were always impoverished and lowly. By contrast, some buyers can be identified owing to a prodigious presence in the Ur III legal and economic documentation, including the well-known entrepreneur SI.A-a to name but one example.

The sale itself was a formal event that usually took place at the household of the buyer (Steinkeller 1989: 41). The transaction involved the physical participation of the sellers or parents, multiple witnesses, and a person who would act as a guarantor.[9] The purpose of this temporary function of guarantor is never made explicit, but from the sources we can infer that he or she was somebody who vouched for availability of the child, especially promising that the child had not been pledged to another party. The guarantor also acted as a hypothetical co-seller, inasmuch as he or she could be implicated along with the seller in the event of any conflict following the sale. Often the guarantor belonged to the nuclear family of the child, perhaps a parent or sibling (e.g., FAOS 17 46) who promised to personally replace the child as a slave in the event that another household issued a claim. Guarantors are less frequently named in sale records involving adults or persons who were already enslaved before the time of sale, as far as can be determined from the available evidence. The function appears to be associated with sales involving the creation of slavery and is thus restricted to the sale of children or unmarried young women, who, legally speaking, had the same status as children.[10] The need for such a function in the sale of children and unmarried women also perhaps suggests that child sale was not an option to most debt-ridden families and occurred only under very specific circumstances. Presumably, buyers and creditors were wary of buying a child

---

[8] Receipts of sale by mother: FAOS 17 42, 46, 49. Disputes involving the sale of children by the mother: *NG* 35, 53, 55.

[9] Sumerian lu$_2$-gi-na-ab-tum$_2$, on which see Falkenstein 1956–57: vol. 1, p. 126; Steinkeller 1989: 80–90 and his commentary on text 127.

[10] See FAOS 17 25 and 33 (involving the sale of an unmarried woman). FOAS 17 33 includes gab$_2$-gi-in sag-kam "guarantor of the slave," the function of which is unclear. Steinkeller (1989) renders the term, "guarantor of the head," understanding sag as "head" rather than "slave" and perhaps alluding to the guarantor's job of attesting to the quality and health of the slave.

from a family in dire financial circumstances given the likelihood that other creditors might attempt to claim the child.

At the event of sale, payment for the new slave was made in full, with occasional exceptions.[11] Ownership of the child, and the child him- or herself, was then transferred or delivered to the buyer and his household. Ritual acts accompanied this phase of the sale and symbolized the physical transfer of the slave to the new household. One sale receipt from the city of Nippur uses an expression of legal symbolism, stating that the buyer made the enslaved girl "cross a wooden pestle," representing the full transfer.[12] Indeed, many of these sales did involve the crossing of socioeconomic and political boundaries for these children from an insolvent house to one with the means and standing to collect.

The sale records imply that, at some moment during the transaction, the parties swore oaths promising not to contest the status and transfer of the child in the future. When the sale activity was complete, a document was drawn up to record the pertinent information and the transaction was theoretically complete. Unless specific provisions were drafted to release the child at a certain time, any children born of the slave would traditionally be considered the property of the buyer and his household. Many of the documented slaves did eventually bear children. In the case of young women, it is likely that the children were fathered by the household head himself, evidenced by cases in which slave women and household heirs disputed the status of her children after the death of the household head (see below).

A final observation about sale records is that the contracts pertaining to child sales imply a buyer's indifference about the child personally, which by extension indicates a dislocation between the child and his or her ability to perform service for the household from the buyer's point of view. For example, a sale document from Nippur reports that a girl named Allani was sold into enslavement for 5 shekels by her brothers. The document stipulates, "they (i.e., her brothers) will be enslaved if she ceases to work" (FAOS 17 45). Despite being named in the document, the girl was regarded as interchangeable by her new owner, at least at the time of sale or from the point of view represented in the document.

In summation, records of child sales suggest that enslavement could emerge from two situations aside from birth. In the first case, parents sold or pledged children when the household encountered a financial emergency, seeking a remedy by turning to another household to make the sale or collected an advance. In the second, children were implicated in enslavement when members of two different households engaged in financial or business relationships and one party could not uphold his or her side of the contract. The records of child sales indicate that the sale of children and young adults was a one-way and permanent transaction, severing the blood ties of the children, stripping them of their birth status and family affiliations, and transforming them and any potential offspring into what we might call household "chattel." If we continue to trace the life-courses of people pledged or sold into enslavement and supplement this picture with the information from court records, we discover a more complicated picture of slavery.

---

[11] FAOS 17 25 deals with the sale of a young, unmarried woman, stating that, "out of the price, 2 shekels are paid" (line 7). The court records *NG* 176 cases 1 and 2 deal with settled disputes over the non-payment of money for slaves. See also *NG* 63, 65, 66, 131, and 207 case 1, for other examples from Girsu, and *NG* 48, 49, 51, and Molina 2008: no. 9 for examples from Umma.

[12] FAOS 17 41 line 8: giš gin₇ i₃-na-ra-bala. The document reports the sale of an unmarried woman, with a guarantor present. See Steinkeller 1989: 34ff. on this clause, which appears in a number of slave sales.

COURT RECORDS AND CONTESTATIONS OF LIFE-COURSES

Court records from the Ur III period contain summaries of public proceedings during which disputing urban elites presented cases before third parties in pursuit of resolution or settlement. Like the sale records, these documents strictly adhere to an administrative template, presenting the following sets of information in part or full: (1) the names of disputants; (2) the object, person, or entitlement under dispute and stock declarations or statements made by the disputants; (3) the prehistory of the case, with mention of earlier court sessions, events, or transactions; (4) the evidentiary measures presented by the winning party; (5) a decision or settlement, if one was reached; (6) provisions or stipulations about the settlement; (7) oaths, usually cementing promises among the parties not to return to court again; (8) lists of officiating parties, including judges and other high-ranking figures from urban society; and (9) the date.[13]

Of course, court records pose the same limitations as sale records, reporting only brief periods of activity out of what were often prolonged, labored conflicts and cumbersome household or family transitions. Disputes could persist for decades, with disputants resurfacing in courts multiple times and before several groups of arbitrators in pursuit of resolution or a confirmation of conditions. Although conflicting perspectives are evident in the dispute and audit records, the presentation of information in court records is one-sided, with emphasis on the party who won the case. The scribes who composed these records reduced complex networks of people and interests to basic casts of characters, conflating elaborate conflicts into stock paradigms of buyer versus seller, slave versus master, or brother versus brother. Consequently, the ambiguities and events that sparked disputation are not readily apparent in the documents and must be inferred by a close reading of the case and the references to past proceedings and events.

Judging from past events mentioned in the texts, many disputes emerged within the context of public audits of massive household estates.[14] Both dispute proceedings and household audits corresponded to household transition or turmoil, death of the household head, financial emergency, or other kinds of crises that demanded evaluation of the household assets and a public clarification about the precise status and entitlements of household members, including the slaves. Resolution and audit proceedings were therefore consequential social acts by which household members or assets were reconfigured, dissolved, or dispersed into new households.

Among the issues of contention during household transitions and disputes were slaves. Despite the unambiguous language and finality expressed in sale records, ensuing confusion and controversy about the exact terms and conditions of slave sales seems to have been common because the majority of documented court cases from this period — possibly upwards of 65 percent (Culbertson 2009) — deals with disputes about the status, sale, and ownership of domestic slaves.[15] The court documents provide a partial view of what happened to children who were born or sold into enslavement with private households, showing that a variety of conditions and social courses could result from household enslavement. Broadly speaking, slaves appear in two capacities in the documents of relevance to our discussion.

---

[13] Overviews of Ur III records and their construction are available in Falkenstein 1956–57; Molina 2000; and more recently Culbertson 2009 for a full list of publications.

[14] Examples include *NG* 99, 211, and 213.

[15] See Falkenstein 1956–57: vol. 1. This high percentage is partially explained by the fact that there are no lawsuits or court records dealing with immovable property, which predominate in records from the adjacent Sargonic and Old Babylonian periods.

In the first situation, slaves were implicated in court proceedings as the subject of disputes between two or more elites, such as a buyer and seller from different households or between siblings from the same household who stood to inherit after the death of their mother or father. Despite the fact that people retained written records of sales and contractual agreements about the slaves, the court records indicate frequent disagreement and misunderstanding over the terms of sales. Amid the confusion, parties present for sale transactions and oaths, including guarantors, reconvened before judges to argue about the legitimacy and conditions of enslavement.[16] In some disputes, the point of conflicts was whether the sale or payment occurred (e.g., *NG* 196 case 1; see also Molina 2008: no. 10), or whether the slave was delivered to the new household after the payment was made. Court proceedings were used to establish that both payment and delivery occurred in attempt to prevent further claims and misunderstandings (e.g., *NG* 176 case 2 or *NG* 207 case 1).

As sellers, blood parents of enslaved children attempted to retract the sale of their children or claim that they never received payment. For example, *NG* 45 reports that a woman appeared before judges and denied selling her daughter and receiving 5 shekels in payment, but witnesses and written documentation overturned her claim; the judges made the woman swear an oath promising not to claim her daughter again. *NG* 47 similarly reports that a man named Kamu denied receiving 6 shekels as payment for his daughter,[17] but the verdict of the case is broken. In the court record *NG* 48, from Umma, a man denied selling his son for the relatively small amount of 2/3 shekels of silver eight years after the fact, but the court denied the claim for unspecified reasons.

At stake in some disputes was the matter of whether enslavement explicitly involved labor, the requirement to work off a fixed amount of debt, permanent residency in the household as a dependent, unfree servant, or ongoing performance of some other unspecified function (*NG* 7; Sigrist 1995: 612 and no. 2). For example, one dispute record reports that, even though a young enslaved woman somehow paid off her debt and was therefore relieved of enslavement, she was still to remain attached to the household in a transitional status while performing domestic service until her owner's death.[18] The case reported in Molina 2008: no. 2 indicates that a woman left her enslavement without completing her term and headed to another household. The sellers therefore had to refund the 5 shekels paid for her. The death of the household head who purchased the slave was of central concern to this question as many disputes center upon the question of whether the enslaved child was designated to remain in the household until the owner died (e.g., *NG* 58).

Disputes among family members about the inheritance of household slaves are also among the cases concerning slaves. In attested cases, widows fought their sons, daughters, or stepchildren over who would inherit the slaves of the deceased husband/father (*NG* 28), and one case involves investigation of which person bought the slave (*NG* 99).

In the second situation under which slaves appear in court records, slaves are actors in the dispute, appearing in court on their own behalf. Disputes over the inheritance patterns of slaves and their children were common and surfaced in court upon household transitions brought on by the death of the household head. *NG* 7, 33, and 34, for example, involve disputes

---

[16] In *NG* 45, in which the sale record is produced in court to demonstrate the existence of sale witnesses followed by the summoning of those witnesses, and Molina 2008: no. 8; see also ibid., no. 3 for a registration of the death of the guarantor, possibly drafted in anticipation of future conflict.

[17] Probably five to six years before, given the partial names of judges in lines 10–11 who were prevalent during the middle of Šhu-Sin's reign (Culbertson 2009: 127).

[18] UET 3 51. On this matter, see Falkenstein 1956–57: vol. 1, p. 95. See Kleber's discussion of *paramone*, this volume.

between slaves and their masters' heirs. In these examples, male and female slaves argued before judges that they were to have been freed upon their master's death, but were unable to corroborate their claims (via witnesses or written documents) in order to prove that their owner had indeed provided freedom upon his death. In similar cases resulting from the death of the household father, widows were prompted to dispute their husband's heirs over the fate of household slaves (e.g., *NG* 7, 28, 83, 99), usually implicating witnesses to the purchase of the slaves or agreements struck with the household head over inheritance plans.

In *NG* 37, an allegedly enslaved girl named Ninzagesi pled before judges that her father did not sell her. The girl was confirmed to enslavement after witnesses contradicted her testimony and her owner swore an oath declaring that the sale took place. Similarly, *NG* 35 reports that a girl named Etamuzu challenged her enslavement to the household of a high-ranking cook, reportedly stating, "I am not your slave-girl (geme)" before the judges (line 9), only to be contradicted by her mother, Atu, who also attended the proceedings and corroborated the sale of her daughter (see *NG* 36 for a similar case).

Several court records contain stock first-person denunciations of personal enslavement, purporting to give the voice of a disputing slave with the construction: "The slave so-and-so appeared before judges and said, 'I am not a slave'" or "I am not so-and-so's slave."[19] These declarations are intriguing given that the entitlement to participate in the urban court system as a disputant was not guaranteed to all members of Ur III provincial communities, let alone to slaves. Whether or not these slaves were indeed afforded the opportunity to represent him- or herself in real-life proceedings will remain unknown to us; both the Ur III dispute resolution system and the textual documentation it yielded were intended to protect the interests of elites. Yet there are several references in the court records to slaves who claim to possess sale records or other forms of written proof attesting to the conditions of their enslavement, and there is at least one case in which a slave girl actually produces a document in court (*NG* 205; see also Sigrist 1995: no. 1).

Many documented court sessions occurred long after the sale and, in many instances, the slave must have become a grown adult by the time they appeared before judges. The court records make reference to the dates of these alleged sales, and, in a few instances where dates are cited we can reconstruct the amount of time elapsed since the child was sold or enslavement was established:[20]

Court Record	*Documented Period of Contested Enslavement*
NG 31	20 years
NG 34	15 years
NG 41	5 years
NG 48	8 years
NG 65	10 years
NG 67	6 years
NG 70	4 years?
NG 71	13–14 years
NG 88	10 years
NG 192	20 years
NG 205 case 1	36 years

---

[19] *NG* 32, 33, 34, 35; BM 106451; and Sigrist 1995: no. 1.

[20] *NG* 41 deals with enslavement as punishment for murder, not sale.

It should be noted that these figures represent only the time elapsed between the cited date of the sale and the cited date of the specific court document that concerns a dispute over the sale. The actual duration of enslavement, conflict, or ambiguity may have been much longer than these figures admit. In most of these cases, the lag between sale and disputes represents the time between initial acquisition of the slave and the death of his or her buyer. In the context of public disputes and audits and corresponding upheaval of the household and competition among members, enslaved members of the household seized opportunity to contest their enslavement, to varying degrees of success. The death of the household head prompted slave and non-slave family members to determine inheritance patterns and articulate the precise ownership of the household assets, including the slaves. This must be the case with Irišaga, an enslaved man who was purchased and then given to the buyer's son. Thirty-six years later, the buyer having died, his other children sued their brother for rights over Irišaga, taking the matter before governors at least three times before they were finally compelled to cease (as far as we know). In other situations, the conflict seems to have been ongoing over the years, as in the case of the male slave Ahuma, who is cited as having protested his enslavement in court at least three times (see *NG* 33 and 34) over a course of more than fifteen years.

It seems facile and anachronistic to assume that enslaved disputants spent years contesting their enslavement in pursuit of an abstract notion of "freedom." A variety of other reasons for contestation can be hypothesized. For example, some enslaved people seem to have retained the identity of their former household even after sale or transfer, possibly harboring connections to their blood families for decades after the separation. The court records indicate an ambiguity of slave status, identifying household slaves according to their blood parents (i.e., sellers), often[21] providing patronymics of male slaves even if also identifying the owner. Ahuma, for example, is called "Ahuma son of Lumarza, slave (arad) of Kudamartu" (*NG* 33). Female slaves are given a partronymic if their father is alive; if a mother sold her daughter, no patronymic appears in the court records and the relationship is only clear by context. In addition to maintaining previous social and legal identities, other bonds may account for the motivation to leave enslavement. One court record involves a young man's unsuccessful attempt to free his enslaved sister, implying that familial ties were not severed during the sale (Molina 2008: no. 7).

In addition to disputation in court, another manifestation of confusion over the nature and terms of enslavement involves escape. Court records make reference to slaves who fled house, city, and region, and one court record reports that a man escaped as far away as Anshan in Iran, where he was found and captured (Molina 2008: no. 4). Other cases of flight are less extreme and involve situations in which the slave simply left the household under the impression that his or her service had been completed or was supposed to be temporary (Molina 2008: no. 2). Escaped slaves were returned if found, and court proceedings solidified the (re)enslavement before the community. Clearly, many purchased domestic slaves at least fostered an expectation of return and there were different methods for pursuing freedom.

Returning to the issue of house-born slaves, children of enslaved parents were also considered slaves. Despite having been born into the status, children of household slaves nonetheless contested their enslavement in court and this was also undertaken when the household head died. The results of these cases varied. In one case, for example, a male slave lost the dispute because, according to the document, he was born and raised in the household (*NG* 32). In other similar situations, the children of purchased slaves were freed as a result of a plea in

---

[21] Not always: *NG* 45.

court (e.g., *NG* 99, *NG* 205 case 3, and Molina 2008: no. 5). Among these instances, however, the parents of the newly freed children were rarely freed as well, and thus the group remains with the elite household as a subsidiary family of mixed statuses.

Not all enslavements involved futile attempts to detach from a household. Children sold to private households could reach eventual release, and several records attest to the termination of slave status. One record indicates that a slave was ultimately returned to his or her parent's household while still a child (e.g., Molina 2008: no. 5). In other situations, however, the released slave was awarded the status of a freeborn adult. In *NG* 75, for example, an adult man named Ursagub and his children are declared free before the court and community, and the text explicitly states that Ursagub is "returned" to the status of a free citizen (see also *NG* 76).[22] In other examples of this kind of "manumission," the freed slave remains in his master's household, where he is regarded as eligible for inheritance of household property upon the death of its head.

CONCLUSIONS

Reading two corpuses of sources against one another, on the basis of these piecemeal excerpts of enslavement, we find that the initial enslavement-through-sale of young, unmarried individuals could result in years of uncertainty, resistance, and dispute. Misunderstandings about the fate of household slaves is evident in the exhaustively preemptive language of the sale documents, while records of court proceedings confirm that disagreement was nonetheless frequent, not only among slaves and owners but also among non-slave household members.

Some enslavements ended with the transformation of the slave into a semi-free member of the household or a free person who was eligible to start a new household. It is not possible, given all these examples and possible results of enslavement, to characterize the sale of individuals into slavery as a full "social death," as Orlando Patterson (1982) claimed. That is, household enslavement did not necessarily entail the loss of family ties, identity, social affiliations and opportunity, and honor, as demonstrated by the court documents discussed here. While the condition of household enslavement did not guarantee upward mobility, it did afford slaves the opportunity to participate in a restricted court system and occasionally led to a non-slave status with elite affiliations. Above all, the sale of children into slavery could propel the slave through different social contexts over the course of his or her enslavement, and in some situations, the slave had a degree of control over their fate if he or she seized opportunity to argue in court at key moments in the household's history. In short, the different paths taken by un-free children in elite households were varied and defy any universal characterizations.

A number of variables and conditions seemed to have directed the course of the household slave. On the one hand, the sale of a child to an elite household meant the slave had a protected status, which could be extended to the offspring of the child in later years, as a confirmed member of a household. For some household slaves, this affiliation granted access to judges and the entitlement to plead cases in court. Occasionally this participation resulted in the release of the slave and/or his or her children, a break from the normal inheritance pattern. On the other hand, the sale of a child entailed the potentially traumatic separation of a child

---

[22] *NG* 75 lines 22–23, literally, "as if he is 'returned to the previous status of freeborn.'" On this terminology, see Lafont and Westbrook 2003: 197.

from their blood family, accompanied by a loss of inheritance rights, and, one must assume, possible exposure to abuse or violence.

Given that many children were sold in the context of financial crisis, their fate may have been improved through their sale. The idea of an unsettling double potential of child domestic slavery — that is, possible abuse, degradation, and social death, versus possible mobility, safety, or opportunity — can be detected in ancient and modern records about domestic slavery in a variety of contexts, from debates about whether the *mui tsai* (female domestic slaves) custom in Hong Kong represents the enslavement of girls or a philanthropic tradition that saves them from poverty and social oblivion,[23] to debates about brutal conditions and social possibilities of household slavery in ancient Rome.[24] In these cases, we find nothing short of a variety of experiences and perspectives about household slavery.

ABBREVIATIONS

BM	Signature of the British Museum, London
FAOS 17	Steinkeller 1989
Iraq 41	George 1979
MVN 6	Pettinato 1977
NG	Falkenstein 1956–57
UET 3	Legrain 1937

BIBLIOGRAPHY

Adams, Robert McC.
    2010   "Slavery and Freedom in the Third Dynasty of Ur: Implications of the Garshana Archives." *Cuneiform Digital Library Journal* 2010/2.

Campbell, Gwyn; Suzanne Miers; and Joseph C. Miller, editors
    2009   *Children in Slavery through the Ages*. Athens: Ohio University Press.

Culbertson, Laura
    2009   Dispute Resolution in the Courts of the Third Dynasty of Ur. Ph.D. dissertation, University of Michigan.

Diakonoff, Igor M.
    1987   "Slave-Labour vs. Non-Slave Labour: The Problem of Definition." In *Labor in the Ancient Near East*, edited by M. A. Powell, pp. 1–4. American Oriental Series 68. New Haven: American Oriental Society.

---

[23] Pedersen 2001; Pomfret 2008; Poon 2009. While some British imperial officials and interest groups viewed the selling of young girls into domestic service as slavery, various local officials defended the custom, arguing that it was a charitable, philanthropic tradition that offered poor girls a better life and protected status as legal members of a household. The alternative — no home and no legal status — was far worse, they argued. A web of competing interests of course informed all these perspectives, and the voices of the *mui tsai* are less represented. It is known that not all *mui tsai* were given education and a comfortable life, many of them facing abuses, violence, and restricted freedoms.

[24] Laes 2008, especially pp. 257 and 262f.

Falkenstein, Adam
  1956–57   *Die neusumerischen Gerichtsurkunden.* 3 volumes. Bayerische Akademie der Wissenschaften, Philosophisch-Historische Klasse. Abhandlungen, n.F., 39, 40, and 44. Munich: Verlag der Bayerischen Akademie der Wissenschaften.

Gelb, Ignace J.
  1979   "Definition and Discussion of Slavery and Serfdom." *Ugarit-Forschungen* 11: 283–97.

George, A. R.
  1979   "Cuneiform Texts in the Birmingham City Museum." *Iraq* 41: 121–40.

Heimpel, Wolfgang
  2009   "The Location of Madga," *Journal of Cuneiform Studies* 61: 25–62.

Laes, Christian
  2008   "Child Slaves at Work in Roman Antiquity," *Ancient Society* 38: 235–83.

Lafont, Bertrand, and Raymond Westbrook
  2003   "Neo-Sumerian Period (Ur III)." In *A History of Ancient Near Eastern Law*, Volume 1, edited by R. Westbrook, pp. 183–226. Handbook of Oriental Studies, Section One, The Near and Middle East 72. Leiden: Brill.

Legrain, Leon
  1937   *Business Documents of the Third Dynasty of Ur.* Ur Excavations, Text 3. London: Harrison & Sons.

Manning, Patrick
  1990   *Slavery and African Life: Occidental, Oriental, and African Slaves Trades.* Cambridge: Cambridge University Press.

Molina, Manuel
  2000   *La ley más antigua: Textos legales sumerios.* Pliegos de oriente, Textos 5. Madrid: Editorial Trotta.
  2008   "New Ur III Court Records Concerning Slavery." In *On the Third Dynasty of Ur: Studies in Honor of Marcel Sigrist*, edited by P. Michalowski, pp. 125–43. Journal of Cuneiform Studies Supplement Series 1. Boston: American Schools of Oriental Research.

Patterson, Orlando
  1982   *Slavery and Social Death: A Comparative Study.* Cambridge: Harvard University Press.

Pedersen, Susan
  2001   "The Maternalist Moment in British Colonial Policy: The Controversy Over 'Child Slavery' in Hong Kong 1917–1941." *Past and Present* 171: 161–202.

Pettinato, Giovanni
  1977   *Testi economici di Lagas del Museo di Istanbul*, Part 1: *La. 7001–7600*. Materiali per il vocabolario neosumerico 6. Rome: Multigrafica Editrice.

Pomfret, David M.
  2008   "'Child Slavery' in British and French Far-Eastern Colonies 1880–1945." *Past and Present* 201: 175–213.

Poon, Pauline Pui-ting
  2009   "The Well-Being of Purchased Female Domestic Servants (*mui tsai*) in Hong Kong in the Early Twentieth Century." In *Children in Slavery through the Ages*, edited by G. Campbell, S. Miers, and J. C. Miller. Athens: Ohio University Press.

Siegel, Bernard J.
  1947   *Slavery during the Third Dynasty of Ur*. Memoir Series of the American
              Anthropological Association 66. Menasha: American Anthropological Association.

Sigrist, Marcel
  1995   "Some di-til-la Tablets in the British Museum." In *Solving Riddles and Untying Knots:
              Biblical, Epigraphic, and Semitic Studies in Honor of Jonas C. Greenfield*, edited by
              Z. Zevit, S. Gitin, and M. Sokoloff, pp. 609–18. Winona Lake: Eisenbrauns.

Steinkeller, Piotr
  1989   *Sale Documents of the Ur-III Period*. Freiburger Altorientalische Studien 17. Stuttgart:
              Franz Steiner.

Studevent-Hickman, Benjamin
  2006   The Organization of Manual Labor in Ur III Babylonia. Ph.D. dissertation, Harvard
              University.

VerSteeg, Russ
  2000   *Early Mesopotamian Law*. Durham: Carolina Academic Press.

Waetzoldt, Hartmut
  1972   *Untersuchungen zur neusumerischen Textilindustrie*. Studi economici e tecnologici
              1. Rome: Istituto per l'Oriente.

Westbrook, Raymond
  1995   "Slave and Master in Ancient Near Eastern Law." *Chicago-Kent Law Review* 70:
              1631.

  1998   "The Female Slave." In *Gender and Law in the Hebrew Bible and the Ancient Near
              East*, edited by V. H. Matthews, B. M Levinson, and T. S. Frymer-Kensky, pp. 214–
              38. Journal for the Study of the Old Testament, Supplement Series 262. Sheffield:
              Sheffield Academic Press.

Wilcke, Claus
  2007   *Early Ancient Near Eastern Law: A History of Its Beginnings; The Early Dynastic
              and Sargonic Periods*. Winona Lake: Eisenbrauns.

4

DOMESTIC FEMALE SLAVES DURING THE OLD BABYLONIAN PERIOD

ANDREA SERI*

The Old Babylonian period spanned some 400 years from around 2000 to 1595 B.C. It encompassed first a number of independent kingdoms in competition with each other until King Ḫammurabi of Babylon established a hegemonic territorial state over Mesopotamia after defeating all his rivals. Problems preserving the cohesion of such an extensive realm were already apparent under his son and successor Samsu-iluna, who from as early as his eighth regnal year had to face a number of revolts in the southern and northern areas of his domain. For the Assyriologist the period is exceptional in that it is one of the best-documented epochs of ancient history. In fact, several thousand cuneiform administrative and legal tablets and letters record institutional and private transactions. This abundance of documents, however, correlates to a number of methodological problems that I mention from the outset, for they influence our interpretations of the past and of ancient slavery in particular. There is the difficulty of the uneven distribution of the evidence related in part to the fact that not all archaeological sites or levels were excavated. Perhaps the most conspicuous example of this situation is that there are few tablets from the city of Babylon, the very capital of the kingdom, because that stratigraphical layer is under phreatic water (see Klengel 1978). In addition, a great number of tablets became available through the antiquities market and any information about archaeological context or provenance is missing, whereas prosopographical analyses help reconstruct ancient archives only occasionally. But even when archival groups can be identified, their place of origin may remain unknown. Furthermore, records were discarded in antiquity when transactions had expired. We have to keep in mind, therefore, that our evidence is partial and fragmentary.

Those comments pertaining to the availability of written sources apply to all kinds of Old Babylonian records, and to such limitations one should add specific issues related to the group of documents that I discuss in this paper. My corpus of primary sources for this study consists of tablets mentioning female slaves dated to the reigns of Ḫammurabi (ca. 1792–1750 B.C.) and his son Samsu-iluna (ca. 1749–1712 B.C.), although I also consider evidence dated to other kings when pertinent. All the records come from Babylonia, that is, from the lands of Sumer and Akkad according to ancient scribes. I have not included references to slaves belonging to institutions such as the temple or the palace. Instead, my documents deal with slaves affiliated with domestic households independent of whether the slave owner had connections with those institutions. The tablets under consideration were issued exclusively *by* and *for* the upper classes, and slaves are mentioned mostly in their condition of being commodities

---

* I wish to thank Laura Culbertson for inviting me to participate in the seminar, and, most especially, for the discussions on slaves and other Assyriological matters that we had during her stay at the Oriental Institute. I am grateful to Martha Roth for the comments she made on this work as one of the discussants, to John Brinkman for his remarks on the original paper, and to Norman Yoffee for reading the final version.

49

sold, transferred, hired, or subject of dispute. Female slaves, for example, may appear in lists of objects such as beds, chairs, tables, chests, jars, and grindstones. That is to say, female slaves are listed among household items including furniture, utensils, and clothing that brides received from their parents as their dowries upon getting married. For instance, the female slave Ana-šumiya-libluṭ, together with two shekels of silver, one copper kettle, various garments and headdresses, two baskets, one cow, fifteen sheep, two millstones, one bed, six chairs, one table, and four wooden bowls, was part of the dowry that Nabium-atpalam gave to his daughter Amat-Asalluhi (*TLB* 1 229, Si 3, Sippar). Female slaves are also commonly attested in tablets pertaining to division of property (e.g., BE 6/1 28, Ḫa 29/xi/3, Sippar) and inheritance (e.g., BE 6/2 26, Si 6/vi/14, Nippur) that may further include more slaves, real estate, and various other assets.

Slave sale contracts, for their part, provide relatively basic personal information about slaves alongside the price that the buyer paid. Particulars include sex, expressed by the terms "male" or "female" slave (Gelb 1982), his or her name, and clarification of whether this was a house-born slave or one brought from another city or territory. Sometimes the document indicates that the slave was healthy. One recurrent concern in this regard seems to have been that the slave did not suffer from epilepsy (Stol 1993: 132–41), as mentioned in paragraph 278 of the Laws of Ḫammurabi (Roth 1997: 132) and in a number of sale contracts.[1] The information from tablets recording manumissions or fugitive slaves is equally laconic, although a number of letters do provide certain colorful remarks. It is perhaps due to the scarcity of details that there is no comprehensive study of Old Babylonian slavery, and that the few articles dealing with Old Babylonian slaves concentrate on foreign slaves, slave prices, and runaways, or on female slaves as depicted in the various Mesopotamian collections of laws (e.g., Farber 1978; Charpin 1992; Westbrook 1998; van Koppen 2004; van Koppen and Lacambre 2008/09).

The characteristics of most sources then allow only modest goals for the historian of ancient Mesopotamia, for they frustrate any attempt at writing history from below or at rescuing the voice of the oppressed. This is the case because even when slave statements may be quoted in certain tablets, those statements are but standard formulas imposed upon the slave to suit the conventions of legal procedures. Or else they consist of the report of a figure of authority mediated through the offices of the scribe's stylus. The limitations of Old Babylonian sources show that it would be extremely difficult — if possible at all — to study certain topics that are among the interests of other ancient historians. I am specifically thinking of questions discussed in the last three decades or so such as class struggle (e.g., de Ste. Croix 1981; Talbert 1989), slave rebellions and revolts (e.g., Bradley 1989; Urbainczyk 2008), the recreation of the realities of slave experiences (Bradley 2005), or the avoidance of slaves and their history in the writings of ancient and modern scholars (duBois 2008).

Old Babylonian slave documents are not descriptive like, for instance, those passages in Columella's *De Re Rustica* referring to slaves and, as a result, they do not provide thorough explanations and rich details. Nevertheless, there are a number of productive avenues to study certain aspects of domestic female slaves even though undocumented problems have to remain unexplored. In this paper I present evidence that contributes to the understanding of the role and position of domestic female slaves in Old Babylonian society. I use the term "domestic" to refer to family households and consequently to female slaves employed

---

[1] Thus, for example, in CT 8 43c (Ḫa 18/ix/24), TCL 1 147 (Ae "h"/iv/1), CT 8 27a (Ae "m"/i/6), VAS 7 50 (Ad 7/ix/15), VAS 7 53 (Ad 20/vii/27), TCL 1 156 (Ad 37/xii/11), *ARN* 122 (date broken).

in private houses. This remark is important because whereas the Latin word *domus*, from which the term "domestic" comes, refers to houses and households in the sense of "home," in ancient Mesopotamia the term "house" (Sumerian e_2, Akkadian *bītum*) can designate both a family house and household as well as an institutional administrative unit. The distinction is particularly relevant when one considers slaves originated as prisoners of war who were put to work in state institutions (Leemans 1961). This is the case, for example, with women brought to the city of Uruk around Samsu-iluna's ninth year and employed as weavers in an institution denominated "house of the weavers" (e_2 uš-bar). Based on the extant records, in the following pages I address three issues related to domestic female slaves: the ways in which women became domestic slaves, the activities that they performed, and the treatment that they received from their owners.

* * *

The first question is how did a domestic slave become such. According to our sources, a female slave could enter a private household under a number of different circumstances. Female slaves could be obtained by purchase from local or external sources through merchants or through particular owners. There are a number of tablets in which private slave owners sell their female slaves to other particulars. For example, a certain Šēp-Sîn characterized as her owner, sells a female slave and her child, a house-born slave, to Ilšu-nāṣir (YOS 12 275, Si 7/xii/7). In documents from the city of Sippar, the acquisition of slaves by *nadītu*-women, devotees of the god Šamaš, is not unusual.[2] Thus, for instance, Annunītum-ummī, a house-born female slave, was sold by her owner, the *nadītu* Amat-Mamu, to another *nadītu* (OLA 21 2, Si 8/xi/13). Aside from transactions between particulars, slaves were also purchased from merchants. In a letter addressed to an Ibbi-Ilabrat, a man asks for silver to pay a merchant who had sold him a female slave (CT 2 27a = AbB 2 94). Yet in another letter, the writer instructs his addressee to look for a healthy and good-looking female slave and to send her to him (VAS 16 65 = AbB 6 65). The intermediary role of merchants is apparent from a missive in which Išme-Adad comments that he and his brothers had sold a female slave to a merchant and that later he ransomed that slave girl (PBS 7 119 = AbB 11 119). Merchants were also mainly responsible for trading female slaves brought from faraway kingdoms and regions such as Subartum (e.g., AbB 12 32) in northern Mesopotamia (see, e.g., Finkelstein 1955; Leemans 1950), or from other cities within the kingdom (e.g., VAS 29 5, Si 5). These examples indicate that commercial transactions pertaining to female slaves can involve sales from private owners or merchants; whereas slaves can be house-born (*wilid bītim*) or acquired from other sources not related to private households. Letters and sale contracts may eventually reflect the buyer's preference for healthy and good-looking female slaves (e.g., *ABIM* 20, VAS 16 65 = AbB 6 65, CT 43 51 = AbB 1 51, CT 44 63 = AbB 1 139).

---

[2] *Nadītu* were a class of Mesopotamian women attested from various cities such as Sippar, Nippur, and Kiš who were devotees of particular deities. The institution of the *nadītu*-women existed only during the Old Babylonian period. *Nadītu*-women had religious obligations such as participation in religious festivals, but they also engaged actively in economic activities, lending silver and grain, renting, buying, and selling real estate. *Nadītu*s of Šamaš in the city of Sippar lived in a building complex called *gagûm*, usually translated as "cloister." See, for example, Harris 1964; Janssen 1991; Stone 1982; and Yoffee 2005: 116–21.

Female domestic slaves were also acquired through a number of family circuits that encompassed gifts, donations, and inheritance rather than sales. Wealthy women could receive female slaves as part of their dowries upon getting married. As already mentioned, in such documents slaves are listed among other household items. That slaves were valuable assets in a dowry seems to be implied in a letter in which Šamaš-māgir tells Sîn-erībam that his daughter is getting married and that he does not have anything to give her. Šamaš-māgir's subsequent request that Sîn-erībam should buy and send him two male and three female slaves suggests that he will presumably give some or perhaps all of those slaves to his daughter as part of her dowry (YOS 2 9 = AbB 9 9). Other women belonging to wealthy families received slaves from their parents when they entered the service of a particular deity. One of the tablets, for example, mentions that the parents of Mārat-erṣetim gave her a female slave named Saniq-qabûša in lieu of fields and a house when Mārat-erṣetim was appointed as a *qadištu*-woman (CT 48 2, Ḫa 30/Ø/Ø).[3] This document was issued because ten years after that same female slave had given birth to a daughter, the cousins and the brothers of the *qadištu*-woman brought forward a claim concerning the slave and her daughter. But the elders of the city of Akšak and Sardai examined the document in which Mārat-erṣetim had been granted the female slave, and, as a result, they confirmed that both slaves belonged to Mārat-erṣetim and that her relatives had no basis for the claim. It is not without interest that what is possibly the original tablet (and its envelope) recording the donation of the slave Saniq-qabûša to Mārat-erṣetim has come down to us (VAS 8 69 and 70, tablet and envelope respectively). A number of similar documents record female slaves bequeathed to women and men by their parents.[4]

Other tablets show that female slaves were not only given by parents to their children, but that sometimes the situation was the reverse. Occasionally, when a mother receives a slave from her children, the document stipulates that the slave should support and take care of her new mistress as she grows old. Thus a document from the city of Ur states that three siblings gave a female slave named Ištar-ummī-eništi to their mother in lieu of an allowance for food and clothing. The tablet also contains a clause affirming that if the woman marries, the sons will take the female slave away (UET 5 95, Ḫa 33; see Westbrook 1988: 133). This provision seems to suggest that should the mother marry after the slave was given to her, the slave shall be returned to her children, presumably because her husband should support her instead. There is a similar text in which a woman gives a female slave to her mother. The document states that as long as this woman is alive, the slave shall maintain her, but when she dies it is her daughter who will inherit the properties of her mother (UCP 10 105 line 7, no date). Female slaves bequeathed by relatives also include a case in which Sîn-pilaḫ gives the female slave Mutī-baštī to his wife Šaddašu. This tablet warns the children of Sîn-pilaḫ against suing Šaddašu and also says that any children Mutī-baštī may bear in the future will belong to Šaddašu (VAS 8 15–16, Ḫa "i").

Female slaves could enter a household in other more intimate capacities to be the wife of a man who might have been already married to another woman. For example, a document from the city of Sippar contains the purchase of a female slave by a couple (CT 8 22b, Ḫa 12/

---

[3] The exact function of the *qadištu*-woman is still poorly understood. The title appears in the Laws of Ḫammurabi. In Sippar they seem to have been devotees of the god Adad. See, for example, Renger 1967; Harris 1975: 328–31; and Westenholz 1989.

[4] For example, in MHET III 2/2 243 (Ḫa 32), MHET III 2/2 255 (Ḫa 34), CT 4 1 + MHET III 2/2 328 (Ḫa), YOS 8 71 (RS 59), and in MHET III 2/2 248 (Ḫa 32), where Rēš-Šamaš the son of Sîn-tayyār receives two plots of land, a house, an urban plot, male and female slaves, four oxen, and seven cows.

ii/3). Here, Bunene-abī and his wife Bēlessunu bought Šamaš-nūrī from her father for five shekels of silver, and although she is not characterized as a slave, the purchase price paid to obtain her clearly indicates that she is one. The contract adds that Šamaš-nūrī will be a wife to Bunene-abī and a slave to Bēlessunu, and that if in the future Šamaš-nūrī tells Bēlessunu "you are not my mistress," Bēlessunu can sell her (see Westbrook 1988: 56 n. 65). A slightly different situation occurs in another document from Sippar, where Aḫāssunu acquired Sabītum from her father Aḫūšina and her mother Aḫātani (CT 48 48, Ḫa 16). According to the tablet, Sabītum is a slave to Aḫāssunu and a wife to Warad-Sîn, who was seemingly Aḫāssunu's husband (Harris 1974: 367). As was the case in the previous tablet, if Aḫāssunu should find reasons to do so, she could sell Sabītum. It is worth noting that, unlike Šamaš-nūrī, Sabītum was not purchased but she was "taken" from her parents. Moreover, the document affirms that Sabītum's parents received her full betrothal price (*terḫatum*). It is not unlikely that marrying a second wife may have been related to the fact that the first wife could not bear children. A poorly preserved tablet mentions that Ilšu-abušu bought a female slave named Lamassani from her owner Ammī-sumu, and that he married that slave (CT 48 61, no date).[5] There is another case where Amat-Šamaš, a *nadītu* of Šamaš from Sippar, acquired with her own silver the female slave Aya-gāmilat and gave her to her brother Šamaš-ḫāzir as a wife. The contract then specifies that Šamaš-ḫāzir will continually support his *nadītu* sister as long as she is alive (TCL 1 90, Ḫa 33/iv/Ø).

Tablets dealing with division of property usually list female slaves as one of the items that are being divided and transferred to one of the parties involved in the transaction. These include a variety of cases. There is a most interesting lawsuit document dated to Rīm-Sîn of Larsa, a king who was a contemporary of Ḫammurabi, in which the female slaves and other property that had belonged to Elmēšum are the objects of a dispute. The parties involved in the litigation are her husband, who had presumably divorced her before she died, and her nephew Sîn-šeme, who was the son of her brother Sîn-iqīšam. The authorities had previously taken away Elmēšum's properties from her former husband and had subsequently given her assets to Sîn-šeme (VAS 18 1, RS 55/vi/10). That at least some of the property had reached Elmēšum from her family seems to be implied by an extant document issued thirty years earlier (VAS 18 101, RS 25). In a less complicated document from Sippar recording the division of the paternal property among four brothers, real estate and male and female slaves are included among the assets divided (BE 6/1 28, Ḫa 29/xi/3).

There are also numerous cases in which female slaves are transferred from parents to children as part of their inheritance. In those contracts, slaves belonging to the head of a household become the property of his or her heirs. Several instances pertain to *nadītu*-women, who could receive slaves and other properties from their father's inheritance, and in due term *nadītu*s could transfer their own properties to designated heirs. For instance, the well-off *nadītu* Narāmtum received from her father's inheritance four female slaves, two oxen, four cows, thirty one-year-old sheep, one cargo wagon, two millstones, two beds, and five chairs. The tablet also specifies that she should not set free or sell the slaves, but she is allowed to transfer them to any of her brothers as it pleases her (CT 48 33, Ḫa 34/ii/14). Undoubtedly this clause was meant to secure that this woman's share of the paternal inheritance will return to members of her paternal estate once she died. The inherited goods of another *nadītu* are

---

[5] The interpretation of this document is not without difficulties, and different interpretations have been suggested. See, for example, Westbrook 1988: 79 and Harris 1975: 343.

known because of a lawsuit. In this case, Bābilītum approached the judges with a claim about the paternal inheritance and her brothers were accordingly summoned. After reviewing the pertinent documentation, the judges assigned her ten male and female slaves, three oxen, two millstones, one copper vessel, and four minas of silver that her father had given to her, but that apparently her brothers had retained in their power (CT 6 7a, Si 5/xii/5).

Examples of *nadītu*-women who in turn left their slaves and other goods to their own heirs are numerous. To illustrate this situation one could mention the inheritance tablet of Šāt-Aya daughter of Šamaš-ilum, who declared another *nadītu*, Amat-Mamu the daughter of Ša-ilišu, as her heir. In this case Amat-Mamu received a field and a house located in the cloister. The tablet continues with the property that Šāt-Aya left to her brothers. This includes two small fields, three female slaves, one cow, and six sheep, which she had previously received from her father. The final part of the document mentions that as long as Šāt-Aya is alive, Amat-Mamu will continually provide her with a number of items. This material support is the obligation that Amat-Mamu has acquired as an heir who is not a blood relative of Šāt-Aya (CT 2 41, Ḥa 38/vi/13). This shows, once again, that the inheritance Šāt-Aya received from her paternal estate, including the female slaves, had to return to her kinship group, but that anything else the *nadītu* acquired by putting her own capital to work could be assigned to non-family members. A simpler case of inheritance involved three small fields, a house in the cloister, and a female slave that the *nadītu* Munawwirtum left to Ipqu-iliša, possibly her adoptive daughter (CT 8 5a, Ḥa 36/vi/11).

Another class of women of special status like the *nadītu*, the *kulmašītu*, was similarly related to religious activities and may appear among those receiving female slaves as part of an inheritance.[6] One of these *kulmašītu*s was granted one house, one female slave, one bed, and one chair. All these she can take with her upon getting married but the document clearly states that her inheritance and her estate belong to her brothers alone (CT 8 50a, Ḥa 2). As we have seen with a *nadītu* inheritance, this is yet another proviso to keep family property within the heirs of the paternal estate after a female heir who had married and enjoyed the inheritance while alive had died. That some of these *kulmašītu*s were rich and that their inheritance could be the matter of dispute is clear from a document from Sippar (OLA 21 95, Si 22). In this instance, the *kulmašītu* Inbuša had left to his half-brother Warad-Sîn three fields, two house plots, one male, and three female slaves. But three other people, including a *nadītu* of Šamaš, raised a claim about this property, which was dismissed by the judges of Sippar after they inspected all the inheritance records. Finally, as the last example of inheritance documents including female slaves among various assets, I mention a large tablet from Nippur pertaining to the division of an inheritance of a wealthy family among four brothers which also consists of temple prebends and privileges of the offices of *kalû* and *pašīšu* priests (BE 6/2 26, Si 6/vi/14).

Female slaves, as one would certainly have expected, appear in written records simply because they belonged to rich people whose properties could became contested by family members, heirs, or other parties. The selected examples chosen and presented above show the variety of situations by which a female slave could have entered a household. Thus, besides purchases there were other family mechanisms by which slaves were transferred from one

---

[6] The *kulmašītu* appears in §181 of the Laws of Ḥammurabi, mentioned together with the *nadītu* and the *qadištu* as women dedicated to a deity by their fathers. For their role and further attestations, see Renger 1967: 185–87.

family member to another. On certain occasions, as we have seen, the transferring of a female slave to take care of an elderly mistress seems to have been done to take this responsibility away from direct family members who would donate a slave to fulfill their family duties. It is well known that temporary enslavement because of debt was a possibility during the Old Babylonian period, and this seems to have been the fate of the daughter of Abizu. According to a letter, Abizu had purchased a female slave from the diviner Ibni-Marduk but had not paid him her full price (TCL 18 102 = AbB 14 156). As a result the diviner put Abizu's own daughter in jail for one month and, if our understanding of the phraseology is correct, Ibni-Marduk seems to have considered Abizu's daughter as a temporary slave who would eventually be released (see also Veenhof 2005: 147).

* * *

The second question I address pertains to the kinds of jobs female domestic slaves did and the kinds of activities in which they were involved, even if sometimes this may not have included labor in the strict sense. Such an enquiry is perforce restricted by the characteristics of our sources. This is so because there is no systematic description or regulation concerning the duties of domestic slaves in texts from the Old Babylonian period. Nevertheless, economic and legal records as well as letters provide a few insights regarding a number of these issues. As we have already seen, female slaves appear frequently in dowries because they were bequeathed to brides and newly married wives as one of many other domestic items that young women would need to run their own households. One has to assume then that these female slaves must have been assigned to perform domestic chores such as housekeeping, cleaning, doing laundry, grinding flour, and taking care of children. This supposition is mostly based on common sense; however, some of these tasks seem to have indirect support in the extant records. For example, in a very brief missive, the writer asks the correspondent to give a female slave to do domestic work (*šipir* e₂) to a man so that he can bring her to Larsa (AbB 14 226 line 8). Similarly, a very fragmentary tablet mentions that a female slave was caused to live in the house of Eteyatum and his wife Erištum as a house servant, *ēmiqtum* (CT 48 7, date broken).[7] That female domestic slaves may have ground flour can be inferred from the attestations of millstones in dowry documents, but also from a text from the north in which a woman requests of her father a female slave so that she herself will not have to grind flour (*OBT Tell Rimah* 160: 22).

Domestic female slaves were sometimes entrusted with the well-being of family members that needed assistance, either because they were very young or because they were growing old. For instance, certain female slaves acted as the wet nurse of the family children or of the children of a different household, as becomes clear from a lawsuit from Larsa (*Contribution* 143, Ḫa 41/xii/3). In this case, Kullupat was a female slave in the house of Nūr-ilišu and was possibly hired by Ṣillī-Ištar to feed his daughter Aḫāssunu. The document starts by noting that Dādâ the son of Nūr-ilišu took Aḫāssunu from her wet nurse Kullupat at the city gate of

---

[7] Due to the scarce extant attestations of the term *ēmiqtum* during the Old Babylonian period, it is not clear to me what activities the role of an *ēmiqtu* entails. *CAD* E: 149b translates this word as "a household servant," and *AHw.* I: 214b renders it as "Pflegerin." Note that in VAS 16 7 (= AbB 6 7) a woman called Amat-Adad addresses a letter to a man and refers to herself as *ēmiqtaka* "your *ēmiqtu*," but there is nothing to let us suspect that this woman was a slave.

Larsa. The baby's father, Ṣillī-Ištar, kept looking for his daughter and he finally found her in the house of Dādâ, the son of Nūr-ilišu. Then Ṣillī-Ištar approached the official Sîn-iddinam, and Dādâ's wife Aḫātum was summoned. In front of the authority, Aḫātum declared that the girl Aḫāssunu was not Ṣillī-Ištar's daughter, but that she was the daughter of Kullupat, a female slave in the house of Aḫātum's father-in-law, namely, Nūr-ilišu. In his turn, Ṣillī-Ištar declared that Aḫāssunu was his daughter, that the girl was not a slave, and that he had left her in the house of Aḫātum's father-in-law with the slave Kullupat for nursing. The official Sîn-iddinam then made Ṣillī-Ištar swear that Aḫāssunu was indeed his daughter; whereas Aḫātum swore by the gods Šamaš and Marduk and by King Ḫammurabi that she would not bring forward a claim concerning this case. It is interesting that it is the woman Aḫātum and not her husband or her father-in-law who actively participated in the trial. This may imply that household women were in charge of domestic slave's affairs. Or perhaps she had plans to make Aḫāssunu pass as her own daughter or even as a slave.

Men during the Old Babylonian period were allowed to take a second wife under certain circumstances, including childlessness, misconduct, or disease of the first wife, among other reasons (see Westbrook 1988: 107–09). From a number of available documents it is certain that the second wife or the concubine could be a slave, as mentioned in the previous section. In that respect, and granting that we accept that — unless the document contains a manumission or an adoption clause — the new wife retains her condition of slave, we can pose then that slaves were employed as wives to bear children, to raise them, and to perform other related marital duties. There is furthermore an interesting letter referring to a male slave from the city of Larsa (TCL 18 153 = AbB 14 207). As is usually the case, letters tend to be difficult to interpret because we miss the background knowledge that the sender and the addressee had. This tablet mentions a lawsuit of a certain Šamaš-tappê and the fact that the mother of the mounted messenger had born him to her second husband after she had divorced her first husband. The letter has some lines missing and ends with the following statement: "Such an [act] has never occurred in Larsa. A father with sons does not adopt his slave son" (see Veenhof 2005: 189). With the proviso that this interpretation is speculative, it seems possible to suggest that the slave son whom the father in our letter adopted was born to a domestic slave who was the master's concubine.

Other female slaves were entrusted with the care of their aging mistresses. As already discussed, in one case the three sons of Tarībum gave a female slave to their mother for her support instead of an allowance for food and clothing (UET 5 95, Ḫa 33); whereas in another example, a daughter gave a female slave to her mother to maintain her as long as she was alive (UCP 10 105, no date). In other instances, however, the situation was different in that the slave was first freed and then adopted by her former owner. A tablet from Sippar pertaining to a *nadītu*-woman records that the female slave Maḫartum is the (adopted) daughter of Lamassī, the *nadītu* of the god Šamaš, and that Lamassī has freed her (*TJDB* 15.954, Si 2). The document continues with the statement that as long as Lamassī is alive, her daughter Maḫartum will support her, and that she belongs to the god Šamaš. An additional clause establishes that none of Lamassī's brothers or relatives will raise a claim concerning Maḫartum and that if anyone does so, s/he will pay one mina of silver. A tablet issued some thirty-three years later, possibly in the city of Dilbat, states that Iddin-Lagamal set free Gimillum and his sister Kurrītum and gave them to his wife Tašmētum-mātī for adoption (BIN 7 206, Si 33). Gimillum and Kurrītum will support Tašmētum-mātī as long as she is alive, and in the future the children of Iddin-Lagamal shall not claim them. After the oath by the god Uraš and by King Samsu-iluna, the tablet affirms that should Gimillum and Kurrītum tell their mother that they do not acknowledge her as such, Tašmētum-mātī has the right to sell them as slaves. As a last example, I wish to mention an earlier document dated to Hammurabi's father, Sîn-muballiṭ. Here Aḫātum the daughter of Nūr-Adad adopted and freed Warad-Tutub and Bēlessunu (VAS 8 55, Sm). As was the case with the previous tablets, this one also stipulates that the adopted children will support Aḫātum as long as she is alive, and that once she has died no one shall raise a claim against them.[8]

Other activities that domestic female slaves performed seem to have included running errands for their masters. This evidence comes mostly from various letters. In one case, a certain Sîn-māgir tells his correspondents: "Whatever you need is with me. Let a female slave come to me so that I can have her bring it to you" (PBS 7 51 = AbB 11 51). Similarly, the writer of another missive affirms "I am dispatching Quttuttu, your female slave, to you: have (her) bring me the emmer that you had consented to (give) to me..." (PBS 7 120 = AbB 11 120). For his part, Ilī-uṣranni tells Munawwirtum that Ayatiya, the female slave of Warad-ilišu, had brought him a cloak and headdresses, and that now Ilī-uṣranni is sending that same slave to Munawwirtum with five minas of wool (CT 44 58 = AbB 1 134). This letter is important because whereas Ayatiya is characterized as a female slave ($geme_2$), the writer had previously mentioned male and female servants (*ṣeḫru* and *ṣeḫertu* respectively), which shows that Ayatiya is indeed a "slave" and not a "servant," as the terms $geme_2$ (*amtum*) and arad (*wardum*) are sometimes translated (e.g., Frankena 1966: 93). There is also a message that Erīb-Sîn sent to Šamaš-nāṣir in which he says that "she who brought you the tablet is a slave of a *nadītu*" (CT 29 12 = AbB 2 142). As I understand them, these instances imply that at least certain domestic female slaves were trusted to the extent of letting them have some freedom of movement to leave the household, if only for brief periods. Of course, such a privilege must have depended on the slave's docility and reliability, because we know that they could escape and, in fact, fugitive slaves are attested in the written sources.

The trust that seems to be implied in allowing female slaves to run errands outdoors and the possibility of having them talk to other people may have also been an opportunity of gathering gossip that female slaves could pass onto their owners. This seems to be the implication in a letter that Lu-Haia sent to a woman called Ana-bēltim-taklāku (AbB 12 181). After the greeting formula the man complains: "My son did not tell me and my female slave did not tell me, but a stranger told me that their eldest son had intercourse with you. (This is) what he told me and what he swore to me by the god Ningišzida" (see van Soldt 1990: 143). Unfortunately, the tablet is fragmentary, but it is apparent that Lu-Haia was expecting to hear the news from his son or from his female slave and that he was making a point that neither of them informed him of this situation. This shows then that it was not unusual that female slaves would report this kind of gossip to their masters and mistresses. Whether Ana-bēltim-taklāku was Lu-Haia's daughter, his sister, or his wife is not clear, but any of these possibilities is likely.

* * *

---

[8] As with adoptions of female slaves, in certain adoptions of male slaves there is a clause protecting the slave from future claims by the adopter's family. Furthermore, in the case of male slaves, there is occasionally a clause that guarantees his status as the eldest heir should other sons join the family. See Obermark 1991: 30.

The third question I want to consider deals with the treatment female slaves received from their owners and with tracing the interactions between them whenever possible. When addressing this topic, it is important to remember that there were different types of slaves in the ancient Near East and that those differences had a direct connection with the sources of slavery. Thus, for example, a slave could be an outsider who was forced into slavery after being captured as a prisoner of war and after being brought to the enemy's territory. A slave could also be imported from faraway regions and kingdoms and carried to a different destination by merchants. Or else, a slave could be a native-born individual, in which case there were various possibilities: the slave could be a house-born slave, a minor sold into slavery by his or her parents, a self-sold adult, or somebody who became a temporary slave because of a defaulting debt (see Mendelsohn 1946). All these cases are well attested for the Old Babylonian period. Although our sources are silent in this respect, one could suspect that those differences may have influenced the ways in which masters and slaves interacted. In this sense it is possible to hypothesize, for example, that typically a house-born slave would have been more docile than a prisoner of war forcefully brought as an outsider into a different city. Preferences for, say, house-born, local, or imported slaves may have depended on the tasks the buyer had in mind for a particular slave, and also on the market availability. This can be illustrated with a passage from a letter in which Anum-pī-Šamaš instructs Ibni-Adad to buy a female slave if she is a house-born and if she is a weaver (VAS 16 4 = AbB 6 4).

Owners undoubtedly regarded their slaves as commodities, as investments, and as labor force. As merchandise a slave could be bought and sold for an amount of silver that seems to have depended on current values, on political circumstances, and on the personal characteristics of the slave. Numerous slave sale contracts issued during the Old Babylonian period bear witness to that fact. The slave owner would also become the master of the children that were born to a female slave while she was the property of that owner (e.g., *TS* 35). This is clear from sale contracts in which female slaves are sold together with their infants (e.g., MHET III 2/3 444, Si 27). Occasionally, female slaves were taken as pledges by the creditors of their masters and would be returned to the original owner once the debt was cancelled (e.g., CT 29 13 = AbB 2 154; AbB 10 5, UET 5 336, *Bus. Doc.* 74). The economic value of slaves is also apparent from the fact that they usually appear alone or among other valuable assets in lawsuits (e.g., VAS 8 102, Ḥa 4; CT 6 47b, Ḥa 24; OLA 21 24, Ḥa 40; CT 6 7a, Si 5; CT 45 37, Si 27). Domestic female slaves could also be a source of extra income for their owners when they were contracted by third parties. For example, a certain Apil-Amurru hired three female slaves from *nadītu*-women for harvest time and their wages were paid in barley (VAS 9 109+110, Ḥa 35).

Aware that slaves represented an investment and the acquisition of capital, a person who intended to buy one tried to make sure that the slave was healthy, and an owner must have taken the necessary precautions to prevent that a slave died or escaped. Certain documents refer to the death of a slave, but unfortunately the circumstances are not necessarily fully stated. For example, a letter mentions that a female slave that was supposed to be sent to Babylonia died when the merchant dealing with her entered Arrapha (CT 2 49 = AbB 2 87); whereas another female slave was reported to have died while she was imprisoned (*Contribution* 122). As far as I know, the death of domestic female slaves was not recorded in any sort of administrative records, unlike the decease of state slaves, who were registered as dead assets, as is clear, for instance, from documents belonging to the house of prisoners of war in Uruk. Similarly, references to fugitive domestic slaves can appear in letters, but individual owners did not seem to have kept records of runaways. As is the case with deceased slaves, mentions of fugitives tend to be laconic and the details provided are usually kept to a minimum. For instance, in a letter that Ḫammurabi sent to one of his officials he affirms that the sons of Siyyatum wrote to the king complaining that one of the female slaves of their house (saḡ-geme₂ *ša bi-ti-ni* "a female slave of our house") ran away with her daughters and was now in the house of Ilī-māgir in Bad-Tibira (AbB 13 18). The details of this case are not explained, but the king leaves some room for doubts regarding whether the female slave belonged to the claimants and whether she was indeed a runaway.

Fugitive slaves are recorded either because they were being searched for or because they were found. Whether runaways were ever successful escaping their masters remains unknown, for in the Old Babylonian period scribes would not have recorded those small personal victories. However, one wonders about the real chances of success of life-time slaves who had possibly little connection with free people who could have helped them, unless this help simply implied a swap of masters. The reasons why a slave would flee must have been diverse and must have depended on many personal circumstances and on the type of slave in question, but what prompted a slave to escape was most likely related to unhappiness, mistreatment, or exploitation. Once again, these are the kinds of facts scribes did not record, but there are occasionally some hints that let us trace certain mistreatments. There are a few meager attestations to illustrate this situation, such as the case of a slave woman who died while imprisoned (e.g., *Contribution* 122), and also the mention of female slaves beaten and then recommended to be put in fetters (e.g., CT 43 27 = AbB 1 27), or the example from another letter where a person suggests that slaves should be beaten and put on a leading rope (TLB 4 7 = AbB 3 11). Sexual offenses against female slaves seem also to have taken place.[9]

Running away, however, was not the only way out of slavery. As briefly mentioned above, female slaves were occasionally adopted by their owners. We have seen, for instance, that a *nadītu* of Šamaš had freed and adopted a female slave who was supposed to support her adoptive mother as long as she was alive, and there is a clause preventing possible future claims against the freed slave after her adoptive mother dies (*TJDB* 15.954, Si 2). The terms of the adoption of a slave by another *nadītu* dated to the great-grandson of King Samsu-iluna are different (BE 6/1 96, Aṣ 17). Here the *nadītu* Erišti-Aya freed and adopted a female slave together with her infant daughter and the slave will similarly have to support the elderly *nadītu*, as in the previous example. However, the provision of no future claim is more elaborate in this case, for it states that when Erišti-Aya dies the slave is free, will be on her own, and that none of the children of the *nadītu* or those of her brother Kalūmum shall have a claim against the adopted slave and her daughter. To provide yet a different example representative of the nuances of slave adoptions, I mention an undated document also from Sippar in which a certain Taddinam adopted the female slave Šīmāt-Erra (TIM 5 5). The tablet mentions that when Taddinam has died, neither the father of Šīmāt-Erra nor the brothers of Taddinam shall have a claim upon the former slave. Despite formulaic differences, these examples suggest that after the female slave was set free and adopted, there was still a dependency bond between her and the adoptive parent, which entails the responsibility of supporting and maintaining the former owner and new parent. Only after the adoptive parent dies is the slave supposed to be free from any form of dependency.

---

[9] There is, for example, an early Old Babylonian letter found in Lagaš that mentions two female slaves that were raped (TCL 1 10). See also the study by Benno Landsberger (1968).

Interestingly, the arrangement was settled in such a fashion that it brought about a benefit for both parties involved. By setting free and adopting a slave, the previous owner obtained a security for support in old age, whereas the slave would have the gain of complete freedom once her obligations were terminated by the death of the owner. Manumission then did not imply an economic loss for the owner. On the contrary, it constituted an additional benefit. The economic disadvantage was then for the heirs of the owner who would not be able to count the manumitted slave among their inheritance assets. Other cases, however, may not have been so convenient for the former slave. For example, in an undated document, Mārat-Araḫtum is declared daughter of Aḫātani, the mother of the *rēdû*-soldier Gimil-Marduk (CT 48 49). That Mārat-Araḫtum was a slave is apparent from the mention of the smashing of the pot, which was legal terminology used in certain manumission contracts that may have further involved some sort of ceremony (see Roth 1979: 105–14; Malul 1988: 40–76). The tablet also stipulates that Mārat-Araḫtum shall support her adoptive mother Aḫātani as long as she is alive, and further adds that Mārat-Araḫtum was given to Gimil-Marduk as his wife. In other words, unlike the other instances mentioned earlier, the bond of Mārat-Araḫtum and her previous owner remained after her mistress died because she was married to the son of her adoptive mother (see Donbaz and Yoffee 1986: 51–52).

* * *

The study of slavery during the Old Babylonian period remains an underexplored subject, even though this is one of the best-documented epochs in ancient history. Perhaps one of the most challenging limitations for such a research enterprise resides precisely on the character and nature of the extant written sources, which consist mainly of administrative, economic and legal documents, and letters. Among these records, slave sale contracts are numerous, but aside from very precise information pertaining to the name, to providing minimal personal particulars, price, and the names of seller and buyer, they give few details regarding the person being traded. Whereas lawsuit, manumission, and adoption tablets may provide some more specifics, they were written down because either the transaction recorded implied a certain degree of exceptionality or because that same transaction could be the subject of future disputes (see, e.g., Beckman 1996). In my analysis of female domestic slaves, I have kept the references to the Laws of Ḫammurabi to the minimum possible because I am more concerned about how things functioned than about how things should have been. This approach, however, does not mean that I disregard Mesopotamian laws or that I consider them as an irrelevant primary source. It was simply meant to provide a different perspective relying on scattered documents brought together by the modern scholar rather than on that sort of ancient collage that the Laws of Ḫammurabi represent.

The picture drafted in this article is a mosaic made of different pieces of information, bearing different colors and nuances, coming from different cities, encompassing a period of about eighty years. Because slave documents do not represent all the kingdom's areas and periods, possible local traditions and temporal variations were regrettably overlooked. Yet, despite the risks of putting together such a composite, I hope this kind of approach, even when faulty, will help pose new questions and broaden our understanding of slavery during the Old Babylonian period. My criterion for considering specific female slaves as "domestic" was their attestations in contexts that suggest relatively clearly their affiliation with domestic households, families, and family life. As we have seen, aside from purchase, there were a number of other family circuits by which slaves could have been transferred from one household to another. This included gifts, dowries, division of property, lawsuits, and inheritance. Female domestic slaves could also be taken as pledges. Questions regarding the tasks and activities that domestic female slaves performed are difficult to trace because the sources barely provide that kind of information. The available evidence suggests that they were in charge of various chores such as housekeeping, cleaning, grinding flour, wet-nursing, taking care of children and of elderly people, and, occasionally, running errands outside the household. Although poorly documented, the harsh conditions that certain slaves must have endured seem to have prompted them to escape. But we know that at least some of them could have hoped for other alternatives to obtain freedom such as adoption and full manumission after the adoptive parent died. From the point of view of economic history, domestic female slaves may not have been the main force of production in Old Babylonian Mesopotamia; that fact, however, does not make them less important.

ABBREVIATIONS

Kings

Ad	Ammi-ditana, king of Babylon
Ae	Abi-ešuḫ, king of Babylon
Aṣ	Ammi-ṣaduqa, king of Babylon
Ḫa	Ḫammurabi, king of Babylon
RS	Rīm-Sîn, king of Larsa
Si	Samsu-iluna, king of Babylon
Sm	Sîn-muballiṭ, king of Babylon

Bibliographic

AbB 1	Kraus 1964
AbB 2	Frankena 1966
AbB 3	Frankena 1968
AbB 6	Frankena 1974
AbB 9	Stol 1981
AbB 10	Kraus 1985
AbB 11	Stol 1986
AbB 12	van Soldt 1990
AbB 13	van Soldt 1994
AbB 14	Veenhof 2005
ABIM	Al-Zeebari 1964
AHw.	von Soden 1965–81
ARN	Çığ, Kızılyay, and Kraus 1952
BE 6/1	Ranke 1906
BE 6/2	Poebel 1906
BIN 7	Alexander 1943
Bus. Doc.	Waterman 1916
Contribution	Boyer 1928
CAD	The Chicago Assyrian Dictionary of the Oriental Institute of the University of Chicago
CT 2	Budge 1896

CT 4	Budge 1898a
CT 6	Budge 1898b
CT 8	Budge 1899
CT 29	Budge 1910
CT 43	Figulla 1963
CT 44	Pinches 1963
CT 45	Pinches 1964
CT 48	Finkelstein 1968
MHET III 2/2	Dekiere 1994
MHET III 2/3	Dekiere 1995
OBT Tell Rimah	Dalley, Walker, and Hawkins 1976
OLA 21	van Lerberghe 1986
PBS 7	Ungnad 1915
TIM 5	van Dijk 1968
TS	Jean 1931
TCL 1	Thureau-Dangin 1910
TCL 18	Dossin 1934
TJDB	Szlechter 1958
TLB 1	Leemans 1956
TLB 4	Frankena 1965
UCP 10	Lutz 1931
UET 5	Figulla and Martin 1953
VAS 7	Ungnad 1909a
VAS 8	Ungnad 1909b
VAS 9	Ungnad 1909c
VAS 16	Schroeder 1917
VAS 18	Klengel 1973
VAS 29	Klengel and Klengel-Brandt 2002
YOS 2	Lutz 1917
YOS 8	Faust 1941
YOS 12	Feigin 1979

BIBLIOGRAPHY

Al-Zeebari, Akram
    1964   Altbabylonische Briefe des Iraq-Museums. Ph.D. dissertation, Westfälische Wilhelms-
                Universität, Münster.

Alexander, John Bruce
    1943   *Earlier Babylonian Letters and Economic Texts.* Babylonian Inscriptions in the Col-
                lection of J. B. Nies 7. New Haven: Yale University Press.

Beckman, Gary
    1996   "Family Values on the Middle Euphrates in the Thirteenth Century B.C.E." In *Emar:
                The History, Religion and Culture of a Syrian Town at the Late Bronze Age*, edited
                by M. W. Chavalas, pp. 57–79. Bethesda: CDL Press.

Boyer, Georges
    1928   *Contribution à l'histoire juridique de la 1ʳᵉ dynastie babylonienne.* Paris: Paul
                Geuthner.

Bradley, Keith R.

1989 *Slavery and Rebellion in the Roman World, 140 B.C.–70 B.C.* Bloomington: Indiana University Press.

2005 *Slavery and Society at Rome.* Cambridge: Cambridge University Press. (First edition 1994).

Budge, E. A. Wallis

1896 *Cuneiform Texts from Babylonian Tablets, &c. in the British Museum,* Part 2. London: The British Museum.

1898a *Cuneiform Texts from Babylonian Tablets, &c. in the British Museum,* Part 4. London: The British Museum.

1898b *Cuneiform Texts from Babylonian Tablets, &c. in the British Museum,* Part 6. London: The British Museum.

1899 *Cuneiform Texts from Babylonian Tablets, &c. in the British Museum,* Part 8. London: The British Museum.

1910 *Cuneiform Texts from Babylonian Tablets, &c. in the British Museum,* Part 29. London: The British Museum.

Charpin, Dominique

1992 "Immigrés, réfugiés et déportés en Babylonie sous Hammu-rabi et ses successeurs." In *La circulation des biens, des personnes et des idées dans le Proche-Orient ancien* (Actes de la 38ᵉ Rencontre Assyriologique Internationale, Paris, 8–10 juillet 1991), edited by D. Charpin and F. Joannès, pp. 207–18. Paris: Éditions Recherche sur les Civilisations.

Çığ, Muazzez; Hatice Kızılyay, and Fritz Rudolph Kraus

1952 *Eski babil zamanina ait Nippur hukukî vesikaları = Altbabylonische Rechtsurkunden aus Nippur.* Istanbul: Milli Eğitim Basımevı.

Dalley, Stephanie; C. B. F. Walker; and J. D. Hawkins

1976 *Old Babylonian Tablets from Tell al Rimah.* London: British School of Archaeology in Iraq.

Dekiere, Luc

1994 *Old Babylonian Real Estate Documents from Sippar in the British Museum,* Part 2: *Documents from the Reign of Hammurabi.* Mesopotamian History and Environment Series III, Texts. Ghent: University of Ghent.

1995 *Old Babylonian Real Estate Documents from Sippar in the British Museum,* Part 3: *Documents from the Reign of Samsu-iluna.* Mesopotamian History and Environment Series III, Texts. Ghent: University of Ghent.

Donbaz, Veysel, and Norman Yoffee

1986 *Old Babylonian Texts from Kish Conserved in the Istanbul Archaeological Museums.* Bibliotheca Mesopotamica 17. Malibu: Undena Publications.

Dossin, Georges

1934 *Lettres de la première dynastie babylonienne.* Textes cunéiformes du Louvre 18. Paris: P. Geuthner.

duBois, Page

2008 *Slaves and Other Objects.* Chicago: University of Chicago Press.

Farber, Howard

1978 "A Price and Wage Study for Northern Babylonia during the Old Babylonian Period." *Journal of the Economic and Social History of the Orient* 21: 1–51.

Faust, David Earl

1941 *Contracts from Larsa: Dated in the Reign of Rīm-Sîn.* Yale Oriental Series, Babylonian Texts 8. New Haven: Yale University Press.

Feigin, Samuel I.
1979   *Legal and Administrative Texts of the Reign of Samsu-Iluna.* Yale Oriental Series, Babylonian Texts 12. New Haven: Yale University Press.

Figulla, H. H.
1963   *Cuneiform Texts from Babylonian Tablets, &c. in the British Museum*, Part 43: *Old Babylonian Letters.* London: The British Museum.

Figulla, H. H., and William J. Martin
1953   *Letters and Documents of the Old-Babylonion Period.* Ur Excavations, Texts 5. London: Joint Expedition of the British Museum and of the University Museum, University of Pennsylvania, Philadelphia.

Finkelstein, Jacob J.
1955   "Subartu and the Subarians in Old Babylonian Sources," *Journal of Cuneiform Studies* 9: 1–7.

1968   *Cuneiform Texts from Babylonian Tablets, &c. in the British Museum*, Part 48: *Old Babylonian Legal Documents.* London: Trustees of the British Museum.

Frankena, Rintje
1965   *Tabulae Cuneiformes a F. M. Th. de Liagre Böhl collectae, Leidae conservatae*, Volume 4: *Altbabylonische Briefe.* Leiden: Nederlands Instituut voor het Nabije Oosten.

1966   *Briefe aus dem British Museum (LIH und CT 2–33).* Altbabylonische Briefe in Umschrift und Übersetzung 2. Leiden: Brill.

1968   *Briefe aus der Leidener Sammlung (TLB IV).* Altbabylonische Briefe in Umschrift und Übersetzung 3. Leiden: Brill.

1974   *Briefe aus dem Berliner Museum.* Altbabylonische Briefe in Umschrift und Übersetzung 6. Leiden: Brill.

Gelb, Ignace J.
1982   "Terms for Slaves in Ancient Mesopotamia." In *Societies and Languages of the Ancient Near East: Studies in Honour of I. M. Diakonoff*, edited by M. A. Dandamayev, I. Gershevitch, H. Klengel, G. Komoróczy, M. T. Larsen, and J. N. Postgate, pp. 81–98. Warminster: Aris & Phillips.

Harris, Rivkah
1964   "The *nadītu* Woman." In *Studies Presented to A. Leo Oppenheim, June 7, 1964*, edited by R. D. Biggs and J. A. Brinkman, pp. 106–35. Chicago: University of Chicago Press.

1974   "The Case of Three Babylonian Marriage Contracts," *Journal of Near Eastern Studies* 33: 363–69.

1975   *Ancient Sippar: A Demographic Study of an Old-Babylonian City (1894–1595 B.C.).* Leiden: Nederlands Historisch-archaeologisch Instituut te Istanbul.

Janssen, Caroline
1991   "Samsu-iluna and the Hungry *nadītum*s." *Northern Akkad Project Reports* 5: 3–39.

Jean, Charles François
1931   *Tell Sifr textes cunéiformes conservés au British Museum.* Paris: Librairie Orientaliste P. Geuthner.

Klengel, Horst
1973   *Altbabylonische Rechts- und Wirtschaftsurkunden.* Vorderasitatische Schriftdenkmäler der Staatlichen Museen zu Berlin 18. Berlin: Akademie-Verlag.

1978   "Eine altbabylonische Kaufurkunde aus Babylon." In *Festschrift Lubor Matouš*, edited by B. Hruška and G. Komoróczy, pp. 201–05. Assyriologia 5. Budapest: Eötvös University.

Klengel, Horst, and Evelyn Klengel-Brandt
2002   *Spät-altbabylonische Tontafeln Texte und Siegelabrollungen.* Vorderasitatische
            Schriftdenkmäler der Staatlichen Museen zu Berlin, neue Folge 8, Heft 29. Mainz
            am Rhein: Philipp von Zabern.

Kraus, Fritz Rudolf
1964   *Briefe aus dem British Museum: CT 43 und 44.* Altbabylonische Briefe in Umschrift
            und Übersetzung 1. Leiden: Brill.

1985   *Briefe aus kleineren westeuropäischen Sammlungen.* Altbabylonische Briefe in Um-
            schrift und Übersetzung 10. Leiden: Brill.

Landsberger, Benno
1968   "Jungfräulichkeit: Ein Beitrag zum Thema 'Beilager und Eheschliessung.'" In *Sym-
            bolae juridicae et historicae Martino David dedicatae,* edited by J. A. Ankum, R. Fe-
            enstra, and W. F. Leemans, pp. 41–105. Leiden: Brill.

Leemans, Wilhelmus F.
1950   *The Old Babylonian Merchant: His Business and His Social Position.* Leiden: Brill.
1956   *Tabulae Cuneiformes a F. M. Th. de Liagre Böhl collectae,* Volume 1. Leiden: n.p.
1961   "The *asīru.*" *Revue d'assyriologie et d'archéologie orientale* 55: 57–76.

Lutz, Henry Frederick
1917   *Early Babylonian Letters.* Yale Oriental Series, Babylonian Texts 2. New Haven:
            Yale University Press.

1931   *Legal and Economic Documents from Ashjâly.* University of California Publications
            in Semitic Philology 10. Berkley: University of California Press.

Malul, Meir
1988   *Studies in Mesopotamian Legal Symbolism.* Alter Orient und Altes Testament 221.
            Kevelaer: Butzon & Bercker; Neukirchen-Vluyn: Neukirchener Verlag.

Mendelsohn, Isaac
1946   "Slavery in the Ancient Near East." *The Biblical Archaeologist* 9: 74–88.

Obermark, Peter R.
1991   Adoption in the Old Babylonian Period. Ph.D. dissertation, Hebrew Union College.

Pinches, Theophilus G.
1963   *Cuneiform Texts from Babylonian Tablets, &c. in the British Museum,* Part 44: *Mis-
            cellaneous Texts.* London: The British Museum.

1964   *Cuneiform Texts from Babylonian Tablets, &c. in the British Museum,* Part 45: *Old
            Babylonian Business Documents.* London: Trustees of the British Museum.

Poebel, Arno
1906   *Babylonian Legal and Business Documents from the Time of the First Dynasty of
            Babylon: Chiefly from Sippar.* Babylonian Expedition of the University of Pennsyl-
            vania, Series A: Cuneiform Texts 6/2. Philadelphia: Department of Archaeology of
            the University of Pennsylvania.

Ranke, Hermann
1906   *Babylonian Legal and Business Documents from the Time of the First Dynasty of
            Babylon: Chiefly from Sippar.* Babylonian Expedition of the University of Pennsyl-
            vania, Series A: Cuneiform Texts 6/1. Philadelphia: Department of Archaeology of
            the University of Pennsylvania.

Renger, Johannes
1967   "Untersuchungen zum Priestertum in der altbabylonischen Zeit." *Zeitschrift für As-
            syriologie und Vorderasiatische Archäologie* 58: 110–88.

Roth, Martha T.
  1979   Scholastic Tradition and Mesopotamian Law: A Study of FLP 1287, a Prism in
              the Collection of the Free Library of Philadelphia. Ph.D. dissertation, University of
              Pennsylvania.
  1997   *Law Collections from Mesopotamia and Asia Minor.* Second edition. SBL Writings
              from the Ancient World Series. Atlanta: Scholars Press.

Schroeder, Otto
  1917   *Altbabylonische Briefe.* Vorderasitatische Schriftdenkmäler der Staatlichen Museen
              zu Berlin 16. Leipzig: J. C. Hinrichs.

Ste. Croix, Geoffrey E. M. de
  1981   *The Class Struggle in the Ancient Greek World: From the Archaic Age to the Arab
              Conquests.* London: Duckworth.

Stol, Marten
  1981   *Letters from Yale.* Altbabylonische Briefe in Umschrift und Übersetzung 9. Leiden:
              Brill.
  1986   *Letters from Collections in Philadelphia, Chicago, and Berkeley.* Altbabylonische
              Briefe in Umschrift und Übersetzung 11. Leiden: Brill.
  1993   *Epilepsy in Babylonia.* Cuneiform Monographs 2. Groningen: Styx.

Stone, Elizabeth
  1982   "The Social Role of the *nadītu* Woman in Old Babylonian Nippur." *Journal of the
              Economic and Social History of the Orient* 25: 50–70.

Szlechter, Emile
  1958   *Tablettes juridiques de la 1re dynastie de Babylone conservées au Musée d'Art et
              d'Histoire de Genève.* Paris: Recueil Sirey.

Talbert, Richard
  1989   "The Role of Helots in the Class Struggle at Sparta." *Historia* 38: 22–40.

Thureau-Dangin, François
  1910   *Lettres et contrats de l'époque de la première dynastie babylonienne.* Textes cunéi-
              formes du Louvre 1. Paris: P. Geuthner.

Ungnad, Arthur
  1909a   *Altbabylonische Privaturkunden.* Vorderasitatische Schriftdenkmäler der Staatlichen
              Museen zu Berlin 7. Leipzig: J. C. Hinrichs.
  1909b   *Altbabylonische Privaturkunden.* Vorderasitatische Schriftdenkmäler der Staatlichen
              Museen zu Berlin 8. Leipzig: J. C. Hinrichs.
  1909c   *Altbabylonische Privaturkunden.* Vorderasitatische Schriftdenkmäler der Staatlichen
              Museen zu Berlin 9. Leipzig: J. C. Hinrichs.
  1915   *Babylonian Letters of the Ḫammurapi Period.* Publications of the Babylonian Section
              7. Philadelpha: University Museum.

Urbainczyk, Theresa
  2008   *Slave Revolts in Antiquity.* Berkeley-Los Angeles: University of California Press.

van Dijk, J. J. A.
  1968   *Cuneiform Texts: Old Babylonian Contracts and Related Material.* Texts in the Iraq
              Museum 5. Baghdad: Directorate General of Antiquities.

van Koppen, Frans
  2004   "The Geography of the Slave Trade and Northern Mesopotamia in the Late Old Baby-
              lonian Period." In *Mesopotamian Dark Age Revisited* (Proceedings of an International
              Conference of SCIEM 2000, Vienna 8th–9th November 2002), edited by H. Hunger
              and R. Pruzsinszky, pp. 9–33. Vienna: Verlag der Österreichischen Akademie der
              Wissenschaften.

van Koppen, Frans, and Denis Lacambre
  2008/09   "Sippar and the Frontier between Ešnunna and Babylon. New Sources for the History of Ešnuna in the Old Babylonian Period." *Ex Oriente Lux* 41: 151–77.

van Lerberghe, Karel
  1986   *Old Babylonian Legal and Administrative Texts from Philadelphia.* Orientalia Lovaniensia Analecta 21. Leuven: Departement Oriëntalistiek.

van Soldt, Wilfred H.
  1990   *Letters in the British Museum.* Altbabylonische Briefe in Umschrift und Übersetzung 12. Leiden: Brill.

  1994   *Letters in the British Museum.* Altbabylonische Briefe in Umschrift und Übersetzung 13. Leiden: Brill.

von Soden, Wolfram
  1965–81   *Akkadisches Handwörterbuch.* 3 volumes. Wiesbaden: Harrassowitz.

Veenhof, Klaas R.
  2005   *Letters in the Louvre.* Altbabylonische Briefe in Umschrift und Übersetzung 14. Leiden: Brill, 2005.

Waterman, Leroy
  1916   *Business Documents of the Hammurapi Period from the British Museum.* London: Luzac.

Westbrook, Raymond
  1988   *Old Babylonian Marriage Law.* Archiv für Orientforschung, Beiheft 23. Horn: Ferdinand Berger & Söhne.

  1998   "The Female Slave." In *Gender and Law in the Hebrew Bible and the Ancient Near East,* edited by B. M. Levinson, V. H. Matthews, and T. S. Frymer-Kensky, pp. 214–38. Journal for the Study of the Old Testament Supplement Series 262. Sheffield: Sheffield Academic Press.

Westenholz, Joan
  1989   "Tamar, *qēdēšē, qadištu,* and Sacred Prostitution in Mesopotamia." *Harvard Theological Review* 83: 245–65.

Yoffee, Norman
  2005   *Myths of the Archaic State. Evolution of the Earliest Cities, States and Civilizations.* Cambridge: Cambridge University Press.

SECTION TWO:
THE ISLAMIC NEAR EAST

5

PRELIMINARY REMARKS ON SLAVES AND SLAVE LABOR IN THE THIRD/NINTH CENTURY ʿABBĀSID EMPIRE

MATTHEW S. GORDON, MIAMI UNIVERSITY*

I

Near Eastern urban society relied on slave labor in the early Islamic period (first–fourth century A.H./seventh–tenth century A.D.). Modern scholarship has moved slowly, however, in describing the nature and extent of that reliance.[1] This paper considers the initial careers of two individuals of slave origin, each a member of a well-known cohort of ʿAbbāsid urban society: elite women singers (*qiyān*, sing. *qayna*) and Turkish commanders, the officers of the ʿAbbāsid slave military. In his recent study on Ibn ʿAbd al-Ḥakam (d. 214/829) and early Mālikī slavery law, Jonathan Brockopp (2000: 116–17) observes that modern scholarship has privileged the two cohorts while saying rather little about the much wider phenomenon of domestic slavery (the focus of both Qurʾānic regulation and early Islamic legal writings). Given, in all likelihood, that the great majority of slaves of early ʿAbbāsid society lived and worked in domestic settings — urban households — then the lacuna is obvious.

The larger project of which this paper is a part considers the question of upward social mobility on the part of individuals from each of the two cohorts. The process by which they emerged as political, social, and cultural brokers needs explanation given that upon their entry into the Islamic Near East none could lay claim to social connection or standing. Although their careers cannot be pieced together in full, as I indicate below, a broader reconstruction is possible: the project seeks to identify and describe the likely elements at work at each stage of these careers. The effort involves, in part, making better sense of the linkages between each of the two histories — that of the singers and that of the Turkish officers — and the wider development of ʿAbbāsid-period slavery. To study the careers of singers and commanders, in other words, is to move closer to understanding the place and dynamics of slavery in Near Eastern society of the early Islamic period. These linkages are the subject of the following comments; they concern the first, earliest stage of the two histories.

For evidence, I draw, in good measure, on two extended texts, only the relevant excerpts from which are provided below. The paired texts introduce two individuals, Waṣīf, a Turkish officer, and Maḥbūba, a female singer of unspecified origin (at least on her mother's side). The setting for each of the two careers was imperial (the Arab/Islamic empire under ʿAbbāsid

---

* I wish to thank the participants of the symposium, "Slaves and Households in the Near East," for their responses to the paper. I owe particular thanks to Laura Culbertson (for the invitation) and to Kathryn Babayan, Indrani Chatterjee, and Ehud Toledano (for their insightful comments).

[1] Brunschvig 1960 and Müller 1977– are two excellent if now dated surveys.

suzerainty) and urban (the social fabric of Baghdad and Samarra, the dynasty's principal administrative centers). The indications are that Waṣīf and Maḥbūba belonged initially to large
urban households before their careers were properly launched. It is likely, in other words, that
both spent their youth as domestic servants.

The first text occurs in the *Kitāb al-buldān* of al-Yaʿqūbī (d. 283/897), a work of early
ʿAbbāsid urban geography. It describes the acquisition of young Turkish/Central Asian recruits by the ʿAbbāsid prince, later caliph, Abū Isḥāq al-Muʿtaṣim (r. 218/833–227/842) and
his (later) settlement of them at Samarra, a new capital that he founded shortly after assuming
office. The text indicates that certain of the Turks — all, including Waṣīf, in their capacity
as well-placed military men — played a prominent part in the politics of the new regime
(Gordon 2001). The report also contains a striking reference to the caliph's distribution of
slave women to the Turkish soldiers.

> Aḥmad ibn Abī Yaʿqūb [al-Yaʿqūbī] said: When al-Muʿtaṣim came to Baghdad, re-
> turning from Ṭarsūs in the year in which he was recognized as caliph — this was [A.D.
> 833] — he resided in al-Maʾmūn's palace. Then he built a palace on the eastern side
> of Baghdad and moved there, staying there in the years [A.D. 833, 834, 835, 836]. A
> group of Turks, who were at that time "barbarians," [lit. non-Arabic speakers] were
> with him. [255][2]

> Jaʿfar al-Khushshakī informed me: In the time of al-Maʾmūn, al-Muʿtaṣim used to
> send me to Nūḥ ibn Asad in Samarqand to purchase Turks. I would bring him a group
> of them each year. During al-Maʾmūn's reign [A.D. 813–833], about three thousand
> slaves [*ghulām*, pl. *ghilmān* = young male slaves] were acquired for him. When he be-
> came caliph, he sought them urgently and even bought whatever slaves were in Bagh-
> dad from private citizens. Among those he purchased in Baghdad were a large group
> including Ashinās, who was a slave (*mamlūk*) of Nusaym ibn Khāzim, the father of
> Hārūn ibn Nuʿaym; Ītākh, who was a slave of Sallām ibn al-Abrash; Waṣīf, who was
> a slave armor-maker belonging to the Āl al-Nuʿmān;[3] and Sīmā al-Dimashqī, who
> was a slave of Dhuʾl-Riʾāsatayn al-Faḍl ibn Sahl. When these "barbarian" Turks
> would gallop around on horseback, they would crash into people left and right, so the
> rabble would pounce on them and kill some of them and beat up others. [The Turks']
> blood could be shed with impunity; nothing was done against those committing these
> deeds. This weighed heavily on al-Muʿtaṣim, and he decided to leave Baghdad. [The
> caliph goes on to found Samarra in A.D. 836–838]. [255–56]

The land-grants [in Samarra] for the Turks were kept wholly separate from those
of all the other people. [Al-Muʿtaṣim] kept them segregated so that they would not
be mixed up with the local people and only the people of Farghāna would be their
neighbors. Ashinās and his companions had estates in the place known as al-Karkh.
He was joined by a number of Turkish military officers and men, and he was ordered
to build the mosques and markets. Khāqān ʿUrṭūj and his companions received estates
adjacent to [the palace complex of] al-Jawsaq al-Khāqānī. His companions were ordered to join him and forbidden to be settled within the general populace. Waṣīf and
his companions received estates adjacent to al-Ḥayr; he built an enclosed area named
Ḥāʾir al-Ḥayr around them. The land-grants for all the Turks and the non-Arabs from
Farghāna were kept distant from the markets and the crowded areas of the wide avenues and long streets. [258–59]

---

[2] The numbers in bold type refer to the Arabic text.   [3] *Kāna zarrādan mamlūkan li ʾl-Āl al-Nuʿmān.*

Then [the caliph] purchased slave girls (*jawāri*, sing. *jāriya*) for [the Turks] and had them take wives from among them. He forbade them to marry or to become related through marriage to members of the local populace (*muwalladūn*), and, at the point when their children grew up, they too could marry only one another. Fixed stipends were established for the slave girls of the Turks, and their names registered in the administrative records. Not a one of [the Turks] could divorce his wife or separate from her. **[259]**

Then there were the places for the date-sellers; the slave-market, at an intersection where there were a number of roads branching off, with chambers, upper rooms, and the slave-shops; the police station and main prison; and private residences. There were markets to the left and right on this avenue [offering] a variety of products and manufactured goods. That was just next to Bābak's gibbet. **[260]**

(al-Yaʿqūbī 1892)

The second and later text occurs in the *Murūj al-dhahab* of al-Masʿūdī (d. 345/956), a work that combines features of the universal chronicle and belles-lettres collection. It describes the fate of Maḥbūba, a prominent female singer at the court of the tenth ʿAbbāsid caliph, al-Mutawakkil (r. 232–247/847–861). We learn of her acquisition and rise to prominence, then of her treatment at the hands of Waṣīf and his drinking circle.[4] As seen in two references in the preceding text, Waṣīf had risen from household service to become a member of Samarra's high command; again, al-Yaʿqūbī refers to his acquisition, decades earlier, by al-Mutawakkil's father (al-Muʿtaṣim) from the al-Nuʿmān family of Baghdad.[5] The present text represents Waṣīf high on the social ladder.

> ʿAlī ibn al-Jahm said: When the office of the caliphate passed to the Commander of the Faithful, Jaʿfar al-Mutawakkil ilā Allāh, the notables (*al-nās*) gave him gifts commensurate with their ranking. Ibn Ṭāhir's[6] gift included two hundred slaves, male (*waṣīf*) and female (*waṣīfa*). The gift included a young woman (*jāriya*) named Maḥbūba. She had belonged to a man from [the town of] Ṭāʾif who had seen to her education, refinement, and training in many areas. She acquired facility with poetry which she would sing while performing on the *ʿūd*, excelling in the manner of those gifted persons who do excel. Thus, her relations with al-Mutawakkil grew close: she held a lofty place in his affections unrivalled by any other person. **[281–82]**

> ʿAlī [ibn al-Jahm] continued: Following the murder of al-Mutawakkil,[7] she and many of the [caliph's] slaves became the possession of Bughā the Elder.[8] On one occasion, I visited [Bughā] for a round of drink and good company. [At one point], he ordered the curtain [concealing the performers] wrenched aside and summoned the singers. They

---

[4] This version of the story differs in details from the account in al-Iṣfahānī's *Aghani* (22:204–05). I refer to the latter account below.

[5] I have not been able yet to identify the family (several prominent individuals bearing the name "al-Nuʿmān" lived in Baghdad in this period).

[6] Probably Muḥammad ibn ʿAbdallāh ibn Ṭāhir (d. 253/867), governor of Baghdad through much of the Samarra period.

[7] The famous act of regicide, in Shawwāl 247/ December 861, was carried out by a team of mid-level Turkish officers led by one Bughā the Younger.

[8] Another of the leading Turkish commanders, reported to have been captured in Khurasan with his sons and sent to al-Maʾmūn.

sauntered forward in all manner of jewels and finery; Maḥbūba, without a trace of
either jewels or finery, emerged dressed simply in white.[9] She then sat, her head low-
ered, entirely withdrawn. Waṣīf invited her to sing but she begged off. He said, "But
I implore you," and ordered that an *ʿūd* be given her (lit., "placed against her chest").
Seeing that she had no option but to respond, she pressed the *ʿūd* to her chest and, ac-
companying herself on it, improvised lines of song:

> *What life can bring me pleasure / if I no longer find Ja ʿfar there?*
> *A monarch, I saw him / bloodied and soiled with dust*
> *All who came unhinged [with grief] / or fell ill have long since recovered*
> *Except Maḥbūba who / were she to see death on offer*
> *Would snatch all / that her hand could hold and thus be entombed.*

He continued: Waṣīf grew furious with her [as a result] and ordered her locked up.
She was imprisoned and it was the last that anything was heard of her. **[285–86]**

(al-Masʿūdī 1861–77: volume 7)

Maḥbūba represents the one group, highly trained female entertainers, most of whom
were singers and all of whom, with one or two exceptions, were slaves. Kilpatrick (2003:
47–54), Richardson (2009: 109–10), and Bray (2004) remind us, each in their way, that the
classical Arabic authors are quite particular in what they say of these women. Bray puts it that
the women most often play the role of "heroine, or sometimes villain, of countless romantic
stories" (2004: 136). The information contained in independent stories or "reports" (*khabar*,
pl. *akhbār*) of this kind is, by its very nature, fragmentary and seldom can be substantiated.
It occurs, in any case, as often as not, in deliberately fictional form. Al-Masʿūdī's text bears
out this description: it provides background information on the young singer's appearance and
her subsequent rise to prominence, all related directly to her close relations with the ill-starred
caliph. But, if seemingly credible, the information serves mostly as setting, in this case, for the
account of Maḥbūba's dignified fall from grace. And the aim of such stories is often elusive:
one can as easily read the story as a comment on social types (the boorish, heavy-handed Turk
meets the gutsy but tragic singer) as the record of two individuals' confrontation. There is
little that one can do, in any case, to corroborate either the description of the confrontation
itself or Maḥbūba's fate.

Given the difficulty of reconstructing the individual careers, the effort here is to seek out
broader patterns of description. The women, again, were principally singers although typically they accompanied themselves, with considerable ability, on the *ʿūd* (lute) and other
instruments. Al-Masʿūdī's passage understands, as well, that the singers provided their male
cohort, with their owners/masters usually first in line, with companionship and sexual favors.
His text suggests that matters frequently grew edgy. The scene — the wrenching aside of the
curtain separating the singers from their all-male audience — is not atypical of this brand
of story but the numerous and varied references to the public and highly sexualized role of
the singers might indicate that a *topos* of this kind was "less a fantasy than a gloss applied"
to a social dynamic (Bray 2004: 137). The indications are many that unlike "the veil" of the
free, respectable woman of aristocratic and mid-ranked households, that of the performer was
safely cast aside (Richardson 2009: 111–12). The curtain's rending, with its barely concealed

---

[9] The color of mourning.

suggestion of assault, speaks to a frail, tenuous status on the part of the singers. It is, more specifically, of a piece with numerous other references to violence visited upon the young female slaves. These are hardly surprising given the young women's standing and the apparent role played by coercion, here as perhaps in all forms of slave practice (Blackburn 1988: 271).

The singers became a fixture of ʿAbbāsid high urban culture and, along the way, nurtured networks of personal and professional contacts. Maḥbūba's example suggests that these relationships included close ties to members of the imperial house. Thus much of their activity occurred in and around the caliph's court, in her case that of al-Mutawakkil (who is said elsewhere by al-Masʿūdī to have had a huge appetite, as it were, for young slave women) (Kennedy 2004b: 165). The sources use various terms for the singers, including not only *qayna* (pl. *qiyān*) but also *mughanniya* and the more general *jārīya*, sometimes in combination (e.g., *al-jāriya al-mughanniya*). Given their highly public "face," their close participation in contemporary culture and the range of their contacts, it is appropriate to refer to the *qiyān* as courtesans.

The question of how best to read the Arabic sources arises as well in treating the second group of slaves: represented here by Waṣīf, the group consisted of officers from the predominantly Turkish and Inner Asian regiments of the third/ninth century ʿAbbāsid military (Gordon 2001). The formation of the Turkish regiments occurred on the heels of a grim civil war — a cluster of civil conflicts, in fact, in Iraq but across the provinces as well (Kennedy 2004a: 147–55) — that nearly cost the dynasty throne and empire alike. As part of a wider ʿAbbāsid effort to recover its footing, the newly ascended seventh ʿAbbāsid caliph, ʿAbdallāh al-Maʾmūn (r. 198–213/813–833), assigned the new forces to his younger brother, al-Muʿtaṣim. The Turkish units probably served as the latter's personal guard before taking on responsibilities as a field army (Gordon 2001: 45–46). Al-Yaʿqūbī, as his text suggests, is a principal source on the history of the Turkish forces. He describes their acquisition from elite Baghdadi families in some cases, from a thriving Central Asian slave trade in most others. It was, in part, to accommodate these and his other, non-Turkish troops — the imperial regiments included slave and free forces alike — that al-Muʿtaṣim created the new center at Samarra (Gordon 2001: 47–74).

Some decades into the Samarra period, Waṣīf and others of the Turkish command took the lead in a brief and costly period of unrest. The chaos included rioting on the part of poorly paid troops (Turks and non-Turks) and an assault by Samarran forces (mostly Turks) on the city of Baghdad (251–252/865–866). Taking place simultaneously was a ham-fisted bid for influence by Turkish officers, backed by civilian allies including members of the imperial family. Following their assassination of al-Mutawakkil — for whom Maḥbūba voiced her lament — the Turkish officers sought to promote pliable ʿAbbāsid candidates. The result, a quick turnover of six caliphs, four of whom perished in the process, took place over less than ten years (247–256/861–870) (Gordon 2001: 75–104; Kennedy 2004a: 169–85). The ʿAbbāsid house somehow weathered the violence — the loss of key provinces, often permanent, was probably inevitable — before returning to Baghdad some two decades on. The unrest took a particular toll on the Turkish high command itself: Waṣīf was killed by fellow Turks in 253/867, shortly after the resolution of the Baghdad siege, one in a series of violent deaths suffered by the high command (al-Ṭabarī 1879–1901: 3:1687–88; al-Yaʿqūbī 1892: 2:614). Violence, if usually of a different sort, thus informed the lives of the officers as much as it did the lives of the singers.

In accounting for the histories of the singers and commanders, and, more generally, for third/ninth-century Near Eastern slave practice, there is considerable written and documentary evidence on hand. One might speak of three categories of sources. Early, usually foundational works of Islamic jurisprudence, read in conjunction with the Qurʾān and early works of Ḥadīth, contain many references to slaves and slavery. A second category is the documentary record; of special value in this regard is S. D. Goitein's discussion of slavery as evinced by the Cairo Geniza, and the work of Yūsuf Rāġib which draws upon a wider body of documentary (read: papyrus) evidence. This material generally deals with medieval Egypt but it has the virtue of providing "non-literary" information. Most of the documents date, however, to the fourth/tenth century and later, a question that neither Goitein nor Rāġib address head-on. The two categories of sources, for all of their considerable differences in form, content, and emphasis, have in common a concern with domestic slaves/slavery. Neither, in other words, provides references to, or evidence dealing directly with, the elite singers and commanders.

For this evidence, one must turn to the third — and thus for present purposes invaluable — body of sources, the narrative and literary works produced in Arabic by mostly urban, mostly Muslim scholars from the late second/eighth century on. This is, admittedly, to gloss over the many distinctions within a vast and highly variegated corpus of writing. The works by al-Masʿūdī and al-Yaʿqūbī from which the two extracts are drawn fall into this category, as does a particularly important source on the slave singers, a work as difficult to categorize as the *Murūj:* the *Kitāb al-aghānī* ("Book of Songs") by the fourth/tenth-century writer Abū al-Faraj al-Iṣfahānī (d. 356/967). Of comparable value to the history of the Samarran Turkish military in general, and the careers of the Turkish commanders in particular, is the massive history of al-Ṭabarī (d. 310/923), the *Taʾrīkh al-rusul wa ʾl-mulūk* ("Chronicle of Prophets and Kings").

Again, in eliciting social history from such evidence, and given the near impossibility of piecing together individual biographies, I propose to identify wider patterns. So, for example, the reference to Maḥbūba falls in line with not only a countless number but also a variety of sorts of reference to the presence of the courtesans and the very public character of their profession. A further example regarding enslaved women more generally, each of the texts describes the distribution by a member of the imperial aristocracy of large numbers of slave women. In al-Yaʿqūbī's case, it is al-Muʿtaṣim's assignment of women to the Turkish soldiers, in al-Masʿūdī's case, Ibn Ṭāhir's gifting to al-Mutawakkil of two hundred young slaves (male and female). One can do little to verify either episode; the passage from al-Yaʿqūbī — a reference, after all, to an apparent, large-scale project of social engineering — occurs, so far as I know, nowhere else in the Arabic sources. But one can hardly set such accounts aside. The one reference (al-Yaʿqūbī) provides a plausible, indeed the best explanation for the appearance of the second generation of Samarran Turks (Gordon 2001: 69–70); the second reference (al-Masʿūdī) can be joined to a long series of examples in which slave women end up as gifts. The extent and variety of attestations of this sort certainly suggest conditions on the ground.

The singers and soldiers were clearly distinct from one another as they were from other categories of ʿAbbāsid-era slaves. The distinctions, of gender certainly but also access to decision-making circles — al-Masʿūdī's text, it might be said, understands that members of both groups shared at least some manner of access of this kind — seem obvious. No less a distinction was that of the kind of labor provided by each of the two cohorts (the efforts of each is indicative, of course, of the highly variegated nature of ʿAbbāsid-era slave labor). The fact that the Turkish soldiers wielded force — although clearly not a monopoly of force (the Samarra period might otherwise have been quieter) — are likely to have distinguished their ability to meet their individual and collective needs, notably in acquiring influence. A more difficult question is whether bearing arms allowed them to mitigate the effects of enslavement.

But here the point is that while these distinctions were hardly secondary, in fact quite the contrary, there is reason to stress the common experience of slavery. It is not simply that, in all likelihood, singers and soldiers arrived on the scene with little to distinguish their situation from that of the mass of other young slaves about whom we know next to nothing. It is that slavery, as a determinant, remained constant, even beyond the moment of manumission if and when it occurred.[10]

II

The singers and their counterparts in the Turkish high command gained access to elite standing by moving across sociocultural, legal, economic, and even political boundaries. They did so in part by virtue of their membership in, and, in some cases, creation of, elite urban households. A first step is to locate both sets of individuals at the point of their entry into urban 'Abbāsid society. It involves joining both sets of imperial servants to what looks to have been a flourishing commerce in human beings in the third/ninth-century Mediterranean world.

Given how much remains to be understood about early 'Abbāsid slave history, Michael McCormick's discussion, in *Origins of the European Economy* (2001), is to be welcomed. It puts slavery near the center of a comprehensive argument regarding the economic history of early medieval Europe and the Mediterranean basin. 'Abbāsid-era slavery, he argues,[11] was not simply a link in a trans-regional and vigorous commerce that spanned all coasts of the Mediterranean and the hinterlands to which they gave access. McCormick posits that the Islamic/Arab world of the second/eighth and third/ninth centuries was rather the venue to which most of the slave traffic was directed: "fur, probably, and Frankish swords certainly were exported to the Muslim world. But the thing which Europe was producing in greatest abundance around 800 was Europeans. The strength and beauty of their bodies were in great demand in the expanding economy of the Caliphate, and they had the signal advantage of transporting themselves across the Alps" (2001: 791). European and, by the turn of the third/ninth century, Arab slave traders worked with great energy to meet the "voracious appetite" of Arab/Islamic urban centers for, in this case, "northern" slaves (2001: 759, 768, 776). Cruel and boundless activity, it lent, McCormick argues, powerful impetus to early Europe's economic expansion.

European medievalists are best placed to assess McCormick's central contentions. But clearly he raises questions for specialists in Islamic and Near Eastern studies: for example, how well are we able to map conditions in the Islamic urban world that, if the argument holds, raised the demand for slave (and free) labor to new levels? McCormick draws on a broad number of sources, including Arabic works in translation, among these the writings of Ibn Khordādhbeh (d. 300/911?), al-Jāḥiẓ (d. 255/869), and others. He mostly ignores evidence remaining in the original Arabic, however, which is far less a criticism of a remarkable book than recognition that historians of Near Eastern and Islamic society have much additional material, not to speak of a different and closer vantage point, to bring to bear on a wide-ranging topic (Müller 1977–: 66).

---

[10] References to manumission of individual female singers exist but almost none to individual Turkish commanders. This is not to say, of course, that it did not occur. See Kennedy 2001: 122.

[11] The phrase ("'Abbāsid-era") is mine.

At work are a number of elements. Trade in the late second/eighth and early third/ninth centuries likely assumed the predominant role that conquest and capture had played, in producing an enslaved population/work force, in the first period of Islamic history (Brockopp 2000: 145–46; Crone 1980: 50; Lewis 1990: 9–11). If McCormick's emphasis falls on the busy commerce that moved slaves from particular regions of Europe to the southern reaches of the Mediterranean, much other evidence points to equally vigorous trade moving to the same end point — the urban centers of the Maghrib, Egypt, Syria, Arabia, and Iraq — but along routes moving north across the Sahara and along the Red Sea or south and west from the Caucasus and Transoxiana ('Athamina 2007: 390–91; Brunschvig 1960: 32; McCormick 2001: 759).

Al-Ya'qūbī, elsewhere in his *Buldān*, refers to the building (*dār al-raqīq*) containing the slaves of Abū Ja'far [al-Manṣūr — the second of the 'Abbāsid caliphs]; he describes them as having been acquired across "distant lands" (al-Ya'qūbī 1892: 248). Ibn Hawqal (fl. late fourth/tenth century), an important Arab geographer, mentions slaves, either traded and/ or produced, in a number of locales across the contemporary Islamic world and adjoining regions. He does so often in passing, citing the presence of slaves (and/or activities concerning slaves) alongside that of other products (e.g., furs, agricultural goods, livestock, and so on), each a feature of the given locale (Ibn Hawqal 1964).[12] He does so, one might add, in matter-of-fact fashion; the common marketing of goods and slaves apparently required no particular comment.

In assessing the regional and ethnic complexity of 'Abbāsid slave populations, there is the question of dating: much of the available evidence originates from sources dating to periods subsequent to the third/ninth century. A widely cited text, for example, the mid-fifth/eleventh-century treatise of Ibn Buṭlān (d. 458/1066), a Baghdadi scholar of Nestorian Christian background and physician by trade, is a short handbook on the purchase and physical examination of slaves. It lists at one point the ethnic and regional origins of female slaves, with comments on the physical and "moral" qualities of each of the categories of women (Ibn Buṭlān 1373/1954: 372–78).[13] The range of geographical reference is striking: the list includes women of India, Sind, the Maghrib, several regions of sub-Saharan and coastal Africa, three towns of Arabia (Mecca, Medina, and Ṭā'if), Yemen, Qandahar (Afghanistan), Allān (Caucasus), and the Daylam region (northern Iran). It refers as well to Turkish, Greek (presumably Byzantine), and Armenian women (toward whom Ibn Buṭlān seems testy: Lewis 1990: 137 n. 3).[14]

The references to Waṣīf and Maḥbūba sit well with Ibn Buṭlān's list; the example of each of the two slaves helps in describing the demographic complexity of 'Abbāsid slave traffic. The reference to Turkish women, for example, is to be joined to al-Ya'qūbī's comments on the acquisition of Turkish males, in Central Asia and in Baghdad itself. But, in each case, wrinkles appear. There is, for example — and the problem is greater in the case of the Turkish military recruits than it is, comparatively speaking, for the slave singers — rather little specific evidence regarding the dynamics of acquisition and enslavement. The evidence, a handful of references, largely concerns the delivery of Central Asian slaves by 'Abbāsid governors and other imperial agents (Gordon 2001: 34–36; la Vaissière: 210–11). Unclear is the means by which they came into possession of the slaves. Broadly speaking, however, ethnic tensions,

---

[12] For quick reference, see the excellent index in Kramers and Wiet = Ibn Hawqal 1964.

[13] For partial translations of the Arabic, see Lewis 1987: 243–51 and Mez 1937: 160–62.

[14] Perhaps unrelated is Ibn Hawqal's reference (1964: 2:336) to controversy surrounding the sale of Armenian slaves.

territorial wars, and other forms of conflict endemic to Inner Asia likely produced a steady flow of enslaved individuals and groups (Golden 2001). As in the case of the Ḥijāz (see below), a regional practice of slaving became, by the ʿAbbāsid period, if not much earlier, a sub-system of the global Mediterranean trade.

A related question is whether there was a particular effort to acquire adolescent Turkish males; the question is clearly suggested by the effort itself, that is, to form a new-style military force. A long-held view (Ayalon 1975: 55–56) is that the effort involved the acquisition of recruits young enough to be "shaped" into properly loyal imperial troops. The argument links enslavement to a particular form of service required of the Turkish soldiers: stripped of all other loyalties, they would (somehow) attach themselves dutifully to the caliph and/or his office. The history of the Samarran Turkish military, one that culminated in a terrible confrontation with the caliphate, certainly raises questions in this regard. Many of the recruits were young men but we know of at least one case, that of Bughā the Elder (d. 248/862), said to have been captured with his sons, where it would appear to be the case of an older man (Gordon 2001: 19, 92–94). Waṣīf, for his part, was acquired by al-Muʿtaṣim from a leading household of that city: al-Yaʿqūbī describes him as possessing skills in weapons-making and as "owned" (*mamlūk*). The name is sufficient evidence in itself; standing alone in the manner of most such names, it strips away all reference to background and family attachment.[15] Unsurprisingly, we have no indication of his specific origins apart from the general designation of "Turk." It can be reasonably assumed that Waṣīf was brought to Iraq as a youngster; there is, in any case, no reference anywhere to his having been born there. The point is that he likely joined the ʿAbbāsid military at an older age.

By contrast, Maḥbūba — another single name ("Beloved") with, perhaps, in this case, a sardonic edge — was probably born a slave into a Near Eastern household. The two references we possess are a bit difficult to reconcile: while al-Masʿūdī locates her at a very early point in Ṭāʾif, al-Iṣfahānī identifies her as a slave-girl of mixed Arab and non-Arab origin (*muwallada*) from Baṣra (1412/1992: 22:204–05). Ibn Buṭlān, for his part, refers to Ṭāʾif, along with Mecca and Medina, as venues of slave commerce. He does not include Baṣra but there is good reason for including it in this regard alongside the three Arabian towns. Many sources indicate a practice of slavery in both locales already in the pre-Islamic period, with a number of specific references to well-placed women singers. Maḥbūba thus followed many generations of singers produced in, and sold from, these same towns (Farmer 1929: 36–88 passim). Her example, in other words, suggests that two interrelated patterns remained at work into the ʿAbbāsid period: the integration of a local, Near Eastern sub-system of slavery with the Mediterranean region-wide system, much like that connecting Samarqand and other Central Asian cities with the same broader system, and, here as there, the provision of specific types of skilled slave labor.

The reference to Maḥbūba as a *muwallada* indicates, again, that she was the daughter of a (free) Arab father and non-Arab slave concubine, of either local or foreign origin. That Maḥbūba was subsequently turned over to the slave market would indicate, in turn, that her father, one supposes the head of the household, denied his paternity of her. As a result of her origins and fatherlessness, so to speak, the girl's standing in the household was decidedly tenuous. She was, effectively, left prey to the decision, as such time as it was made, to offer her up for purchase.

---

[15] The point made all the clearer by the particular name (Arabic *waṣīf* "servant, domestic"). On naming of slaves in quite a later period (the Ottoman empire), see Zilfi 2010: 156–58.

Further passages in the *Aghānī* seem to point to a steady traffic in the daughters of (slave) concubines. These brief texts, no more than a few lines in most cases, contain statements of protest, voiced by the slave women themselves, in which they contest their standing. Nagging questions surround the origin and intent of these passages: it would be naive to ignore the likely rhetorical elements at work (Gordon 2009: 266–67). But they may serve as evidence of the girls' treatment, that is, the sale of the young women to slave merchants, and thus rude entry into the slave market, and their subsequent handling. In each case the complaint, on the part of the singer, turns on the same legal point: that because they were the offspring of free males — the father in each case, usually the *paterfamilias*, had produced the child with a slave woman in his possession — they were by law to have free standing. Islamic law also stipulates that the mother acquired a new status — that of the *umm walad* (lit. "mother of a child") — that brought with it legal protections (Richardson 2009: 107). By denying any role on his part, the father-in-all-but-admission was presumably also denying these protections to his one-time companion.

III

The two slaves — the future singer and the commander-to-be — thus joined a large, ethnically (quite) diverse and (often) transient population of slaves subject to a flourishing commerce of the eastern Mediterranean, one operating on the local and trans-regional levels. But what of their subsequent history as denizens of ʿAbbāsid society? The task is to follow the trajectory to elite standing, that is, the later stages of the two histories. Singers and soldiers had much in common to this point, with each other and with the larger mass of more "ordinary" slaves about whom the sources offer little information. But, from here, the common experience — of slavery, at least elements of which persisted from sale to grave — began to give way to the distinct paths followed by members of each of the two cohorts, relative to one another and to that larger slave populace. The task thus requires a balancing of factors, shared and distinct.

At least three elements of the subsequent period of these nascent careers deserve further exploration: the "manufacture" of the singers and soldiers as skilled slaves; the opportunities provided them as a result of formation and education; and the obstacles placed before them that acted, I suggest, in countervailing fashion.

The setting for both histories, again, was both urban and dynamic: the early ʿAbbāsid period witnessed a steady rise in the size and number of towns and cities across the Maghrib and Near East (Wheatley 2001: 33–58). It is unlikely that sufficient evidence will emerge to properly quantify urban slave labor in either region for this period. A related problem with the Arabic/Islamic sources is a tendency, seen above in both texts, to amplify numbers; at best, perhaps, these are used to indicate relative scale. It seems clear, nonetheless, that the majority of slaves of the third/ninth-century Near East served in urban households; such was the case of both Waṣīf and Maḥbūba. Slavery was "deeply embedded in the household system, mitigated against the hardship endured by slaves in societies in which slave labor was a primary relationship of production" (Marmon 1988: 331). Many indications are that even households of modest size owned at least one slave, and the consistency with which the sources — in one anecdote after the next — have a young male (*ghulām*) or female (*jāriya*) slave on hand, providing often mundane services, certainly suggests a ubiquitous presence of domestic slaves.

Urban society employed its slaves in a variety of capacities, and, in many cases, the labor required of them is likely to have been either unskilled (e.g., washing, cleaning, and the mundane forms of food preparation) or, where skills were needed, of a sort that could be acquired along the way (e.g., child-rearing, errand-running, and the delivery of sensitive messages). The skills provided by singers and soldiers were more specialized. In the case of the singers, the sources, as al-Mas'ūdī's passage bears out, refer to the high-level training received by the singers prior to their acquisition by owners and masters. To put it differently, slave traders, responding to market demand, turned their energies in (they hoped) appropriate fashion to the selection and provision of skilled slaves. The sources too often only hint at this facet of the 'Abbāsid-era slave trade. Al-Mas'ūdī refers above to Maḥbūba's training. Arīb al-Ma'mūnīya, perhaps the most celebrated of the early 'Abbāsid singers, is reported similarly to have undergone a thorough education — in the city of Baṣra — in the language arts, poetry, singing, and composition, as well as sundry activities such as chess and backgammon (Gordon 2005: 86).

As one might expect in an imperial setting, the demand for courtesans with their requisite training appears to have been driven by the caliphal court itself: innumerable anecdotes, notably those contained in the *Aghānī* but in all other medieval Arabic belles-lettres works as well, have one 'Abbāsid caliph after another, and the members of their entourages, in close association and in possession of large numbers of trained female slaves. One reading of this material is to relate it to the rise of a dynamic urban society in the early 'Abbāsid period (Bray 2004: 137): taste for the company of the singers was duplicated in fine homes across the imperial capitals, with the imperial court thus modeling at least the one highly visible complex of cultural practice.

Supply of Turkish and Inner Asian military recruits also met specific demand, in this case on the part of the imperial state. The new-style institution, the slave military, appears to have been initiated by al-Ma'mūn and assigned to Abū Isḥāq al-Mu'taṣim (r. A.D. 833–842), prior to his accession to the imperial throne. The young slaves were required to provide skilled labor, in this case, in the use of a variety of arms, particularly it seems, bow and horse. (It might be added that Turkish units, outfitted in fine uniforms, were used for ceremonial purposes as well, and it seems that Turkish boys, much like their female counterparts, were sought out as well by 'Abbāsid society for entertainment, companionship, and sexual favors.) But, to date, next to no information has come to light regarding the formation of the young Turkish military recruits, either as guardsmen (with ceremonial functions) or as field troops.

There are certainly indications that 'Abbāsid society held to perceptions of the Turks as hardy warriors particularly skilled in horsemanship and archery. Modern scholarship has often echoed the point in arguing for the contribution of the Samarran Turkish fighters (Kennedy 2001: 122–23). The problem may be, however, that one is confusing cultural perceptions — however well grounded these might have been in some reality — with the performance of these particular recruits if, in fact, they arrived in 'Abbāsid Iraq as boys. Can one be sure, in other words, that they were of an age to bring appropriate knowledge to their new military service? Or were they taught by older Turkish instructors? The acquisition of Waṣīf and other perhaps older and better acculturated Turks in Baghdad suggests an effort to find individuals on whom al-Mu'taṣim could rely in his dealings with the rank and file, but this falls mostly into the realm of speculation (Gordon 2001: 23–25). It remains unclear how the Turkish forces acquired their martial skills.

The demand for skilled labor marks a significant point of connection between the two elite slave cohorts and the wider current of 'Abbāsid-era slaves. Singers and soldiers, to put it in simple terms, were culled from that same broad slave population. It is difficult to discern the terms by which the young candidates were selected; one can safely assume, I think, a set of judgments that mixed assessment of their physical appearance and mental acuity with assumptions rooted in cultural typecasting. The latter factor, at any rate, is certainly suggested by the catalog of qualities provided by Ibn Buṭlān.

What followed, for future singers and commanders alike, was a process of constant negotiation, or so the evidence would suggest. They were subject, at least to the point of manumission (see above) but probably well beyond it, to realities over which they had little control. They were subject to the demands of the market and the whims of their owners; I have suggested earlier that this may have been far more the case of the singers than the commanders. But slave standing entailed — and, again, manumission appears not to have been a wholly mitigating factor — deracination, social stigma, and forms of legal discrimination. The sources suggest the effects of each of these factors. But, on the other hand, and by virtue of their training and the press of market demand — for high-end cultural production and social intercourse, in the case of the singers, for high-level support in the creation and administration of the new military, in the case of the commanders — the members of both cohorts were provided with potentially unlimited opportunity for access around such obstacles. The end result was elite standing; but the indications — Maḥbūba's disappearance into oblivion and Waṣīf's destruction at the hands of his fellow soldiers — are that even standing of the kind remained highly fragile.

BIBLIOGRAPHY

'Athamina, Khalil

2007   "How Did Islam Contribute to Change the Legal Status of Women: The Case of the *Jawārī*, or the *Female Slaves.*" *Al-Qanṭara* 28/2: 383–408.

Ayalon, David
   1975   "Preliminary Remarks on the *Mamlūk* Military Institution in Islam." In *War, Technology and Society in the Middle East*, edited by V. J. Perry and M. E. Yapp, pp. 44–58. London: Oxford University Press.

Berkey, Jonathan P.
   2003   *The Formation of Islam: Religion and Society in the Near East, 600–1800.* Themes in Islamic History 2. Cambridge: Cambridge University Press.

Blackburn, Robin
   1988   "Defining Slavery — Its Special Features and Social Role." In *Slavery and Other Forms of Unfree Labour*, edited by L. J. Archer, pp. 262–97. History Workshop Series. London: Routledge.

Bray, Julia
   2004   "Men, Women and Slaves in Abbasid Society." In *Gender in the Early Medieval World: East and West, 300–900*, edited by L. Brubaker and J. M. H. Smith, pp. 121–46. Cambridge: Cambridge University Press.

Brockopp, Jonathan E.
   2000   *Early Mālikī Law: Ibn 'Abd al-Ḥakam and His Major Compendium of Jurisprudence.* Studies in Islamic Law and Society 14. Leiden: Brill.

Brunschvig, R.
   1960   "'Abd." In *Encyclopaedia of Islam*. Volume 1, pp. 24–40. 2nd edition. Leiden: Brill.
Bulliet, Richard W.
   1994   *Islam: The View from the Edge.* New York: Columbia University Press.

Crone, Patricia
1980   *Slaves on Horses: The Evolution of the Islamic Polity.* Cambridge: Cambridge
              University Press.

Farmer, Henry George
1929   *A History of Arabian Music to the XIIIth Century.* London: Luzac. Reprinted 1967.

Goitein, S. D.
1967–93   *A Mediterranean Society: The Jewish Communities of the Arab World as Portrayed in
              the Documents of the Cairo Genizah.* 6 volumes. Berkeley: University of California
              Press.

Golden, Peter B.
2001   "The Terminology of Slavery and Servitude in Medieval Turkic." In *Studies on
              Central Asian History in Honor of Yuri Bregel,* edited by D. A. DeWeese, pp. 27–56.
              Indiana University Uralic and Altaic Series 167. Bloomington: Research Institute for
              Inner Asian Studies.

Gordon, Matthew S.
2001   *The Breaking of a Thousand Swords: A History of the Turkish Military of Samarra
              (A.H. 200–275/815–889 C.E.).* State University of New York Series in Medieval
              Middle East History. Albany: State University of New York Press.
2005   "ʿArib al-Maʾmuniyah (797–890)." In *Arabic Literary Culture, 500–925,* edited by
              M. Cooperson and S. M. Toorawa, pp. 85–90. Dictionary of Literary Biography 311.
              Farmington Hills: Thomson Gale.
2009   "Yearning and Disquiet: Al-Jāḥiẓ and the *Risālat al-qiyān.*" In *Al-Jāḥiẓ: A Muslim
              Humanist for our Time,* edited by A. Heinemann, J. L. Meloy, T. Khalidi, and
              M. Kropp, pp. 253–68. Orient-Institut Beirut, Beiruter Texte und Studien 119.
              Würzburg: Ergon.

Ibn Buṭlān, al-Mukhtār ibn al-Ḥasan
1373/1954   *Risālah fī shirāʾ al-raqīq wa-taqlīb al-ʿabīd,* edited by ʿAbd al-Salām Hārūn, pp.
              333–89 (no. 15). Nawādir al-makhṭūṭāt 4. Cairo: Maṭbaʿat Lajnat al-taʾlīf waʾl-
              tarjamah waʾl-nashr.

Ibn Hawqal, Abū al-Qāsim al-Naṣībī
1964   Original translated by J. H. Kramers and G. Wiet as *Configuration de la terre.* 2
              volumes. Paris: Maisonneuve & Larose.

Al-Iṣfahānī, ʿAlī ibn al-Ḥusayn
1412/1992   *Kitāb al-aghānī,* edited by ʿAbd al-Amīr ʿAlī Mahannā and Samīr Jābir. 27 volumes.
              Beirut: Dār al-Kutub al-ʿIlmīya.

Kennedy, Hugh
2001   *The Armies of the Caliphs: Military and Society in the Early Islamic State.* Warfare
              and History. London: Routledge.
2004a   *The Prophet and the Age of the Caliphates: The Islamic Near East from the Sixth to
              the Eleventh Century.* 2nd edition. London: Pearson/Longman.
2004b   *When Baghdad Ruled the Muslim World: The Rise and Fall of Islam's Greatest
              Dynasty.* Cambridge: Da Capo Press.

Kilpatrick, Hilary
2003   *Making the Great Book of Songs: Compilation and the Author's Craft in Abû l-
              Faraj al-Isbahânî's* Kitâb al-aghânî. RoutledgeCurzon Studies in Arabic and Middle-
              Eastern Literature 5. London: RoutledgeCurzon.

La Vaissière, Étienne de
2007   *Samarcande et Samarra: Élites d'Asie Centrale dans l'Empire Abbasside.* Studia
              Iranica, Cahier 35. Leuven: Peeters.

Lewis, Bernard
    1987   *Islam: From the Prophet Muhammad to the Capture of Constantinople*, Volume 2:
                Religion and Society. 2nd edition. Documentary History of Western Civilization.
                Oxford: Oxford University Press.
    1990   *Race and Slavery in the Middle East: An Historical Enquiry*. Oxford: Oxford
                University Press.

Marmon, Shaun E.
    1999   "Domestic Slavery in the Mamluk Empire: A Preliminary Sketch." In *Slavery in the
                Islamic Middle East*, edited by S. E. Marmon, pp. 1–23. Princeton: Markus Wiener.
    1988   "Slavery, Islamic World." In *Dictionary of the Middle Ages*, edited by J. R. Strayer,
                volume 11, pp. 330–33. New York: Charles Scribner's Sons.

Al-Masʿūdī, ʿAlī ibn al-Ḥusayn ibn ʿAlī
    1861–1877   *Murūj al-dhahab wa ʾl-ma ʾādin al-jawhar*. Edited and translated by C. Barbier de
                Meynard and P. de Courteille as *Les prairies d'or*. 9 volumes. Paris: Imprimerie
                Impériale and Imprimerie Nationale.

McCormick, Michael
    2001   *Origins of the European Economy: Communications and Commerce, A.D. 300–900*.
                Cambridge: Cambridge University Press.

Mez, Adam
    1937   *The Renaissance of Islam*. Translated by S. Khuda Bukhsh and D. S. Margoliouth.
                London: Luzac.

Müller, Hans
    1977–   "Sklaven." In *Wirtschaftsgeschichte des Vorderen Orients in islamischer Zeit*, edited
                by B. Spuler, pp. 53–83. Handbuch der Orientalistik. Erste Abteilung, Nahe und der
                Mittlere Osten. Leiden: Brill.

Al-Nuwayrī, Aḥmad ibn ʿAbd al-Wahhāb
    1963–   *Nihāyat al-arab fī funūn al-adab*. Volume 5, pp. 38–116. Cairo: al-Muʾassasah al-
                Miṣrīyah al-ʿĀmmah lil-Taʾlīf waʾl-Tarjamah waʾl-Ṭibāʿah waʾl-Nashr.

Rāġib, Yūsuf
    1993   "Les marchés aux esclaves en terre d'Islam." In *Mercati e Mercanti nell'alto me-
                dioevo: L'area Euroasiatica e l'area Mediterranea*, pp. 721–63. Settimane di studio
                del Centro italiano di studi sull'alto Medioevo 40. Spoleto: Centro Italiano di studi
                sull'alto medioevo.

Richardson, Kristina
    2009   "Singing Slave Girls (*qiyan*) of the ʿAbbasid Court in the Ninth and Tenth Centuries."
                In *Children in Slavery through the Ages*, edited by G. Campbell, S. Miers, and J. C.
                Miller, pp. 105–18. Athens: Ohio University Press.

Al-Ṭabarī, Muḥammad ibn Jarīr
    1879–1901   *Ṭa ʾrīkh al-rusul wa ʾl-mulūk*, edited by M. J. de Goeje et al. as *Annales quos scripsit*.
                15 volumes. Leiden: Brill.

Wheatley, Paul
    2001   *The Places Where Men Pray Together: Cities in Islamic Lands, Seventh through the
                Tenth Centuries*. Chicago: University of Chicago Press.

Al-Yaʿqūbī, Aḥmad ibn Abī Yaʿqūb
    1892   *Kitāb al-buldān*, edited by M. J. de Goeje. Bibliotheca geographorum Arabicorum 7.
                Leiden: Brill.

Zilfi, Madeline C.
    2010   *Women and Slavery in the Late Ottoman Empire: The Design of Difference*.
                Cambridge Studies in Islamic Civilization. Cambridge: Cambridge University Press.

6

AN EMPIRE OF MANY HOUSEHOLDS: THE CASE OF OTTOMAN ENSLAVEMENT

EHUD R. TOLEDANO, TEL AVIV UNIVERSITY

Enslavement in many Islamic societies was intimately connected to the main social, economic, and political unit that permeated and undergirded those societies for centuries — the household. This view has been put forth and debated in the literature over the past decade or so and seems to have been widely accepted.[1] The purpose of this chapter, then, is to explain the enslavement-household **nexus** and its pivotal role in the Ottoman societies of the Middle East and North Africa from the seventeenth century to the nineteenth. To achieve that, we begin with a brief survey of what enslavement was in the Ottoman Empire, to be followed by an analysis of the history of households and how they exploited the labor and sexuality of the enslaved people in them.[2] We are not interested in providing a universal definition of enslavement, which greatly varied from one social and historical context to another. However, a broad-based schema for understanding the Ottoman and Islamic phenomenon is provided below, in order to facilitate a fruitful comparison between that and enslavement in the societies of the ancient world.

THE OTTOMAN EMPIRE AND THE ENSLAVED

There is precious little research on Ottoman enslavement in the period preceding the nineteenth century. Whereas the past two decades have seen an impressive growth in the literature dealing with enslavement and the slave trade in the Empire during the last century of Ottoman rule, only very few studies, all in article format, have appeared on the early modern period. Here we have to rely on the pioneering work of scholars like Halil Sahillioğlu, Halil İnalcık, Ronald Jennings, Alan Fisher, Jane Hathaway, Yvonne Seng, Suraiya Faroqhi, and Madeline Zilfi.[3] Much ground still needs to be covered before a satisfactory picture can emerge, but the good news is that there is no shortage of first-hand and first-rate sources — from court records and government correspondence to narrative accounts. For the early modern period — contrary to the nineteenth century — these have been only very partially tapped: one need only count the small number of court cases adduced in all these studies together in order to realize the task ahead and the promising potential for future research.

---

[1] See, for example, Toledano 1997 and the literature on Ottoman-local elites contained therein.

[2] In putting together this article, I have weaved in revised sections from two earlier publications: Toledano 2007b, and my most recent book, *As If Silent and Absent: Bonds of Enslavement in the Islamic Middle East* (2007a).

[3] For full references to these works, see the notes immediately below. See also: Sahillioğlu 1985; Fisher 1978, 1980, and 1985; Jennings 1987; Zilfi 2000; Hunwick 1999; Seng 1996; Ertuğ 1998; Ayyıldız and Çetin 1996; Faroqhi 2002 (this is a collection of previously published articles, of which nos. 4, 6, and 13, published between 1997 and 2001, are relevant to our discussion). Erdem 1996 also has some interesting observations about pre-nineteenth-century enslavement. On *kul*/harem enslavement in Ottoman Egypt, see Hathaway 1997 and 2003.

The Ottoman Empire was the last and greatest Islamic power of the early modern and modern eras. In many ways, the history of the Middle East between 1517 and 1918 is a chapter in Ottoman history, and Ottoman heritage has lingered in the eastern Mediterranean many decades after the demise of the Empire. While often viewed in the West as the paragon of conservatism and stagnation, the last two decades of intense research have shown that the Ottoman Empire was, through many periods of its long history, a complex and fascinating entity, dynamic and adaptable, pragmatic and resilient, tolerant and accommodating. There were of course periods in which it resembled its negative image in many ways, but the overall account of the teeming and diversified social web under its rule certainly defies that image. The Decline Paradigm of Ottoman history refers to the early modern period, or more precisely to the seventeenth and eighteenth centuries. The dramatic transformation the Empire underwent during that period also had a profound impact upon the social institution of enslavement.

Enslavement was a universal phenomenon, present in almost every known human society and culture. The Ottomans were no exception, and in many ways they followed in the footsteps of earlier Islamic states. The legal essence of enslavement derives from Islamic law, although various Muslim societies developed their own brand of enslavement. Thus, the Ottomans had inherited the basic practice of military-administrative bondage from the Caliphate of Al-Mu'tasim (d. 833) and later the Mamluk Sultanate (1258–1516/7), which they had defeated and replaced in the eastern Mediterranean. From fairly early on in their history, the *kul*, or the slaves of the sultan recruited by child levy in the Balkans, formed the backbone of the imperial army and government. The female cognate institution was known as *harem* slavery, and for much of the early modern period, it was the mainstay of the imperial and elite household network. But other types of bondage co-existed with the *kul*/harem system, namely agricultural, domestic, and menial enslavement.

The main source of enslaved persons in the Ottoman Empire was the large pool of captives taken as spoils of war on the various fronts, including those in Europe. From the fifteenth to the eighteenth centuries, European slaves, mostly from the northeastern shores of the Mediterranean, that is, Greece and the Balkans, were being forcibly transported into the Ottoman Empire and employed there in different occupations. Whereas many of the male captives were used on agricultural estates, others were employed on smaller farms, gardens, vineyards, and orchards. A large number of women reached the harems of the imperial elite and were engaged in domestic service or — in smaller numbers than fantasized by European travelers — used as concubines. The enslaved tended to livestock and fisheries, and worked in bakeries, cotton mills, shipyards, and ports. Some of the servants were trusted with trade and finances, but most of those who labored in an urban setting were simply servants.[4]

In general, the Ottoman system did not favor agricultural enslavement, and the advent of Ottoman rule, as in the case of Cyprus, normally meant the extinction of cultivation by unfree persons.[5] One of the few scholars to have studied Ottoman agricultural enslavement is Halil İnalcık, who showed that enslaved captives were employed on large Ottoman estates up to the sixteenth century, where they were mainly used in rice cultivation and other cash crops.[6] But with the large transformations that the Ottoman Empire underwent in the seventeenth century, agricultural production — alongside the restructuring of other aspects of government, society, and the economy — was reorganized into smaller units, abandoning the large estates

----

[4] Seng 1999: 30.

[5] Jennings 1993.

[6] İnalcık 1979: 30–35; 1982: 88–94.

and their large-scale methods of labor exploitation. In the evolving realities of the Ottoman countryside, agricultural labor in most regions was now organized around a free peasantry, cultivating small tracts of land under a tax regime with several variants. Many of the newly acquired territories were parceled out to low- and high-level military officers in return for taxes and military service as part of the *timar* system. In the early modern period, that system evolved into short-term tax farming by auction (*iltizam*) and later, larger long-term and lifetime tax farms (*malikâne*).[7]

Agricultural enslavement was to be seen again in the Ottoman Empire only in the second half of the nineteenth century, when it was introduced from the outside either as an imported formation or a local response to an external market stimulant. The first instance occurred when the Circassians were deported from the Caucasus by the Russians during the 1850s and 1860s. The refugees were allowed to bring with them to the Ottoman Empire their enserfed cultivators, who entered as families and were settled on land provided by the government. The other case of agricultural enslavement was the temporary rise in the employment of African, mostly Sudanese, laborers in the cotton fields in Egypt during the cotton boom of the 1860s, caused by the American Civil War.[8]

Thus, the other forms of enslavement in the Empire toward the early modern period included domestic service in urban elite households, largely performed by women who were either captured or purchased from southeast Europe, lands lying north of the Black Sea, and — increasingly in the eighteenth century — from the regions between the Caspian and the Black Seas, that is, Georgia and Circassia. Enslaved men from all those regions performed menial tasks such as mining and occasional public works. This variety of functions performed by enslaved persons in Ottoman societies, coupled with the equally varied places of origin from where the enslaved were wrenched, constitute the fabric of Ottoman enslavement as a subject of research and study. Rather than think of these as unrelated, disjointed types of enslavement, we better see them all inhabiting a **continuum**, with varying origins, cultures, functions, and statuses.[9] Indeed, the complexity of the practice makes it necessary to look for a differentiated approach that can accommodate its internal contradictions and seeming intractability: high- and low-status mix, honor and shame appear intertwined, even to a trained eye in non-Ottoman, non-Islamic forms of enslavement.

To better understand the phenomenon we may classify the position of enslaved people according to **six** main criteria, which in turn affected their treatment and fortunes:

- the **tasks the enslaved** performed — whether domestic, agricultural, menial, or *kul*/harem;
- the **stratum of the slavers** — whether an urban elite, rural notability, small-hold cultivators, artisans, or merchants;
- **location** — whether in the core or the peripheral areas;
- **type of habitat** — whether urban, village, or nomad;

---

[7] For an introduction-level survey of the *timar* system, see İnalcık 1989; for a monographic treatment of the transformation into *iltizam* and *malikâne*, see Khoury 1997 and the references to Ariel Salzmann's articles contained therein.

[8] For agricultural enslavement among the Circassians in the Empire, see chapter three of Toledano 2000b.

For agricultural enslavement in Egypt, see Baer 1969. For a related discussion, see also Toledano 2002.

[9] A model for understanding Ottoman enslavement is suggested in my article "The Concept of Slavery in Ottoman and Other Muslim Societies: Dichotomy or Continuum?" (2000a).

- **gender** — whether male, female, or eunuch; and

- **ethnicity** — whether European or Caucasian (and later African).

For the late eighteenth century and later, the following impression clearly emerges from the sources:

- enslaved **domestic** workers in **urban elite households** were better treated than enslaved people in other settings and predicaments;

- the **farther** from the core, the **lower** on the strata scale, and the **less densely-populated** the habitat, the **greater** the chances the enslaved had to receive **worse** treatment.

This brings up the whole issue of how "mild" was enslavement in Ottoman and Islamic societies, as compared to ancient enslavement, or early modern and modern enslavement in the Atlantic and the Indian Ocean worlds. Since we have already dealt with this question on several occasions,[10] we need here only to mention that Madeline Zilfi has recently put to rest the argument by stating and showing unequivocally that it is impossible to sustain the position that the Islamic model was in any way benign.[11]

Before we move on, however, we need to briefly address the question whether the category of *kul*/harem should form part of Ottoman enslavement. Leading Ottomanists have suggested alternative terms to describe the predicament of people in that group, feeling that they cannot properly be lumped together with members of the less-privileged groups of domestic and agricultural slaves in Ottoman society. Metin Kunt refers to the *kul* as "the sultan's servants," whereas Suraiya Faroqhi prefers to call them "servitors."[12] As against that, in her 2003 book *Morality Tales*, Leslie Peirce firmly asserts that "the privileges of elite slavery were temporary." For one thing, she adds, elite slaves were not allowed to bequeath their wealth — or status, I would add — to their offspring, and their wealth reverted to the treasury upon their death (to an extent a loophole was available to them through the mechanism of charitable endowment known as *vakif*/*waqf*). Just as the sultan "controlled his enslaved servants' religious and cultural identity and their material environment," Peirce argues, he also "controlled their right to life, taking it if they were judged to have violated their bond of servitude." She then defines what in her view is "a paradox at the heart of the Ottoman system — that ordinary subjects enjoyed rights denied to those by whom they were governed. One of their rights was immunity from the sultan's direct power of life and death."[13] In her recent book, Madeline Zilfi also considers military-administrative bondage as part of the larger phenomenon of Ottoman enslavement, arguing in fact that it was so central to the Ottoman state as to have been a constituent pillar of Ottoman identity.[14]

Despite the fact that, over the centuries of Ottoman imperial rule, certain aspects of *kul* servitude were gradually being mitigated in practice, Peirce is certainly correct in her observations. In fact, the main changes in the status of *kul*/harem slaves came only in the nineteenth century, whereas in the early modern period we can safely assume their bondage to have been real in the terms described above. As in previous works, here too, my view is that all legally

---

[10] See, for example, for the latest, Toledano 2007a: 19–20.

[11] Zilfi 2010: 13–15, 107–17, and 159–69.

[12] See Kunt 1983 and Faroqhi 1994.

[13] Peirce 2003; all quotes are from page 315.

[14] Zilfi 2010: chapter 4, but more emphatically pp. 13–15.

bonded subjects of the sultan should be treated as enslaved persons also for the purpose of social analysis. This is an integrated, inclusive position, that is, that there was no **difference of kind** between *kul*/harem slaves and other types of Ottoman slaves, although there certainly were **differences of degree** among them but **within** the category of Ottoman slavery.

To complete the story, we should say a few words about the number of persons enslaved within the Ottoman Empire. Clearly, we still need further research before the picture becomes full and clear. Zilfi rightly observes for the end of the nineteenth century that the size of the enslaved population hovered around 5 percent and enslavement was "the practice of a small, privileged minority and as such scarcely reflected the experience of the majority."[15] The overwhelming number of families, she adds, were monogamous, and did not own slaves or employ free servants. This was probably true also for the early modern period, though we still do not possess reliable data for the volume and precise nature of Ottoman enslavement during that time. However, it does seem plausible to assume that the demise of agricultural enslavement reduced the overall number of enslaved persons in the Empire, whereas urban household bondage continued to remain on the same level. At the same time, households became much more important from the seventeenth century onward, both in the metropolitan center and the provinces, forming the backbone of political-social-economic life in Ottoman societies.[16]

For the "long nineteenth century," covering approximately 150 years, figures of the volume of the slave trade into the Ottoman Empire and the size of the enslaved population within its borders have been compiled and published, and despite some legitimate differences, the picture is fairly clear. Scattered data and reasonable extrapolations regarding the volume of the slave trade from Africa to the Ottoman Empire yield an estimated number of approximately 16,000 to 18,000 women and men who were being transported into the Empire per annum during much of the century. Ralph Austen's estimates for the total volume of coerced migration from Africa into Ottoman territories are as follows:[17] from Swahili coasts to the Ottoman Middle East and India — 313,000; across the Red Sea and the Gulf of Aden — 492,000; into Ottoman Egypt — 362,000; and into Ottoman North Africa (Algeria, Tunisia, and Libya) — 350,000. If we exclude the numbers going to India, a rough estimate of this mass population movement would amount to more than 1.3 million people. During the middle decades of the nineteenth century, the shrinking Atlantic traffic swelled the numbers of enslaved Africans coerced into domestic African markets, as well as into Ottoman ones.

Although the regions whence enslaved persons were being captured and sold into the Ottoman Empire had changed dramatically, as we show below, it might be reasonable to argue that — allowing for the expected population growth — overall demand remained fairly steady. With the demise of agricultural enslavement in the sixteenth century, the internal market restructured itself around stable demand for unfree labor in domestic, menial, and household service. Following the significant rise during the sixteenth century in the number of *kul* required by the imperial government, and later the changing structure and functions of the imperial army in the seventeenth, much of the force was no longer servile. Increasingly, the recruitment and socialization of actual *kul* devolved from the sultan's household-court to

---

[15] Zilfi 2004: 29; further assessments are provided in Zilfi 2010: scattered, but for Africa, mainly pp. 117–19, 130–33.

[16] On that, see Toledano 1997.

[17] The following figures are derived from Austen's two articles, 1988 and 1992. Note John Wright's suggestion that the figures for the trans-Saharan traffic were overstated due to the lack of their adjustment to low years and the general irregularity of those slave-trade routes (for a summary of his position and relevant citations, see Zilfi 2010: 132–33).

leading members — *kul* and non-*kul* — in both his central and provincial administration. All in all, the size of the *kul*/harem group was shrinking toward the end of the early modern period.

So we may perhaps venture an educated guess that already in the eighteenth century, *kul*/harem slaves no longer formed a significant part of the enslaved population in the Empire.[18] While not a few of the leading officeholders in the military and the administration were still *kul*, the bulk of both the army and the bureaucracy consisted of free men. If we also allow for a seventeenth to eighteenth centuries lull in agricultural enslavement, then the rest of the unfree labor market should have remained the same into the nineteenth century as well. Many of the women in urban elite households were still *harem*-enslaved, but they would now be taken from different regions. Thus, we may have at least a rudimentary method of reckoning back the numbers of enslaved persons that were being transported into Ottoman territories during the early modern period; we might also be able to then estimate the size of the enslaved population. Until reliable figures can be obtained from archival sources of the early modern period, this will have to be done on the basis of the better figures and estimates we have for the nineteenth century.

We may also say a bit more about the ethnic composition of the enslaved population, or more precisely, about the origins of the men and women who were brought into the Ottoman Empire and enslaved there during the early modern period. Here, Yvonne Seng's work is especially useful, as she maps the ethnic landscape in Üsküdar, what is now the Asian part of Istanbul.[19] She writes that at the beginning of the sixteenth century, approximately 15 percent of that town's 30,000 inhabitants were non-Muslim, and that in public places and commercial areas the languages often heard included "Greek, Armenian, Turkish, Farsi, Kurdish, Slavic, and Central Asian dialects." Greek and Slavic obviously represented people who came from southeastern Europe, but whereas we cannot assume all of them to have been enslaved, it stands to reason that not a few were. Most of the enslaved persons who appear in court records — mainly because they had absconded — point out that they had been captured in the Ottoman campaigns in the Balkans, but also in the Crimean Khanate's incursions into Russia and Poland. Origins of captives listed in court records include Russian (39 percent), Croatian (31 percent), and Bosnian (11 percent), with the remaining 19 percent coming from Hungary, Walachia, and Bulgaria; enslaved Greeks, Circassians, Albanians, and Africans were rare at the time.

THE PATTERN SHIFT OF THE EARLY MODERN PERIOD

It is important to point out that, as we approach the modern period, while enslavement was still sanctioned by the Ottoman state, the government was intervening to check the level of abuse. This trend will become a major feature of nineteenth-century reforms, in which the Tanzimat-state (1830s–1880s) entered decidedly into the enslaver-enslaved relationship to limit the enslavers' entitlement to the labor and body of the enslaved.[20] Until the

---

[18] Zilfi believes that this was not so, and that the impact of the *kul* system remained a major force in shaping the nature of the Ottoman Empire (2010: 107–17).

[19] Seng 1999: 27–28.

[20] On this, see Toledano 2007a: chapter two. When we use the term "state" in the Ottoman context of the early modern period, we do not mean a well-integrated, modern entity, much in the way we think of present-day, or even late nineteenth-century European states. Rather, the Ottoman variant was a "compound" polity, made up of a coalition of the interest-groups that formed its imperial elite. That elite was mostly male and Muslim, multi-ethnic, *kul*/

mid-nineteenth century, and in a similar manner to other "societies with slaves" and "slave societies," the Ottoman state upheld the rights of enslavers and refrained, as much as possible, from intervening in enslaver-enslaved relationships. When it did intervene, this was in most cases to help enslavers recover their absconding slaves, or, conversely, to liberate severely-abused enslaved persons from oppressive enslavers.

Until 1845, the Tanzimat-state was also reluctant to impose its criminal system upon enslaved persons, leaving the responsibility in the hands of slaver owners. However, that changed as part of the growing role the state assumed in criminal matters in general. In August of that year, while reviewing a theft case in which an enslaved African male was accused of stealing from his enslaver, a certain Mustafa Bey, the Council of Ministers decided that unfree offenders should be treated as free ones.[21] They, too, were henceforth to be handled by the state — not by the enslavers as stipulated in the *Şeriat* — and receive the same penalties as free offenders. Having served their term in prison, such enslaved convicts should be returned to their enslavers, the Council ruled.

Toward the latter part of the eighteenth century, the presence of enslaved Africans in the Ottoman Empire was well-established, and communities of enslaved Africans were already then quite entrenched in the Ottoman urban landscape. Their deep roots in Ottoman societies were evident in the series of lodges they established to care for communal needs of both the enslaved and the freed. From the second quarter of the nineteenth century, Africans constituted the vast majority of the enslaved population in the Ottoman Empire. Women were the overwhelming majority among the enslaved, and most of them served in urban elite households as domestic servants. Within about a century and a half, African women — and to a lesser extent also Circassian and Georgian ones — have replaced European men in the Ottoman servile workforce, and agricultural enslavement gave way to household and menial servitude.

As already mentioned above, the main source of enslaved persons at the beginning of the early modern period was war captives. Both the state and individual officers on the battlefield had appropriated the defeated enemy's manpower accessible to them, and then redistributed it on the domestic unfree market. Most of the captives came from southeast European powers, including present-day Russia and Ukraine, but on the eastern fronts, Iranian and Caucasian captives also fell victim to war-related enslavement. Owing to the end of Ottoman expansion in Europe toward the beginning of the eighteenth century — except for few and brief interludes — the supply of enslaveable European men and women has dried up. Similarly on the Iranian front, the 1736 treaty ending the Ottoman-Iranian war also provided for the release of war captives by the Ottomans and the repatriation of enslaved Iranian subjects (which proved quite difficult to enforce internally).[22] With occasional Crimean Tatar raids into Russian and Ukrainian territories, and with Ottoman activities to stabilize control over the western Caucasus, those areas now replaced the former sources for unfree labor in the Empire.

---

harem and freeborn, military-administrative-legal-learned, urban and rural, officeholding and proper-tied, Ottoman-imperial and Ottoman-local. The center of that "composite" polity moved with changing political circumstances from the palace to the seat of the grand vezir and back, with shifting coalitions forming, collapsing, and re-forming among interest groups and leading elite members. This composite polity is reminiscent of the notion of a "classical tributary empire," that is, "segmented, loosely integrated, and partly overlapping forms of power and authority" (see the conference on "Royal Courts and Capitals," Sabanci University, Istanbul, 14–16 October 2005, part of the COST Action "Tributary Empires Compared: Romans, Mughals and Ottomans in the Pre-Industrial World from Antiquity Till the Transition to Modernity").

[21] İrade/Meclis-i Vala/1280/*Mazbata*, 23.7.1845, the Grand Vezir to the Sultan, 5.8.1845.

[22] On this, see also Faroqhi 2002: 101.

This changing trade pattern can also be seen in the geographic origins of the slave dealers who carried out the traffic. Faroqhi argues that in the second half of the eighteenth century, many of them came from central and east Anatolian towns, indicating that the importation areas have shifted to the Caucasus and the regions north of the Black Sea.[23] But the most significant transformation of the trade patterns in enslaved persons reached southward from European and eastern sources — it was the rise, gradual at first, of African lands as the main enslaveable human reservoir for Ottoman markets. Whereas this trend peaked toward the middle decades of the nineteenth century, it was already in evidence during the last quarter of the eighteenth.[24] As our third story clearly shows, communities of enslaved Africans existed already then on Ottoman soil. The interesting point, however, is why free had not replaced servile labor, unlike what had happened when agricultural enslavement disintegrated in the sixteenth century. The reason lies, for the most part, in the structure of the Ottoman-imperial and Ottoman-local elites, at whose heart lay the Ottoman elite household.

HOUSEHOLD, STATUS, AND DEMAND: ECONOMIC OR SOCIOCULTURAL?

During the seventeenth and eighteenth centuries, the household emerged as the basic unit of belonging or attachment throughout the Ottoman lands. Although households surely existed before that period, they nonetheless came to play a distinct role in Ottoman societies as a result of the large-scale transformation that took place in the Empire from the end of the sixteenth century onward. We need not go into the various reasons that caused the transformation, as they have been amply discussed in the literature.[25] Suffice it here to note that a dual process of **localization** and **Ottomanization** was taking hold in the provinces, producing Ottoman-local elites throughout the Empire.[26] In this process, the Ottoman imperial elite was becoming less mobile, with posts being assigned within limited regions, so that specialization according to needs of specific provincial "clusters" were developing within the military and the bureaucracy. They developed strong ties to the local economy, society, and culture, and linked their and their children's future to one province, often to one city. At the same time, local elites — urban and rural notables, *ulema*, and merchants — were seeking to become part of the imperial administration, trying to attain government offices and being Ottomanized in the process. The localizing imperial elite and the Ottomanizing local elites gradually merged into Ottoman-local elites, which better served the interests of both sides.

Of major importance in this process was the household, or rather more specifically in our case, the Ottoman-local household, which served as the social, economic, political, and even cultural unit that facilitated and promoted Ottoman-local integration. In the seventeenth

---

[23] Faroqhi 2002: 259–60.

[24] See, for example, Dr. Frank's eye-witness account of the trans-Saharan slave trade into Egypt at the close of the eighteenth century in Le Gall 1999.

[25] The main contributors to the debate over the transformation of the Empire's governance in that period are: Islamoğlu and Keyder 1987; Owen 1993, especially the chapter entitled "Introduction: The Middle East Economy in the Period of So-Called 'Decline,' 1500–1800," pp. 1–23, 294–99 (notes); Kunt 1983;

Faroqhi 1994: 552–56; Abou-El-Haj 1991; Hathaway 1997: 1, 14, 24 (and throughout the book); Hathaway 2003: 4–6; and Özel 2004 on demographic and economic pressures during the sixteenth and seventeenth centuries. This debate has consequently helped to revise the Decline Paradigm, which is now virtually defunct in Ottomanist discourse, though unfortunately still quite alive outside the field of Middle East studies, and even to some extent within sections thereof.

[26] For more on this, see Toledano 1997.

century, households were being created around leading officeholders in the bureaucracy and within the military. While forming initially around the nuclear and extended family of the founder, from the outset they relied on patronage relationships between the head of the household and a broad array of clients. The essential component of any household were the founder's retainers, who were a sort of militia force, often small, armed, and protecting the interests of the household. A concomitant component were the producers of the household wealth, which enabled its expansion through recruitment and networking. Marriage among the various households was another essential element for forming inter-household alliances to promote common causes and take over income-producing economic assets. Conjugal arrangements provided the sociopolitical cement that bonded household coalitions, or factions as they were often called, and made networking possible. Although essentially a constructed notion, households also had a physical dimension, located in estates, often one or several complexes that housed dozens of individuals, hundreds in the larger ones, who performed a wide variety of functions including command and control, enforcement, financial, service, and trade.

Household heads vied for resources and coalesced locally, usually in a provincial town, where the local governor resided, but they soon realized that it was essential to build a network that would transcend sub-district, district, and even provincial bounds. Truly successful household coalitions had to be also connected to the imperial capital, where officeholders were consolidating their patronage networks through that new-type household. In the seventeenth century, the crucial stepping-stone toward household consolidation — that is, its social reproduction — was the ability to survive the founder's demise, that is, to entrench a multi-generational structure. Until the latter part of the century, many households disintegrated at that stage, leaving the provincial scene to new households and new factions. However, gradually, some households and some factions proved more resilient, better adapted to the changing circumstances at the center and the provinces, and more capable of sustaining the incessant competition over resources. By the end of the first quarter of the eighteenth century, in provinces throughout the Empire, a single household, or rather faction of households, usually emerged as hegemonic, securing for its leader and his lieutenants near-full control of the body politic and the economy. The main offices of state, hence also access to and appropriation of the main income-generating assets, would fall into the hands of members of that household.

All this occurred in a world of intense political struggles that were led and directed — through active networking and by skillful deployment of balancing acts — by members of the imperial and Ottoman-local elites: men and women, both *kul*/harem and freeborn, both in Istanbul and in the provinces. Among the most famous of these households we may mention the Kazdağlıs of Egypt, the Eyübizades of Iraq (mainly in Bagdad and Basra), the Azms of Syria, the Husaynis of Tunis, and the Karamanlıs of Libya. In some cases, hegemonic households would turn in the nineteenth century into local dynasties (Egypt, Tunisia), in others the Tanzimat-state would remove them and take their place (Syria, Iraq). Ottoman political culture was heavily influenced by patterns that evolved during the last two and a half centuries of imperial rule, leaving their mark on political interaction in the successor states of the Middle East for decades after the Empire's demise. The strong link between political and economic interaction, the belief in diversification through placements of family members in competing networks to minimize risk and increase security, the overwhelming impact of patronage politics, the lingering effect of "grandee families," and the presence of both formal and informal dynastic orders are some of the salient features that the Ottoman system bequeathed to modern Middle Eastern and North African societies.

For our purposes here, it is important to examine the ways in which households recruited and socialized new members. The purchase of enslaved persons for various roles was one of the four most important channels of recruitment to imperial-center and Ottoman-local households. The other three modes of recruitment-cum-bonding to a household were biological-kin relationships, marriage, and voluntary offer of loyalty and services in return for patronage. Less prevalent were adoption and suckling relationships, but the sources occasionally do mention them too. Bonding ensured that loyalty and patronage would flow from top to bottom and from the bottom up in households across Ottoman societies, linking people from various elites to non-elite groups and individuals. In that way, society was cohesively undergirded both vertically (within a household) and horizontally (alliances among households). Not infrequently, individuals were bonded to a household through more than one of these ties, as, for example, when one was the purchased *kul*-type (Arabic, *mamluk*) retainer of the household head and was also married to his daughter. Attachment to a household gave an individual protection, employment, and social status. But not less significantly, it gave household members (*kapı halkı*) a sense of belonging and an identity, both social and political.

Thus this system, which encompassed Ottoman political, social, and economic life, kept alive the demand for enslaved persons, whether as its *kul*/harem leadership or its household workforce.[27] To be sure, already during the early modern period, much of the labor in elite households was free, not bonded, but the remaining servility was still so engrained in the system and so indispensable culturally, that is, mainly as status symbol, that it ensured the continuation of demand for enslaved persons in the Ottoman Empire well into the nineteenth century. Despite the major reforms of the Tanzimat, and the prohibition of the slave trade — enforced in earnest only in the last quarter of the century — slavery was not legally abolished until the demise of the Ottoman Empire and the rise of the Turkish Republic.[28]

Thus we end up with the open question: what was the value for Ottoman enslavers in sustaining that constant demand for enslaved labor in urban elite households? It is doubtful whether the real reason was economic: there was a ready and active market for free labor in domestic service, in fact it constituted the lion's share of the labor market as a whole. As previously observed, in the Ottoman social structure of the early modern and modern periods, the basic building block of social, political, and economic networking was the elite household, both at the imperial center and in the provinces. Within that system, elite households emulated the sultan's household-court as much as they could afford to. As long as the essential component of the sultan's household-court continued to include *kul*/harem and domestic enslavement, so did — albeit to a lesser degree — the households of his military-administrative officeholding elite that served him and his composite state. As long as the size of harems, the presence of eunuchs, and the pattern of sociopolitical marriages within the elite persisted, demand for enslaved persons remained stable. In that sense, we can say that what perpetuated Ottoman enslavement throughout the early modern period and into the modern era was its sociocultural value, not its economic worth.[29]

---

[27] For a similar view, though cast in somewhat different terms, see Faroqhi 2002: 149.

[28] On the last phase, see Erdem 1996; on the suppression of the traffic, see Toledano 1998.

[29] As already mentioned above, Zilfi sees the reason for the survival of Ottoman enslavement and the lack of antislavery movement in the Ottoman Empire as emanating from the essential role slavery played in the structure and nature of the Empire. This does not contradict the view stated here, but carries it somewhat beyond the role and importance that I tend to assign to enslavement in the Ottoman Empire.

BIBLIOGRAPHY

Abou-El-Haj, Rifa'at Ali
1991　　*Formation of the Modern State: The Ottoman Empire, Sixteenth to Eighteenth Centuries*. Albany: State University of New York Press.

Austen, Ralph
1988　　"The 19th Century Islamic Slave Trade from East Africa (Swahili and Red Sea Coasts): A Tentative Census." In *The Economics of the Indian Ocean Slave Trade in the Nineteenth Century*, edited by W. G. Clarence-Smith, pp. 21–44. Special Issue of *Slavery and Abolition*, 9/3. New York: Routledge.
1992　　"The Mediterranean Islamic Slave Trade Out of Africa: A Tentative Census." *Slavery and Abolition* 13/1: 214–48.

Ayyıldız, Erol, and Osman Çetin
1996　　Slavery and Islamization of Slaves in Ottoman Society according to Canonical Registers of Bursa between the Fifteenth and Eighteenth Centuries. Unpublished report on work in progress.

Baer, Gabriel
1969　　"Slavery and Its Abolition." In *Studies in the Social History of Modern Egypt*, edited by G. Baer, pp. 161–89. Chicago: University of Chicago Press.

Englund, Robert
2009　　"The Smell of the Cage." *Cuneiform Digital Library Journal* 2009: 4.

Erdem, Y. Hakan
1996　　*Slavery in the Ottoman Empire and Its Demise, 1800–1909*. New York: Macmillan Press.

Ertuğ, Hasan Ferit
1998　　"Musahib-i Sani-i Hazret-i Şehr-Yari Nadir Ağa'nın Hatıratı-I." *Toplumsal Tarih* 49: 7–15.

Faroqhi, Suraiya
1994　　"The Ruling Elite between Politics and 'the Economy.'" In *An Economic and Social History of the Ottoman Empire, 1300–1914*, edited by Halil İnalcık and D. Quartaert, pp, 545–74. Cambridge: Cambridge University Press.
2002　　*Stories of Ottoman Men and Women*. Istanbul: Eren.

Fisher, Alan
1978　　"The Sale of Slaves in the Ottoman Empire: Markets and State Taxes on Slave Sales." *Boğaziçi University Journal* 6: 149–74.
1980　　"Studies in Ottoman Slavery and Slave Trade, II: Manumission." *Journal of Turkish Studies* 4: 49–56.
1985　　"Chattel Slavery in the Ottoman Empire: Some Preliminary Considerations." In *Slaves and Slavery in Muslim Africa*, edited by J. R. Willis. London: Frank Cass.

Hathaway, Jane
1997　　*The Politics of Households in Ottoman Egypt: The Rise of the Qazdaglis*. Cambridge: Cambridge University Press.
2003　　*A Tale of Two Factions: Myth, Memory, and Identity in Ottoman Egypt and Yemen*. Albany: State University of New York Press.

Hunwick, John
1999　　"Islamic Law and Polemics Over Race and Slavery in North and West Africa (16th–19th Century)." In *Slavery in the Islamic Middle East*, edited by S. E. Marmon, pp. 43–68. Princeton: Markus Wiener Publishers.

İnalcık, Halil
1979   "Servile Labor in the Ottoman Empire." In *The Mutual Effects of the Islamic and Judeo-Christian Worlds: The East European Pattern*, edited by A. Ascher, T. Halasi-Kun, and B. K. Kiraly, pp. 25–52. New York: Brooklyn College Press.
1982   "Rice Cultivation and the Çeltukci-Re'âyâ System in the Ottoman Empire." *Turcica* 14: 69–141.
1989   *The Ottoman Empire: The Classical Age, 1300–1600.* New Rochelle: A. D. Caratzas.

Islamoğlu, Huri, and Çağlar Keyder
1987   "Agenda for Ottoman History." In *The Ottoman Empire and the World Economy*, edited by H. Islamoğlu-Inan, pp. 42–62. Studies in Modern Capitalism. Cambridge: Cambridge University Press.

Jennings, Ronald C.
1987   "Black Slaves and Free Blacks in Ottoman Cyprus, 1590–1640." *Journal of the Economic and Social History of the Orient* 30/3: 286–302.
1993   *Christians and Muslims in Ottoman Cyprus and the Mediterranean World, 1571–1640.* New York: New York University Press.

Khoury, Dina Rizk
1997   *State and Provincial Society in the Ottoman Empire: Mosul, 1540–1834.* Cambridge: Cambridge University Press.

Kunt, Metin
1983   *The Sultan's Servants: The Transformation of Ottoman Provincial Government 1550–1650.* New York: Columbia University Press.

Le Gall, Michel
1999   "Translation of Louis Frank's *Mémoire sur le commerce des nègres ay Kaire, et sur les maladies auxquelles ils sont sujets en y arrivant* (1802)." In *Slavery in the Islamic Middle East*, edited by S. E. Marmon, pp. 68–88. Princeton: Markus Wiener Publishers.

Owen, Roger
1993   *The Middle East and the World Economy, 1800–1914.* Revised edition. London: I. B. Taurus.

Özel, Oktay
2004   "Population Changes in Ottoman Anatolia During the 16th and 17th Centuries: The 'Demographic Crisis' Reconsidered." *International Journal of Middle Eastern Studies* 36/2: 183–205.

Peirce, Leslie
2003   *Morality Tales: Law and Gender in the Ottoman Court of Aintab.* Berkeley: University of California Press.

Sahillioğlu, Halil
1985   "Slaves in the Social and Economic Life of Bursa in the Late 15th and Early 16th Centuries." *Turcica* 17: 7–42.

Seng, Yvonne J.
1996   "Fugitives and Factotums: Slaves in Early Sixteenth-Century Istanbul." *Journal of the Economic and Social History of the Orient* 39/2: 136–67.
1999   "A Liminal State: Slavery in Sixteenth-Century Istanbul." In *Slavery in the Islamic Middle East*, edited by S. E. Marmon, pp. 25–42. Princeton: Markus Wiener Publishers.

Toledano, Ehud R.

1997   "The Emergence of Ottoman-Local Elites (1700–1800): A Framework for Research."
         In *Middle Eastern Politics and Ideas: A History from Within*, edited by I. Pappé and
         M. Ma'oz, pp 145–62. London: Tauris Academic Studies.

1998   *The Ottoman Slave Trade and Its Suppression, 1840–1890*. Princeton: Princeton
         University Press.

2000a   "The Concept of Slavery in Ottoman and Other Muslim Societies: Dichotomy or
         Continuum?" In *Slave Elites in the Middle East and Africa: A Comparative Study*,
         edited by M. Toru and J. E. Philips, pp. 159–69. New York: Kegan Paul International.

2000b   *Slavery and Abolition in the Ottoman Middle East*. Seattle: University of Washington
         Press.

2002   "Where Have All the Egyptian Fallahin Gone To? Labor in Mersin and Çukurova
         during the Second Half of the Nineteenth Century." In *Mersin, the Mediterranean,
         and Modernity: Heritage of the Long-Nineteenth Century*, pp. 21–28. Mersin: Mersin
         University Press.

2007a   *As if Silent and Absent: Bonds of Enslavement in the Islamic Middle East*. New Haven:
         Yale University Press.

2007b   "The Shifting Patterns of Ottoman Enslavement in the Early Modern Period: From
         European to African-Caucasian." In *Relazioni economiche tra Europa e mondo isla-
         mico*, secc. XIII–XVIII (atti della "trentottesima settimana di studi," 1–5 maggio
         2006), edited by Simonetta Cavaciocchi. Grassina: Le Monnier.

Zilfi, Madeline C.

2000   "Goods and Mahalle: Distributional Encounters in Eighteenth-Century Istanbul."
         In *Consumption Studies in the History of the Ottoman Empire, 1550–1922: An
         Introduction*, edited by D. Quartaert, pp. 289–311. Albany: State University of New
         York Press.

2004   "Servants, Slaves, and the Domestic Order in the Ottoman Middle East." *Hawwa:
         Journal of Women of the Middle East and the Islamic World* 2/1: 1–33.

2010   *Women and Slavery in the Late Ottoman Empire: The Design of Difference*. Cambridge
         Series in Islamic History. Cambridge: Cambridge University Press.

SECTION THREE:
SECOND AND FIRST MILLENNIUM EMPIRES

NEITHER SLAVE NOR TRULY FREE: THE STATUS OF THE DEPENDENTS OF BABYLONIAN TEMPLE HOUSEHOLDS

KRISTIN KLEBER, FREIE UNIVERSITÄT BERLIN

The aim of this chapter is to review the debated character of *širku*s, people who were dependents of temples in the Neo-Babylonian period (sixth century B.C.) of Mesopotamia. *Širku*s are often characterized as temple slaves, and it is generally held that their fate was better than that of other kinds of slaves because the temple gods, as owners, did not directly exercise rights of ownership. I argue that *širku*s were not slaves, in fact, but are better understood as institutional dependents whose limited freedom, in comparison with free citizens of a Babylonian town, was a result of their social subordination to an institutional temple household. After a brief overview of the status terminology used in the sixth century B.C., I discuss the usage of a combination of various status terms and their legal background. In the second part, I juxtapose major legal, economic, and social features of slaves and *širku*s in Babylonia to show that neither of these approaches allows *širkūtu*, the status of temple dependent or "*širku*-hood," to be subsumed under the category "slavery."[1]

TERMS FOR STATUS, AND THEIR USAGE

Owing to the existence of numerous designations for non-free and manumitted persons in the first millennium B.C., and indeed throughout Mesopotamian history, some clarification of the different terms and their particular nuances is necessary. The designations *ardu* "(male) slave" and *amtu* "(female) slave," though common in many periods of Mesopotamian history, are rarely employed to mean "chattel slave" in the sixth century B.C. In the Neo-Babylonian context, *ardu* and *amtu* rather indicate social subordination in general. Thus, lower-ranking officials call themselves *ardu* of their superiors, while both *ardu* and *amtu* appear as elements in personal names (henceforth PN), in which they express subordination to a deity. *Qallu* (and feminine *qallatu*) is the most frequently used word for "(chattel) slave" in the sixth century. In the fifth century, the term *ardu* regains popularity and replaces *qallu*.[2] The etymology of *qallu* indicates how slaves were viewed within Neo-Babylonian society: *qallu* means "of low standing, of little value" or "small," the antonym of "mighty, powerful."

Zakû (male) and *zakītu* (female), "cleared (from private claims)," denote a freedman or freedwoman. In this period, chattel slaves were not frequently manumitted into autonomy, but were more often inducted into temple service and dedicated to the service of the temple deity. *Zakû* thus often appears in combination with the name of a temple deity, as in *zakītu-ša-Ištar*,

---

[1] On the issue of degrees of slavery and the various statuses that can neither be characterized as slave or free, see Finley's (1964) classic essay, "Between Slavery and Freedom."

[2] Several terms can designate slaves in collectives, such as *lamūtānu*, *amēlūtu*, and *nišē bīti*. They do not denote a legal status but mean merely "servants, domestics."

for example, "freedwoman of Ištar." The corresponding status is *širkūtu*, or "*širku*-ship." The terms *širku* (male) and *širkatu* (female) themselves derive from the Akkadian verb *šarāku* "to present, give as a gift, dedicate." The status of such people was hereditary, and descendants of people who had been dedicated as *širku*s were also ascribed with this status.

The element *banû* in the status term *mār banê* is connected to the adjective meaning "well formed, of good quality." The *Chicago Assyrian Dictionary* translates *mār banê* as (1) "free person, citizen" and (2) "nobleman." However, use of the term *mār banê* is not restricted to freeborn or noblemen. Manumission deeds are called *ṭuppi mār banûti* "tablet of the status of *mār banê*."

Complicating our investigation, it appears that multiple status designations could be applied to the same person at the same time. This is usually the case in transient situations, such as when slaves were manumitted but served in *paramone*, that is, when they served in the household until their master's death. Owners could demand continued service by their slaves even if they had dedicated them to a temple, and persons in such transient states could simultaneously be designated as *qallu/qallatu* and *zakû/zakītu* or *širku/širkatu*. Because *širkūtu* denotes a perpetual servile status, we would at least expect *mār banûtu* (freedom) and *širkūtu* to be incompatible.[3] However, this is not the case. Two Neo-Babylonian legal documents illustrate cases in which the same individual, in both instances a manumitted slave (*zakû*), is called both *mār banê* and *širku*.[4] As a basis for the following discussion, one of the texts, OIP 122 38, is paraphrased here:

> Ištar-abu-uṣur, a former slave and now a freedman (*zakû*) of Ištar-of-Uruk, testified that his former masters had married him to a free woman and manumitted him by writing his *ṭuppi mār-banûti* (tablet of free status). In this manumission deed they determined that he and the offspring from this marriage would be *zakûti* (freedmen) of Ištar. This means that they relinquished their rights of ownership and dedicated Ištar-abu-uṣur to the temple. Most likely he continued to serve his former masters in *paramone*. The marriage was consummated and three children were born. Nine years later, his former mistress attempted to sell him to a creditor of her deceased husband. Ištar-abu-uṣur complained at court. The judges summoned his former mistress who testified as follows: "After we had sealed a tablet for Ištar-abu-uṣur, turning him and the children which Innin-ēṭirat would bear him into *mār banê*'s and freedmen (*zakûtu*) of Ištar-of-Uruk, PN ... seized me and drew up a slave contract for Ištar-abu-uṣur (*riksu ša wardūti*) with me, claiming: 'I am a creditor of your husband.'" The document ultimately states that the judges decided not to change (*enû*) the tablet of Ištar-abu-uṣur's status as a freedman but declared him and his children to be *širku*s.

Thus, the former slave Ištar-abu-uṣur won the lawsuit. The most recent treatment of this text was done by Westbrook (2004), who argued that the slave and master had concluded a

---

[3] The two conditions are mentioned as being distinct in eviction clauses of slave-sale documents, for example (BRM 2 25): *pūt lā širkūti lā šušānūti lā mār banûti lā arad-šarrūti lā amēl bīt sīsê u lā amēl bīt narkabti ša* PN *ardi šuati* ... PN₂ *naši* "PN₂ guarantees with regards to PN, that slave, the absence of *širku*-status, of *šušānu*-status (a type of royal service), of *mār banûtu*-status (freedom), of the status of royal servant, absence of the horse-fief and wagon-fief military service-obligation." If one of the mentioned conditions applied to the sold person, namely, either freedom or some servile condition other than slavery, the sale would be illegal.

[4] The two texts are *Cyr.* 332 (translated in Dandamaev 1984: 192f. and Westbrook 2004: 106) and OIP 122 38. OIP 122 38 was first edited by Roth (1989) and then included in Weisberg 2003. The reading *širkūtu* in line 45 is preferable over Weisberg's (2001 and 2003: 71–73) reading *pirqūtu*; see Westbrook 2004: 102 with notes 8 and 9.

paramone contract[5] in which the slave was manumitted, but still owed future payments in the form of continued service or supplies. If the slave neglected or refused this continued service, then the manumission could be reverted and the *paramonar* re-enslaved.[6] Dedications to a temple, according to Westbrook, were seldom *paramone* arrangements but a gift *causa mortis*, the dedication taking effect only upon the owner's death. Until the owner's death, the slave would legally remain a slave.

To resolve the terminological dilemma posed by the case documented in OIP 122 38, Westbrook suggested that the two ways of releasing a slave, manumission and dedication, were combined. He understood the case as "an immediate manumission with a *donatio mortis causa* to the temple, but in the meantime, *paramonē* for the lifetime" of the former owners of Ištar-abu-uṣur (2004: 106). The logic of giving Ištar-abu-uṣur a temporary freedom and *mār banê* status, according to Westbrook, was to obstruct claims of other creditors — but this is nonetheless precisely what happened in the case under discussion. In other words, the owners surmised that if Ištar-abu-uṣur was a free man serving in *paramone* during the interim period before his owner's death and his own consequent dedication, nobody could lay claims on him. If he were still a slave, according to this logic, he could at the least be pledged or hired out until the owners died and the dedication took effect.

This interpretation is problematic, however, as it suggests that the rights of the slave owners extended to children born of their former slave after his manumission. How could they justly dedicate his future children as *širku*s after he had acquired his status as a free man? The same problem applies to dedicated slave women who bore children. Numerous texts show that children born before the dedication of their parents to temples were in fact slaves and could be claimed by the owners and their heirs. By contrast, all children born after the dedication were considered *širku*s. The dedication must therefore have changed the status of the slave and was not, therefore, a gift *causa mortis*, but a sacred manumission instead. I believe that the dedication of Ištar-abu-uṣur, for example, was effective immediately but that it did not exclude continued service in a *paramone* arrangement.[7] The temple simply accepted the custom of *paramone*. After the death of the master, the former slave would acquire social and legal

---

[5] Also argued in Westbrook 2009: 183f.

[6] The text *Nbn.* 697 (translated in Dandamaev 1984: 438; Westbrook 2004: 104 and 2009: 184) was issued by a man who had manumitted his slave in return for care in his old age. But the slave ran away, abandoning the old master. The master issued the document *Nbn.* 697 to the effect that the former slave, should he be caught, would be re-enslaved and transferred to the master's daughter-in-law, who took it upon herself to provide care for the elderly man in lieu of the slave. We do not know whether the master could justly re-enslave him, but it is likely that a Babylonian court would have decided in favor of the master in such a case. *Paramone* contracts are not attested as separate documents; the conditions of continued service were laid down in the manumission deed. Enslavement was also a penalty in Old Babylonian adoptions should the adoptee refuse his adoptive parents (David 1927: 47–52; cf. an Old Assyrian slave manumission and adoption with this penalty, cited in Westbrook 2009:

183f.). In this case the service arose from status (as a quasi-son or freedman/-woman), not from contract. The relationship between manumitted slave and former master was perceived as binding as a parent-child relationship. This is expressed in Wunsch 2003/04: no. 17. The manumitted slave is to provide his former mistress with food, anointing oil and clothing "like sons (would do)." A similar phrase is found in an Aramaic document from Elephantine (K 5 in Kraeling 1953). The manumitted slave woman and her daughter (whose biological father is the master) promise to support the master and his son "as a son or daughter would support their father." Therefore it is possible that the continued service was an established practice resulting from the social status as freedman. It shows that post-manumission dependency was very strong in Babylonia.

[7] For an overview of paramone in ancient Delphi, see Hopkins 1980: 133–68.

protection from the temple. This was particularly important for women, but also for men who were aliens in the society of their masters. The temple served as a social roof for those who had no or few relatives.

With respect to the case of Ištar-abu-uṣur and his shifting, multiple statuses, Martha Roth suggested to me that Ištar-abu-uṣur was a free man from the point of view of his former owners, but was meanwhile a *širku* from the temple's point of view. Even though this solution assumes a lack of precision on part of the people who drew up the legal documents, I also suggest that the difficulties of this situation are best reconciled if we accept the existence of this lack of precision. *Širku*s were not usually called *mār banê* when the term designates the citizens of Babylonian cities who lived under the social roof of private households. I would assume that in the specific contexts of OIP 122 38 and the similar case documented in *Cyr.* 332, *mār banê* and *ṭuppi mār banûti* had no wider social meaning, and the terms were utilized in a reduced sense of manumission from slavery.[8] Ištar-abu-uṣur was dedicated to Ištar and therewith manumitted. He continued to serve his former masters until they died.

The ostensible dilemma of terminology in our text is also fed by the perception that the temple owned *širku*s much in the same way that private households owned slaves. This leads us to the second part of this chapter, in which I argue that *širku*s were not temple slaves. In fact, these persons were never designated as temple "property" (*makkūru*),[9] but were subordinate members of the temple household owing labor and services to the temple.

ŠIRKŪTU: TEMPLE "SLAVERY"?

In the 1970s a controversy regarding "institutional slavery" versus "serfdom" was led by I. M. Diakonoff on the one side, and I. J. Gelb on the other.[10] The discussion cannot simply be dismissed as ideologically charged; central problems of the very definition of slavery lay at the core of the discussion. While many Western scholars applied a legal approach to their studies of slavery, focusing on salability and personal rights, Russian scholars used an economic definition. According to Diakonoff (1974: 63), the unalienable workers of his "type II," which Gelb called "serfs," were the institutional counterpart of private slaves. Their "somewhat more liberal life condition ... and the preservation by them of some indisputable features of being the subjects of personal rights, were, of course, due to the fact that there was no possibility for constant coercion of each of them on the large territories of state lands, in order to keep them in the condition of complete (i.e., also legal) slavery." He points out that the major factors conditioning their membership to a socioeconomic class are extra-economic coercion of labor and deprivation of property in means of production.

Both Gelb (1972) and Diakonoff (1974: 58f.) listed a number of distinct and common features for slaves and "serfs." I want to similarly overview the features of slaves and *širku*s, but with a larger textual basis while restricting my investigation to the Neo-Babylonian period.

---

[8] Wunsch (2003/04: 208) interpreted this passage similarly, understanding *mār banê* here as "non-slave."

[9] Contrary to Dandamaev 1984: 483 and 510 — in both passages *makkūru* does not pertain to the people at stake but to real estate or silver respectively.

[10] In his seminal work *Slavery in Babylonia* (1984), M. A. Dandamaev distinguishes "dependent social groups" (p. 585ff.) and slaves but nevertheless envisiges *širku*s as "temple slaves." On pages 67ff. he summarizes previous approaches to the problem of a definition of slavery with special respect to the ancient Near East. See also Finley 1981: chapter 8 on various servile statuses in ancient Greece.

I introduce a few new aspects to my overview in order to include a social definition of slavery, specifically that put forward by O. Patterson (1982). At the core of Patterson's definition of slavery stands the dishonored condition of the slave. Slavery, according to Patterson, is the absence of rights of birth. This natal alienation applies not only to foreign captives, but also to their children because they remain without social affiliation in the society in which they live. That is, slaves have no claims on their parents and children. Slavery is an alternative to death, but not life in a social sense since the affiliations and possibilities of free persons are denied. The following preliminary overview of the conditions of *širku*s and chattel slaves considers the social and familial affiliations of both slaves and *širku*s, but it should be noted that much further study is needed here to reach quantified results and clarify details.[11]

(1) Major sources: Neo-Babylonian documentation indicates that prisoners of war who were sold as slaves presumably made up a major source of private chattel slavery. Individuals born into slavery were not infrequent, but exact quantifications are not available. Regarding temples, it is known that the king dedicated prisoners of war to temples (Kleber 2008: 260–64), but birth certainly played a larger role in the creation of temple personnel. *Širku*-status was also created by the dedication of slaves by their masters as pious acts, the transfer of private slaves to the temple in lieu of debts, and the dedication of children in times of famine.[12]

(2) Physical marks: Slaves received a branding of the name of the owner onto his or her hand or face. Similarly, when slave owners dedicated their slaves to temples, they marked the slave with the symbol of the temple deity (Dandamaev 1984: 488f.). Born *širku*s were unmarked under normal circumstances, but branding with the symbol of the deity was done to captured fugitive *širku*s.[13] Otherwise, *širku*s were registered in temple ledgers but bore no physical mark indicating their condition.

(3) Names: Naming practices are another measure of the social place of non-free persons. In the Neo-Babylonian period, members of the elite bore a given name, a father's name, and a clan or family name. *Širku*s were identified by a given name and father's name only, and they did not have family names, with the possible exception in the case of one Gimillu, son of Innin-šumu-ibni (Jursa 2004: 116–19). The personal status of *širku*s often goes unmentioned in the documentation; only when it was relevant for particular circumstances surrounding the *širku* was the designation written down. Slaves, meanwhile, went by their given name plus "slave of PN (name of their owner)."

(4) Family life: Although records of sales of slave families exist, most slaves were sold alone, and sometimes slave women and their children were sold without a father (Cardellini 1981: 213–19, esp. p. 218). Sale records thus indicate that most slaves had no family life or were stripped of their family affiliations at the time of sale (see Culbertson, this volume). By contrast, *širku*s could pursue a normal family life. Temple officials did not interfere with marriages between *širku*s of the same temple (Wunsch 2003: 15). However, mixed-status marriages posed a problem, and the temple prohibited any type of marriage that would endanger or complicate its control over its dependents.[14] Mixed-status marriages are attested, but the

---

[11] After the Chicago symposium, Andrea Seri pointed out to me an unpublished Harvard dissertation on *širkūtu* by Asher Ragen (2007), who came to similar results.

[12] For examples, see YOS 7 17 (dedication as a pious act), YOS 7 164 (transfer in lieu of debts), and YOS 6 154 (famine).

[13] For example, see YOS 3 125.

[14] According to *Dar.* 43, *širkatu*s were prohibited from giving their children up for adoption to *mār banê*. Fear of losing control over temple dependents is also the most likely interpretation of YOS 7 56, in which a (free?) man from the city of Kiš and a *širkatu* of Ištar of Uruk were prohibited to meet each other again.

offspring of such marriages always became *širku*s.[15] *Širku*s had the right to rear their own children. We have to imagine their mothers mostly as housewives, because women feature rarely as recipients of rations in their own right (Jursa 2008: 390). They may, however, have a weaving assignment, a traditional women's work that was usually done at home.

(5) Lodging: The majority of chattel slaves were probably domestics who lived and were fed in the household of their masters. Some slaves, especially those who had a peculium (property allotment held on behalf of the master),[16] lived independently. *Širku*s, however, had more freedom regarding their living arrangements. They could reside in the city or the countryside. The city-based *širku*s lived in family houses in town that they owned or rented.[17] Plot sizes ranging from 24 to more than 150 square meters indicate small to medium-sized residences, probably depending on the size of the family (which is not given by the available sources).

(6) Manumission: While slavery could end in manumission, symbolized by the drafting of a *ṭuppi mār banûti* ("tablet of the status of *mār banê*"), *širkūtu* was a perpetual status. Both statuses were hereditary.

(7) Salability: *Širku*s, including those who were dedicated freedmen still serving in their former master's household, could not be sold — one of the major obvious differences from chattel slaves.

(8) Freedom of movement: Neither slaves nor *širku*s had full freedom of movement. Some *širku*s' professions, like that of a herdsman, often entailed sojourns far away from the hometown, but such trips were always under the authority of their temple officials. *Širku*s frequently escaped while they were conscripted to labor on construction sites. The working conditions were obviously extremely harsh there (Kleber 2008: 132f.).

(9) Ownership of private property: Diakonoff (1974: 64 n. 40) claimed that the institutional dependents decisively did not own property. If they had something, it was a peculium that ultimately belonged to the temple, and therefore *širku*s were slaves in his opinion. More study is needed here, but it is at least certain that *širku*s could possess movable property, including slaves,[18] houses,[19] and livestock. They could not own prebends, but ownership of prebends was strictly a prerogative of the traditional elite anyway. *Širku*s are nowhere attested as owning agricultural land; most likely they did not. Their movable property was inherited by their sons. When in arrears, *širku*s were held responsible with their property up to the amount of the debt.

(10) Sustenance and employment: *Širku*s who were directly employed by the temple received rations consisting of barley and dates. In records of such disbursements, only men appear as recipients. The monthly rations attested from the second half of Nebuchadnezzar's

---

[15] Thus, a slave owner whose slave is married to a *širku* loses claim to the offspring of that marriage. In marriages between free persons and *širku*s, the children are *širku*s, too. This inheritance pattern has to be held against the religious background of *širkūtu*: nobody can risk offending the city's patron deity. The gods' rights outrival any private claims. This applies to custodial claims not only on people but also on property. When a defaulted debtor's estate is sequestrated, the temple's receivables are collected first, and only then are the claims of private creditors met.

[16] The peculium of private slaves is treated by Ronan Head in his dissertation (2010).

[17] On ownership, see YOS 7 2; on rent, see BM 114551 (3 1/4 shekels of silver per year). The size of the houses is unknown.

[18] PTS 2308 is a hiring contract of a slave woman of a *širku* who hires her out to a private free woman. The hire of the slave is exceptionally called *idu* here instead of *mandattu*.

[19] YOS 7 2: A house of a *širku* had been confiscated by the temple as payment for his arrears. The house is now rented out to a man, who, according to his father's name, could be the son of the defaulted debtor.

rule onward were enough to meet the caloric needs of a man, a woman, and two small children. *Širku*s were free to exchange a part of the barley and dates for other foodstuffs, like vegetables, fish, and oil on the market. The "ration" thus became more like a wage in kind.[20] Other *širku*s rented temple property, like livestock or gardens,[21] or worked as bird catchers or fishermen in the temple's area of influence. These *širku*s most likely did not receive rations but lived off the profit from their occupations instead. They had to deliver a fixed quantity of produce to the temple, but anything they could achieve beyond that was legally theirs.

*Širku*s had all sorts of professions: they could work as administrative personnel in the temple, porters, craftsmen, herdsmen, animal tenders in stables, or bird catchers. Not all of them served the temple full time. The case of a *širku* baker who was pledged by his father to a private woman to work off a debt shows that the temple did not claim the full working capacity of *širku*s.[22]

(11) Labor and service obligations: Both slaves and *širku*s were subjected to coercive labor as a result of their status. *Širku*s were liable to perform labor for the temple. Male children counted as workers from the age of six onward (Jursa 1995: 8f.). While *širku*s worked for the temple, they could be hired out to work for third parties as well. In these cases, the temple official responsible for the conscription of *širku*s received a compensation called *mandattu*,[23] similar to the compensation paid to slave owners by the slaves or employers for the slave labor. This is terminologically different from the wage of a free person, or *idu*.

Matters get complicated when it comes to defining the exact nature of these obligations. Temples functioned as extensions of the state, and the crown utilized the administrative structure of temples to organize service obligations and taxation. In the Neo-Babylonian period, the traditional tax exemptions that free inhabitants of some major Babylonian cities enjoyed until the Neo-Assyrian period had obviously been reverted. Freemen were subjected to render public services, subsumed under the term *ilku*. The basis on which these duties were levied was ownership of landed property and prebends (Jursa 2009). Slaves were not required to perform these services in their own right.[24] The service obligations were manifold, including military service, transport duties, labor on public building projects, and payments in kind or silver. *Širku*s also had to perform *ilku* obligations, including military service.[25] While that much is known, many details still need to be clarified. We do not know whether *širku*s served as persons in their own right, that is, as subjects of the king, or whether they performed as personnel of the temple that served the king as an institution. The service on military campaigns was not organized by the temple but by the provincial administration. Other *ilku* duties, such as the labor obligation called *urāšu*, to which free men and *širku*s were subjected alike, could be organized by temples. It seems, however, that *širku*s had additional service obligations toward the temple, which resulted from their status. This included the work on royal building

---

[20] On the Neo-Babylonian ration system, see Jursa 2008, especially pp. 410f.

[21] YOS 7 47 refers to labor in a garden.

[22] Scheil 1915.

[23] NCBT 1153: the *dekû* (mobilization officer) of the *širku*s of Ištar acted as lessor. In YOS 17 9, the *qīpu*, the highest temple official who supervised a labor gang of *širku*s on royal building projects, received the payment. The compensation for a *širku* who is absent from work is called *mandattu* in BM 114586, for example.

[24] Note the interesting document from Neirab (Dhorme 1928: nos. 8/9), in which three brothers request that their slave perform military service with them on behalf of a fourth brother. The passage is broken, but it seems that he was released from slavery in return.

[25] See Kleber 2008: 201–31; for the other obligations of the temple toward the crown, see ibid., pp. 75–133.

projects in gangs of temple workers (*dullu ša šarri*) and other work assignments (perhaps grinding flour and weaving). It is lamentable that we cannot assess the temporal scope of these service obligations.

This table summarizes the major features discussed above:

Category	*Širku*	*Chattel Slave*
Major sources	birth, dedication	prisoners of war, birth
Physical mark	no	yes
Father's name	yes	no
Family life	yes	rare
Lodging	owned or rented houses	master's household, outside
Manumission	no	yes
Salability	no	yes
Hiring out	*mandattu*	*mandattu*
Freedom of movement	no	no
Property ownership	movable property and houses	peculium
Sustenance, work	wage-like rations or profit from entrepeneurship (with temple property)	rations or profit from entrepeneurship (with peculiuim)
Coercive labor	temple service, *ilku* obligations (part time)	service to owner
Military service	yes	no

The table above elucidates that the two statuses differ most in social features: *širku*s enjoyed a family life, the absence of dishonorable physical marks under normal circumstances, and the absence of the horrors of a sudden disruption of their lives by sale. In addition to the fact that the majority of them were born as *širku*s, the decisive factors in Patterson's social definition of slavery, particularly natal alienation, would not apply to *širku*s. Regarding economic features, both *širku*s and slaves were subjected to labor obligations as a result of their status, but the labor obligation of *širku*s was not necessarily full time.

It should be added here that *širku*s' lives differed from one another as greatly as slaves' lives did. Just like slaves, they could lead a miserable and oppressed life, but some of them occupied very high positions in the economic administration of the temple. Men such as the aforementioned Gimillu, son of Innin-šumu-ibni,[26] were not poor. Nevertheless, nobody will deny that *širku*s were economically exploited. Still, if we subsume *širkūtu* under the broad heading of slavery, we not only lose complexity but also risk blurring a major social distinction, as well as important legal and economic differences. In almost every society of the ancient world, one finds distinct categories of the servile population who live as institutional dependents but are not slaves. At the same time, no society created a collective designation for this group comparable to the broad term "slave"; different groups bore different status terms.

---

[26] Jursa 2004 is the most recent treatment of Gimillu's career.

It is a task of future research to clarify their specific legal, social, and economic conditions and the nature of their dependencies.[27]

ABBREVIATIONS

BM	Signature of the British Museum, London
BRM 2	Clay 1920
Cyr.	Strassmaier 1890
Dar.	Strassmaier 1892–97
Nbn.	Strassmaier 1887
NCBT	Signature of the Newell Collection of Babylonian Tablets, Yale University
OIP 122	Weisberg 2003
PTS	Signature of the Princeton Theological Seminary
YOS 3	Clay 1919
YOS 6	Dougherty 1920
YOS 7	Tremayne 1925
YOS 17	Weisberg 1980

BIBLIOGRAPHY

Baker, Heather D.
2001   "Degrees of Freedom: Slavery in Mid-First Millennium B.C. Babylonia." *World Archaeology* 33/1: 18–26.

Dandamaev, Muhammad A.
1984   *Slavery in Babylonia: From Nabopolassar to Alexander the Great (626–331 B.C.).* Revised edition. Edited by M. A. Powell and D. B. Weisberg, translated by V. A. Powell. DeKalb: Northern Illinois University Press.

David, Martin
1927   *Die Adoption im altbabylonischen Recht.* Leipziger rechtwissenschaftliche Studien 23. Leipzig: Theodor Weicher.

Diakonoff, Igor M.
1974   "Slaves, Helots and Serfs in Early Antiquity." *Acta Antiqua Academiae Scientiarum Hungaricae* 22: 45–78.

Cardellini, Innocenzo
1981   *Die biblischen "Sklaven"-Gesetze im Lichte des keilschriftlichen Sklavenrechts: Ein Beitrag zur Tradition, Überlieferung und Redaktion der alttestamentlichen Rechtstexte.* Bonner biblische Beiträge 55. Königstein: Hanstein.

---

[27] Finley (1981: 148) claimed that status in ancient Greece should be analysed by "envisaging status (or freedom) as a bundle of privileges" and that a definition of any particular status should be made "in terms of the possession and location of the individual's elements of the bundle." The same applies to the manifold status terms of ancient Near Eastern societies.

Clay, Albert T.

1919　*Neo-Babylonian Letters from Erech*. Yale Oriental Series, Babylonian Texts 3. New Haven: Yale University Press.

1920　*Legal Documents from Erech, Dated in the Seleucid Era (312–65 B.C.)*. Babylonian Records in the Library of J. Pierpont Morgan 2. New Haven: Yale University Press.

Dougherty, Raymond Philip

1920　*Records from Erech, Time of Nabonidus (555–538 B.C.)*. Yale Oriental Series, Babylonian Texts 6. New Haven: Yale University Press.

Finley, Moses I.

1964　"Between Slavery and Freedom." *Comparative Studies in Society and History* 6/3: 233–49.

1981　*Economy and Society in Ancient Greece*. London: Chatto & Windus.

Gelb, Ignace J.

1972　"From Freedom to Slavery." In *Gesellschaftsklassen im alten Zweistromland und in den angrenzenden Gebieten: 18. Rencontre Assyriologique Internationale, München, 29. Juni bis 3. Juli 1970*, edited by D. O. Edzard, pp. 81–92. Bayerische Akademie der Wissenschaften. Philosophisch-Historische Klasse, Abhandlungen, n.F., 75. Munich: Bayerische Akademie der Wissenschaften.

1976　"Quantitative Evaluation of Slavery and Serfdom." In *Kramer Anniversary Volume: Cuneiform Studies in Honor of Samuel Noah Kramer*, edited by B. L. Eichler, pp. 195–207. Alter Orient und Altes Testament 25. Kevelaer: Butzon & Bercker.

Head, Ronan

2010　The Business Activities of Neo-Babylonian Private "Slaves" and the Problem of Peculium. Ph.D. dissertation, Johns Hopkins University.

Hopkins, Keith

1980　*Conquerors and Slaves: Sociological Studies in Roman History*. Cambridge: Cambridge University Press.

Jursa, Michael

1995　*Die Landwirtschaft in Sippar in neubabylonischer Zeit*. Archiv für Orientforschung, Beiheft 25. Vienna: Institut für Orientalistik.

2004　"Auftragsmord, Veruntreuung und Falschaussagen: Neues von Gimillu." *Wiener Zeitschrift für die Kunde des Morgenlandes* 94: 109–32.

2008　"The Remuneration of Institutional Labourers in an Urban Context in Babylonia in the First Millennium B.C." In *L'archive des Fortifications de Persépolis*, edited by P. Briant, W. Henkelman, and M. W. Stolper, pp. 387–427. Persika 12. Paris: De Boccard.

2009　"On Aspects of Taxation in Achaemenid Babylonia: New Evidence from Borsippa." In *Organisation des pouvoirs et contacts culturels dans les pays de l'empire aché-ménide*, edited by P. Briant and M. Chauveau, pp. 237–69. Persika 14. Paris: De Boccard.

Kleber, Kristin

2008　*Tempel und Palast: Die Beziehungen zwischen dem König und dem Eanna-Tempel im spätbabylonischen Uruk*. Alter Orient und Altes Testament 358. Münster: Ugarit-Verlag.

Kraeling, Emil G.

1953　*The Brooklyn Museum Aramaic Papyri: New Documents of the Fifth Century B.C. from the Jewish Colony at Elephantine*. New Haven: Yale University Press.

Patterson, Orlando

1982　*Slavery and Social Death: A Comparative Study*. Cambridge: Harvard University Press.

Ragen, Asher
  2007   The Neo-Babylonian Sirku: A Social History. Ph.D. dissertation, Harvard University Press.

Roth, Martha T.
  1989   "A Case of Contested Status." In DUMU-É-DUB-BA-A: *Studies in Honor of Åke W. Sjöberg*, edited by H. Behrens, D. Loding, and M. Roth, pp. 481–89. Occasional Publications of the Samuel Noah Kramer Fund 11. Philadelphia: University of Pennsylvania Museum Press.

Scheil, Par V.
  1915   "La libération judiciaire d'un fils." *Revue d'assyriologie et d'archéologie orientale* 12/1: 1–13.

Strassmaier, Johann N.
  1887   *Inschriften von Nabonidus, König von Babylon (555–538 v. Chr.).* Babylonische Texte 1–4. Leipzig; E. Pfeiffer.
  1890   *Inschriften von Cyrus, König von Babylon (538–529 v. Chr.).* Babylonische Texte 7. Leipzig: E. Pfeiffer.
  1892–97   *Inschriften von Darius, König von Babylon (521–485 v. Chr.).* Babylonische Texte 10–12. Leipzig: E. Pfeiffer

Tremayne, Arch.
  1925   *Records from Erech, Time of Cyrus and Cambyses.* Yale Oriental Series, Babylonian Texts 7. New Haven: Yale University Press.

Weisberg, David B.
  1980   *Texts from the Time of Nebuchadnezzar.* Yale Oriental Series, Babylonian Texts 17. New Haven: Yale University Press.
  2001   "*Pirqūti* or *širkūti*? Was Ištar-ab-uṣur's Freedom Affirmed or Was He Re-enslaved?" In *Studi sul Vicino Oriente antico dedicati alla memoria di Luigi Cagni*, Volume 2, edited by S. Graziani, pp. 1163–77. Naples: Istituto universitario orientale.
  2003   *Neo-Babylonian Texts in the Oriental Institute Collection.* Oriental Institute Publications 122. Chicago: The Oriental Institute.

Westbrook, Raymond
  2004   "The Quality of Freedom in Neo-Babylonian Manumissions." *Revue d'assyriologie et d'archéologie orientale* 98: 101–08.
  2009   "Slave and Master in Ancient Near Eastern Law." In *Law from the Tigris to the Tiber: The Writings of Raymond Westbrook*, edited by F. R. Magdalene and B. Wells, pp. 161–216. Winona Lake: Eisenbrauns.

Wunsch, Cornelia
  2003   *Urkunden zum Ehe-, Vermögens- und Erbrecht aus verschiedenen neubabylonischen Archiven.* Dresden: Islet.
  2003/04   "Findelkinder und Adoption nach neubabylonischen Quellen." *Archiv für Orientforschung* 50: 174–244.

8

SLAVERY BETWEEN JUDAH AND BABYLON: THE EXILIC EXPERIENCE

F. RACHEL MAGDALENE, UNIVERSITÄT LEIPZIG; AND CORNELIA WUNSCH, UNIVERSITY OF LONDON*

Much scholarly work has been done on the institution of slavery[1] as documented in the Hebrew Bible and the corpus of Neo-Babylonian[2] documents. From these studies and others, we know that the authors of the Hebrew Bible attempted to distinguish in various ways the Israelite practice of slavery from that of its neighbors (see, e.g., Exod. 21:2; Lev. 25:36–37, 39; and Deut. 23:16 [Eng. 23:15]).[3] Until recently, no first-hand information (legal records) from exilic and early post-exilic period legal practice concerning this subject was known. Now, however, documents from communities of exiled Judeans in rural Babylonia, reflecting at least four generations, have come to light.[4] These important texts, herein referred to as the "Judean

* Translations of ancient texts, unless otherwise noted, are those of the authors. Research for this article has been funded in part by the U.S. National Endowment for the Humanities and its award of a Collaborative Research Grant for the authors' project, "Neo-Babylonian Trial Procedure," with Bruce Wells. The 2010–2011 Bridwell Library Scholars Fellowship of the Perkins School of Theology, Southern Methodist University, provided additional support for this undertaking to F. Rachel Magdalene. Any views, findings, conclusions, or recommendations expressed in this publication are those of the authors alone and do not necessarily represent those of the National Endowment for the Humanities, the Bridwell Library, or Bruce Wells. We wish to thank additionally Laurie Pearce, who has also worked on the Judean corpus; Laura Culbertson, who organized the conference related to this volume at the Oriental Institute of the University of Chicago; and Bruce Wells, who organized the conference "Jerusalem in Babylonia: New Discoveries from the Exilic Period" at Saint Joseph's University, at which we also presented some of these ideas.

[1] A growing bibliography on slavery in the ancient and modern world exists. In his seminal work, Patterson (1982) surveys this institution both diachronically and comparatively across cultures. It includes some material on Mesopotamia, but mostly from the third and second millennia B.C., and relies on the works by Mendelsohn (1949) and Driver and Miles (1956, 1960) that are, in certain respects, incomplete or outdated. Furthermore, for the Neo-Babylonian period, the English edition of Dandamaev's (1974) monumental work was not yet available, and, consequently, much information could not be incorporated. For an overview about the sources for the Neo-Babylonian period, Dandamaev's (1984) English version is essential, as it conveniently gathers and presents a vast amount of textual evidence, even though the literature has increased considerably in the past twenty-five years and some aspects require a fresh approach. For a very brief survey of Neo-Babylonian slave law, see Oelsner, Wunsch, and Wells 2003: 928–33. The literature on slavery within the Hebrew Bible is vast. We can only refer here to a few of the more recent works (see, e.g., Baltzer 1987; Jackson 1988; Chirichigno 1993; Matthews 1994; Westbrook 1995, 1998; Van Seters 1996, 2007; Schenker 1998; de Menezes 1999; Carmichael 2000; and Mooney 2008).

[2] We use the term "Neo-Babylonian" here to cover not only the period when the Neo-Babylonian kings held political control over Mesopotamia (612–539 B.C.) but also to include the first half-century of Achaemenid Persian rule until the end of Darius I's reign (539–486 B.C.), as both periods, despite the dynastic change, share in Babylonia proper similar socioeconomic features and are well documented.

[3] This is noted, for example, by Dandamaev (1992: 65).

[4] These texts are dispersed in museum and private collections, such as the Diaspora Museum, Tel Aviv, the Schøyen collection, and the Moussaieff collection. Only a few tablets have been published thus far, by Joannès (1999) and Abraham (2005/06, 2007).

texts," describe life and legal events during what the Bible calls "the captivity"[5] and scholars often call "the Babylonian captivity."[6] They document a crucial period in Jewish history about which we have known quite little. These new texts offer us, not only critical socio-historical insights into what it was like to live in exile, but also key legal historical information about this period. Seven such documents reflect the institution of slavery among the Judeans. This article, therefore, discusses the documents from this corpus that contain references to slaves and asks three primary questions:

1)   What do these documents reflect about the institution of slavery in the Judean exilic community?

2)   Is this practice more consistent with practices described in the Neo-Babylonian corpus or in the Hebrew Bible?

3)   What does this evidence mean in regard to the biblical allusions of Israelites being slaves in Babylonia during the exile?[7]

We must admit that this is just an initial foray into these significant texts and their implications for biblical law. Before we address the relevant texts, we describe the corpus of texts from which they derive.

The publication of the bulk of material is under way; see Pearce and Wunsch (forthcoming; text numbers are cited with the prefix IMMP) and Wunsch (forthcoming; with the prefix JWB). We wish to acknowledge the problem of working with unprovenanced tablets that have been split between museums and private collections. The same holds true for the bulk of Neo-Babylonian archival material, most of which was acquired by European and American museums in the nineteenth and early twentieth century from individual dealers and collectors or through uncontrolled or undocumented licensed excavations and now forms part of their collections. Thus, Assyriologists working in the field are faced with the lamentable lack of stratigraphic information for almost all Neo-Babylonian archival texts and have to make up for this shortcoming with a great deal of work on developing auxiliary methods to reconstruct the original archival groups on the basis of internal criteria (such as prosopographical work) and acquisition details. For examples of results achieved by such procedures, see, for example, Jursa 2005, which provides an overview of the archival background of the entire material known thus far; or Waerzeggers 2005, for a detailed study concerning the Borsippa archives. In regard to the Judean texts, no doubt exists in regard to the authenticity of the documents. Furthermore, these texts appear to be of great historical import and require competent, careful, and responsible publication in

order to avoid misleading information or speculation about their contents. Such a body of information should, therefore, not remain inaccessible to scholars and the public.

[5] See, for example, 2 Kings 24:15: "He carried away Jehoiachin to Babylon; the king's mother, the king's wives, his officials, and the elite of the land, he took into captivity from Jerusalem to Babylon"; and Jeremiah 20:6: "And you, Pashhur, and all who live in your house, shall go into captivity, and to Babylon you shall go; there you shall die, and there you shall be buried, you and all your friends, to whom you have prophesied falsely."

[6] See, for example, Kaufmann 1977; Barstad 1997; and Jones 2004.

[7] The authors are well aware that socioeconomic realities for persons of the same legal status may differ widely, and, conversely, persons of different legal status may find themselves under similar circumstances; that the concept of slavery goes beyond legal ramifications; and that the institution may serve particular functions in various societies. In regard to the fundamental precept of slavery, we follow Finley (1989: 77), who sums up the three essential components of slavery as "the slave's property status, the totality of the power over him, and his kinlessness." For further on our rationale, see Wunsch and Magdalene forthcoming, chapter 1.

THE CORPUS OF TEXTS

The deportation policies of the Neo-Assyrian and Neo-Babylonian empires have been extremely consequential to the history of Israel and to biblical studies as a scholarly field. When the Neo-Assyrians conquered the Northern Kingdom in 722–721 B.C., they deported population groups from Israel to other areas of the Neo-Assyrian empire. Similarly, the Babylonians conquered the Southern Kingdom in 587–586 B.C. and also engaged in a series of major deportations of the population. This second episode, the so-called Babylonian captivity, figures prominently in the Hebrew Bible. The biblical report about the deportation of the Judean population was not substantiated by historical records until the early twentieth century, when some texts were discovered that contain first-hand information concerning the political events recorded in the Bible.[8] Yet, much is still to be done, especially in regard to the social history of the Judeans in exile. We must assume that the large majority of the deported population did not experience the same conditions as the Judean king and his immediate circle, which have been documented.[9] Commoners were probably only brought into Babylon to be employed in large building and similar infrastructure projects. We have assumed that most of them were distributed over the country and, in each locale, settled together with other population groups of which we know from cuneiform texts, such as the settlements of Gezerites, Hindaneans, and Arabs. Thus far, the primary evidence for descendants of common Judean deportees were texts from the Murāšû archive that date about one hundred years later and reflect personal names of West Semitic and Hebrew origin, even containing Yahwistic elements, among the witnesses.[10] In these texts, Judeans occur at the margin; they are usually not the parties of the transaction, but rather witnesses or people mentioned in passing. This textual lacuna has allowed a great deal of speculation but little real historiography to take place.

This situation now has changed thanks to new evidence that shows Judeans as the main protagonists and archive holders within a cuneiform corpus. Only a few of these texts have been published to date. The corpus contains approximately two hundred legal texts from settlements of Judean communities and their neighbors, dwelling in otherwise unattested localities of rural Babylonia, and the records illustrate the administrative and business relations among those population groups; the texts are written in Neo-Babylonian cuneiform and usually have identifiable Babylonian scribes. This is true, far into the Persian period, even where all the parties and most of the witnesses have Hebrew names. The texts date from the time of Nebuchadnezzar through Xerxes, but they are distributed unevenly over time. They start with two isolated texts from the time of Nebuchadnezzar; there are a few from the reign of Nabonidus; and the majority were written during the rule of the first three Persian kings. The

---

[8] The German archaeological excavation at Babylon yielded administrative texts that made reference to the Judean king Jehoiachin being held as a hostage or prisoner in the Babylonian capital, where he and his entourage were maintained by rations given by the crown administration, obviously spending some time there (Weidner 1939). This helped to substantiate the biblical report of 2 Kings 24:12–15. Three years ago, Jursa (2008) discovered a text in the British Museum that mentions the high Babylonian *rab ša-rēši* official Nabû-šarrūssu-ukīn, who is known as Nebošarsekim (*nbwšrskym*, as already expected by Vanderhooft

[1999: 151]) from Jeremiah 39:3. It is a receipt for a substantial amount of gold that was delivered to the Esangila, the main sanctuary of Babylon, on Nabû-šarrūssu-ukīn's behalf in the tenth year of Nebuchadrezzar, about eight years before the events recounted in Jeremiah 39 (dating to 587 B.C.) that refer to Nebošarsekim as a participant in the siege of Jerusalem.

[9] See note 8 concerning King Jehoiachin.

[10] See further Coogan 1976a, 1976b; Zadok 1979, 2002. For more on the Murāšû archive, see Donbaz and Stolper 1997; and Stolper 1985, 1992, 2001.

tablets taper off at the beginning of Xerxes' rule, but a few continue after year two of Xerxes, which is the cut-off point of most known private archives from Babylonia.[11] In contrast to the Murāšû archive, these tablets are much earlier and cover, not only the early post-exilic period, but also part of the exilic period proper. While they are contemporary with the well-documented Neo-Babylonian private archives, as well as temple archives from Babylonia, in their contents and business profile, they show similarities with the later Murāšû corpus. They therefore represent a crucial link between these various archives.

The prosopography allows us to reconstruct up to four generations of Judeans as the protagonists in one archival group and two or three tiers in several others. Thanks to Babylonian record practice, the dates are clearly discernible in most cases. Most of the place names, however, do not help to locate their place of origin, as they either do not occur in other corpora or are known already from other sources but nonetheless cannot be located. Two groups of texts focus most prominently on the towns of Našar (or Bīt-Našar, named after an individual) and Āl-Yāḫūdu (or Judah-town),[12] respectively, and attest to a few individuals who appear in both of them. The third group relates to Bīt-Abī-râm (again derived from a personal name) and displays a faint link to the other two groups. Some other place names are less often attested and otherwise unknown. A few tablets are either drafted in Babylon or mention it, but this is inconclusive, as the parties appear to have traveled there to deal with administrative, juridical, or business matters. Borsippa is mentioned once in connection with the personal affairs of one official, which, again, does not tell us anything about the origin of the archive itself. This leaves the three localities of Karkara, Nippur, and Keš,[13] which point to the region beyond Nippur toward the east and southeast, at the Tigris corridor, in roughly the same area that is later reflected at the fringes of the Murāšû texts.

This region, well known from third- and second-millennium texts, suffered considerably during the time of the Assyrian battles with Elam. Nebuchadnezzar and his successors apparently took measures to revive and repopulate the whole area beyond Nippur to make it economically viable again. The Persian kings must have followed this economic and political strategy, especially in view of the fact that the region touched upon main routes linking Babylonia and Persia (it is unlikely that they did it out of devotion for Babylonian deities and their ancient cult centers, which may have been a key impetus for the Neo-Babylonian kings). In this context, the settlement of Judean deportees appears as one example among many others. Large irrigation projects were undertaken, canals were dug and along their course emerged new outposts, such as the "king's town at the new canal," that still refer to their recent establishment by name. Thus we may surmise that significant groups of Judeans were deported to an area to the east and southeast of Nippur, to the north of Uruk where, after completion of the necessary infrastructure work, they received lands along the waterways, allotted in parcel units of *ḫanšê* "fifties" and were liable as to the obligation to pay taxes and to render either military or corvée service for a certain period per year.[14] The texts further allude to the fact

---

[11] See Waerzeggers 2003/04.

[12] One of the earliest attestations actually says Āl-Yāḫūdaya, which clearly indicates that the place name derives from a gentilic.

[13] Spelled *ki-e-šu₂*[ki]; one might at first consider this as an irregular orthography for Kiš, given the fact that there is no evidence for Keš in the second and first millennia apart from being mentioned in a Nabonidus

inscription. There are, however, texts from the later Achaemenid period issued at Keš (Wunsch forthcoming) that display both syllabic as well as logographic spellings and therefore prove that this place had a functioning temple until at least five generations after Nebuchadnezzar.

[14] On these obligations, see further van Driel 2002: 155–85; and Jursa 2009: 237–69.

that populations of different ethnic and geographical background were transplanted and settled as homogeneous groups according to their origin.

The Judeans' main occupation was agriculture, mainly grain and date palm cultivation. When these settlers arrived and land parcels were measured out to them, they all apparently started from a more or less equal basis. As we follow the archive over three more generations, we notice signs of increasing affluence and wealth in some families, with some of their members climbing the administrative ladder up to a certain point (such as to foreman and summoner of workmen for corvée services[15] or the position of the headman of the village[16]), while others struggle to make ends meet. A certain social polarization among the population can, therefore, be observed. The successful individuals are the ones who left their mark in the archives. As we will see, Judeans engaged in business with outsiders and made active use of Babylonian legal instruments, even applying them to matters of private law, such as marriage, inheritance, and property transfer. In the context of this article, we examine Judean attitudes regarding slave ownership in comparison to the biblical laws regarding slavery.

THE BIBLICAL LAWS OF SLAVERY

We know from studies on slavery in the Hebrew Bible that the authors of the Hebrew Bible attempted to distinguish in various ways the Israelite practice of slavery from that of its neighbors.[17] Moreover, the Hebrew Bible differentiates between chattel slaves (e.g., Lev. 25:46; Qoh. 2:7) and Hebrew debt slaves, who became such via distraint (e.g., Lev. 25:35–38; 2 Kings 4:1), selling themselves into slavery (e.g., Lev. 25:39–43), or being sold by their parents into slavery (e.g., Neh. 5:5).[18] Chattel slaves were typically foreigners acquired by

---

[15] Akkadian [lú]*dēkû*. Stolper (1985: 83) describes the role and title of *dēkû* as "marshaling the taxes and services incumbent on land holders" and provides attestations of individuals bearing this title in the Murāšû corpus. Individuals with Hebrew names are attested in this role, for example, Yāḫû-ezer, son of Ṭūb-šalam (IMMP 12) and Abdi-Yāḫû, son of Barak-Yāma (Joannès and Lemaire 1999: 27–28 [no. 2]).

[16] Written [lú]EN.NAM; Joannès and Lemaire 1999: 27–28 (no. 2).

[17] See, for example, Greengus 1998: 9 n. 28; and Frymer-Kensky 2003: 1007. Although aware of the issues, due to space limitations we do not discuss herein the problem of the apparent conflicts between the slave provisions of the biblical Covenant Code, Holiness Code, and Deuteronomic Code, and the various diachronic solutions to these conflicts. See, among others, Paul 1970; Phillips 1984; Matthews 1994; and Levinson 2006.

[18] In the ancient Near East generally, impoverished persons might voluntarily give up their free status if this were the only guarantee for survival in times of famine. Family members might also be pledged and sold, although families were generally reluctant to sell members and, if done, only in satisfaction of an outstanding debt. This is to be distinguished from the situation wherein a person is under distraint due

to a pledge in a secured debt instrument, that is, debt slavery. As Westbrook (2003: 41) states: "At first sight, the situation of a free person given in pledge to a creditor was identical to slavery: the pledge lost his personal freedom and was required to serve the creditor, who exploited the pledge's labor. Nonetheless, the relationship between pledge and pledge holder remained one of contract, not property. Since the creditor did not own the pledge, he could not alienate him, nor did property of the pledge automatically vest in the creditor. It was in the nature of a pledge that it could be redeemed by payment of the debt, at which point the human pledge would go free. During the period of his service, failure of the pledge to fulfill his duties led to contractual penalties, not punishment under general disciplinary powers of the master." Westbrook (1995: 1639) also states: "Where slavery was created by contract, especially where a self-sale was involved, the rule of status could be affected in an analogous way [that is, to marriage contracts]. The terms of the contract could ameliorate the slave's condition, making it closer to other types of servile condition such as pledge...." The slavery provisions of the Hebrew Bible tend to group these types of slavery into the category of debt slavery and distinguish them from chattel slavery as discussed above.

purchase (e.g., Lev. 25:44; cf. Gen. 37:28; 39:1–6; Ps. 105:16–18), in war (e.g., Deut. 20:10–14; Num. 31:25–41), through raids (cf. 2 Sam. 3:22),[19] and house-born slaves (Gen. 15:3), but they might also be taken from the resident alien population (e.g., Lev. 25:45; 1 Kings 9:15–21; cf. Isa. 14:2).[20] The Hebrew Bible does not envision Hebrews owning Hebrew chattel slaves (e.g., 1 Kings 9:22).[21] Surprisingly, Deuteronomy 23:16–17 (Eng. 23:15–16) even provides protections for escaped slaves: "Slaves who have escaped to you from their owners shall not be given back to them. They shall reside with you, in your midst, in any place they choose in any one of your towns, wherever they please; you shall not oppress them."[22]

Special protections are granted for Hebrew debt slaves. For example, the status of one who had sold himself into slavery, where the creditor or owner was also a Hebrew, was that of a hired workman, not a chattel slave (Lev. 25:39–42, 46). Deuteronomy 5:14 states in addition: "But the seventh day is a sabbath to the Lord your God; you shall not do any work — you, or your son or your daughter, or your male or female slave, or your ox or your donkey, or any of your livestock, or the resident alien in your towns, so that your male and female slave may rest as well as you" (see also Exod. 20:10).

Terms of release are also provided for the Hebrew debt slave (whether or not serving a Hebrew or an alien) but not for the alien chattel slave (cf. Lev. 25:46 with Lev. 25:47–51). Generally, if an individual sold himself to another Hebrew, he had to pay the amount or work it off (Neh. 5:8), but in the seventh year release was granted as a matter of law (Exod. 21:2; Deut. 15:12, cf. verse 18), as well as in the Jubilee Year (Lev. 25:10–11, 40). This provision establishes the period of time by which the law presumed the debt to be paid.[23] The slave did not have to pay for his release, rather the creditor was to give the slave a gift presumably to enable him to reestablish his household (Deut. 15:13–14). If an individual sold himself to a foreigner, he would have to be released when the slave or his relatives could pay the redemption amount (Lev. 25:47–52). Redemption was not, however, always possible (Neh. 5:3–5), nor was release always done appropriately (Jer. 34:8–17).[24] Female slaves, alternatively, were generally not released in the seventh year like male slaves, but they could not be sold off to a

---

[19] "In all societies where the institution acquired more than marginal significance and persisted for more than a couple of generations, birth became the single most important source of slaves" (Patterson 1982: 132). Yet, we do know that slaves could be acquired through war and raids in the ancient Near East. See further Westbrook 1995: 1640–43. Any attempt to rank or quantify the various sources of slaves in either ancient Israel or Neo-Babylonian Mesopotamia on the basis of cuneiform sources is futile, although Dandamaev (1992: 63–64) makes a valiant attempt. We do, however, have some information about the relative ranking in importance of sources for the slave supply in the Roman Empire. Harris (1999: 62), in response to Scheidel (1997: 159–69), maintains: "The sources which most require consideration are: (1) children born to slave-mothers within the Empire; (2) persons enslaved in provincial or frontier wars; (3) persons imported across the frontiers; (4) the 'self-enslaved'; and (5) infants abandoned at places within the Empire." Debt slavery was a significant problem in ancient Israel (2 Kings 4:1; Neh. 5:5).

Enslavement by Hebrews of other Hebrews via kidnapping was, however, prohibited (Deut. 24:7; Exod. 21:16; cf. Exod. 20:17).

[20] On the distinction between Hebrew and foreign slaves, see further Hezser 2005: 29–31.

[21] Cf. van der Ploeg 1972: 87.

[22] This reverses the typical ancient Near Eastern requirement of slave return (see, e.g., Laws of Hammurabi §§16–20; Hittite Laws §§22–44; and Greengus 1997: 9 n. 28. Vasholz (1991), Nelson (2002: 280), and Hiers (2002: 48) all suggest that this provision is meant to apply only to slaves escaped from other nations, although Nelson (2002: 280) also maintains that verse 16 alone might have first been a general slave law that did apply to the Israelites.

[23] Cf. Law of Hammurabi §117, wherein a debt slave may go free after only three years of service. See further Magdalene forthcoming.

[24] See further Chavel 1997.

foreigner (Exod. 21:7). If, however, the slave was not a concubine or if she was to be given to a son in marriage and he deprived her of the basic necessities and conjugal rights, she could go free without any payment to her master (Exod. 21:8–11). Other possibilities for release of male debt slaves were also available (see, e.g., Deut. 15:1–3).

Moreover, the biblical law prohibits the charging of advance interest and the antichretic pledge, wherein the interest owed on the debt is offset by the labor of the slave or detainee in the case of Hebrew-Hebrew debt relations.[25] Leviticus 25:36–37 instructs: "Do not take interest in advance or otherwise make a profit from them [one's kin], but fear your God and let them live with you. You shall not lend them your money at interest taken in advance, or provide them food at profit." Although this provision addresses charging kin any pre-paid interest, it is typically seen, when read with Exodus 22:24 (Eng. 22:25) and Deuteronomy 23:18–20, as a general prohibition on the charging of interest to any Israelite or use of the antichretic pledge.[26]

Some of these passages, such as those that prohibit making a Hebrew a chattel slave, the Jubilee Year release, and not returning runaway slaves to their masters, seek to change some aspect of the practice of slavery in the greater ancient Near East by softening certain usual practices.[27] Let us investigate whether we can observe the operation of any of these biblical laws in the texts from the Judean archive.

TEXTS THAT MENTION SLAVES IN THE JUDEAN MATERIALS

Although only seven texts in the Judean corpus mention slaves, we can glean from them some helpful information about the practice of slavery in these communities. We begin with slaves in debt-related documents and then turn to the transfer of slaves through various other means. Our format examines more fully one or two examples in each of these two groups and summarizes the key points of the other texts.

The first example, JWB 9, is, in most respects, an ordinary Neo-Babylonian promissory note for twenty-one shekels of silver that was drafted in the twelfth year of Darius' reign in a small place called Adabil — of unknown location, but certainly not far from Āl-Yāḫūdu. The creditor Enlil-iqīša,[28] son of Liblut, bears a traditional Babylonian name, and the theophoric element of his first name points toward Nippur, which was the center of Enlil's cult. The debtor Aḫīqam, son of Rapa-Yāma, is known as the central figure in one group of Judean texts. He is obliged to repay the silver in eight months and pledges a slave woman by the name of Ilā-bî (either a West Semitic or Arabic name) under the condition of antichresis, that is, the

---

[25] An antichretic pledge is one whereby a creditor replaces any interest payment that might be associated with repayment of a loan through the use (and the benefit or income obtained thereby) of the pledge (Zaccagnini 2003: 609). Thus, it involves to some extent advance interest.

[26] See, for example, Chiltron 1992: 115. Cf. Proverbs 28:8. As Hiers (2002: 72) indicates: "Here 'brother' probably means fellow-Israelite, perhaps female as well as male." See also Levine 2004: 425. On Neo-Babylonian secured debt instruments and the antichretic pledge, see Oelsner 2001 and Wunsch 2001.

We make comparisons with the Judean corpus against the materials discussed in these articles.

[27] See, for example, the discussions in Jackson 1988: 86, 91; and Westbrook 1995: 1639.

[28] Many of the personal names in the Judean texts, in particular the syllabically written non-Akkadian ones, exhibit spelling variants that make them difficult to be rendered phonetically as well as correct grammatically, especially when it is not clear in which language they originate. We can offer at this time only a tentative reading of several of these names.

interest accruing on the silver is to be offset by the labor of the slave woman. This debt note follows the normal formula and structure for Neo-Babylonian loan documents of this kind. Thus, we may assume that some of the Judeans owned slaves and used them in antichretic pledge situations. In respect to the latter, we observe the biblical prohibition against antichretic pledges in Leviticus 25:36–37, although, here, the Judean is the debtor, not the creditor.

The slave woman is not only described by her name but also bears a tattooed inscription on her wrist of the name of one Kalbaya, son of Ammâ, who we may presume from this mark was her previous owner. We can observe here that the prior owner has an Akkadian name in combination with a West Semitic patronym. This wrist inscription is mentioned in the contract because it is important for the creditor to prove his rightful possession of the slave, should the previous owner, or someone else in, or of, his name, attempt to claim the slave woman as his own, or should she herself assert belonging to someone else. In antichretic situations, the slave is supposed to serve the creditor at his location, which in the case of Enlil-iqīša is probably at some distance from Aḫīqam's locale, so that any legal issue could not be resolved easily. This clause also indicates that the slave woman is not homebred: Aḫīqam came into the possession of her either by the regular means of purchase, inheritance, or dowry acquisition from his wife. The clause is legally important because it affirms that the debtor holds title to the slave and would be able to prove this, despite the contradictory inscription on her wrist.

This clause is followed by a stipulation that is quite exceptional from both a Neo-Babylonian and biblical legal perspective because it says that the creditor does not guarantee against the death or escape of the slave woman. We do not usually find such a provision among the customary contractual clauses of contemporary Neo-Babylonian promissory notes with a slave pledge. Its inclusion may be prompted by the fact that the creditor intends to take the slave woman with him, either to his home base or as a travel companion, and that she might be able to escape more easily as compared with living in a regular settlement, where some household member or neighbor might catch her. The contract also stipulates that the debtor has to replace any item stolen by the slave woman from the creditor's house. This suggests that debtor and creditor are not well acquainted and that the creditor suspects that the slave woman might behave mischievously against him on behalf of her owner. The creditor, therefore, tries to ensure that the debtor does not abuse the situation.

Text JWB 42 shares some similarities to the above tablet. The document was executed in (Bīt)-Našar, in the fifth year of Cambyses. It is a debt note of twenty shekels of silver to be repaid in two months, which is owed by Zabdia, son of Nabû-zēr-ibni, and his wife Sinqia to Arīḫi and Šum-iddin, sons of Bēl-zēr-iddin. Zabdia's name is West Semitic; Sinqia, his wife, has either an Akkadian or West Semitic name; one of the creditors is named Arīḫi (of unknown meaning but known from the Judean corpus); and the other creditor has a typical Akkadian name.

The pledge is, according to the text, their "Egyptian slave woman" Nanaya-baḫī. The theophoric element relating to the goddess Nanaya is popular in West Semitic names, but the final element, -baḫī, is Egyptian. This raises questions as to her ethnic background. Was she Egyptian by birthplace but not ethnicity? Was she ethnically Egyptian, or is Egypt the place to where she was first sold, and her name was then (at least partially) changed? Or was she born in Babylonia to owners of Egyptian descent? We cannot know.

Text IMMP 5 is a slave rental in combination with a pledge. It is executed in Āl-Yāḫūdu, in the eighth year of Nabonidus. The slave owner is Ṣidqi-Yāma, who bears a Yahwistic name and is the son of Šillimu. The slave's renter also bears a Hebrew name: Šikin-Yāma (known in biblical sources as *šqnyh*[*w*]),[29] son of Hinnamu. The slave who is the subject of the contact is called Puhullā, which may be a Hebrew name. If this is correct, one might then surmise that the slave was a Judean, but, as is possible with the Egyptian slave woman above, he may simply have received a new name when he was acquired by his present owner.[30]

It seems that the slave's owner owes nine *kur* (ca. 1,620 liters) of barley to the slave's renter, which the owner promises to deliver after the next harvest (in eight or nine months). The slave serves as security for this claim. During the term of the debt, the slave's wages will be six shekels for thirteen months. As soon as his wages are paid, the slave will be at the disposal of the creditor. While the renter covers the cost of the slave's food, the owner provides one garment for the slave. The slave's wages are quite low, as one could normally expect at least one shekel per month, which in this case would amount to thirteen shekels. Thus, it appears that the interest on this barley loan is being deducted from the slave's wages. The rental contract, therefore, in part disguises an antichretic pledge,[31] which is a common Neo-Babylonian practice.[32]

This is significant because we seem to have a Judean master owning a transferable chattel slave, who also may be a Judean, although we cannot be absolutely certain.[33] Furthermore, we apparently have here a Judean using another Judean for an antichretic pledge. Such a situation is not envisioned by biblical law.[34] There is also no stipulation explicitly exempting the slave from work on the Sabbath as commanded in Deuteronomy 5:14.

IMMP 42 is a receipt concerning a debt note issued upon delivery of the commodities owed in Āl-Yāhūdu, in the thirteenth year of, we believe, Darius's reign. The creditor is a slave woman by the Akkadian name Nanaya-ultarah (whose owner's name is not preserved). The deliverer is again Ahīqam, the archive holder, acting on behalf of three individuals, with Akkadian, Hebrew, and West Semitic names respectively.[35] The text voids the pertaining debt note should it re-appear in the house of the slave woman. Interestingly, we observe here a slave woman conducting business.

Turning now to non-loan-related transactions, IMMP 45 is a duplicate of the transaction in Abraham 2007 which, fortunately, helps, at least in part, to reconstruct some of the lost passages in each individual copy. This contract relates details of an inheritance division after

---

[29] *šknyh*: Ezra 8:3, 5; 10:2; Nehemiah 3:29; 12:3; 1 Chronicles 3:21, 22; *šknyhw*: 1 Chronicles 24:11; 2 Chronicles 31:15.

[30] Martin (1993: 113–15) describes well the difficulty of studying the Jewish practice of slavery in the Roman period. Some Jews took Greek or Roman names; some non-Jews took what were once believed to be Jewish names, but which we have discovered are not necessarily such; and slaves, freedmen, and free persons are often difficult to distinguish in various records. This, coupled with the practice of renaming of slaves, can make it extremely difficult or impossible to determine the ethnicity of slaves and their owners. In our texts, thanks to the archival context, at least the ethnicity of either one or both of the parties is beyond doubt.

[31] This contract contains additionally a contractual liquidated penalty: ten shekels are to be paid by the party who breaks the contract.

[32] For the Neo-Babylonian practice, see Oelsner 2001 andWunsch 2001.

[33] It is possible that slaves owned before the exile were deported with their masters; it is also possible that slaves were acquired while the Judeans were in exile.

[34] We would note here the presence of a slave with a West Semitic name, Barīk-il, in Strassmaier 1887: no. 1113, in a lawsuit about this individual's status. He had been acquired for silver by his previous owner, at least twenty-one years earlier, and then sold. He claims instead to be of *mār banûti* (free) status, but fails to prove it. Dandamaev (1984: 443) assumes that he is "a Jewish prisoner of war." Wallis (1964) also believes that he is a deported Judean, although in the absence of a Yahwistic theophoric element this name should be understood as West Semitic.

[35] Kinâ, son of Ahū; Šabbatāya, son of Bana-Yāma; and Nātina, son of Rahi-il.

Aḫīqam's death and was issued in Babylon in the sixteenth year of Darius. Aḫīqam is the archive holder we met earlier, and in this record we find his five sons — split into two groups, doubtless according to their mothers — dividing their assets. We may therefore assume that Aḫīqam had two wives, either consecutively or at the same time. The recorded distribution involves slaves. His sons Nīr-Yāma and Yāḫû-azza receive the slave woman Nanaya-piḫḫī and ten vats (probably for beer production) as their share, while his other sons, Ḫaggai, Yāḫû-ezer, and Yāḫû-šû, receive the male slave Abdi-Yāḫû and eight vats. Once again, we observe that one of the slaves has a Judean name, but we do not know for certain whether he is, in fact, Judean. The brothers also agree to keep the pertaining implements and utensils as their jointly held property and to divide the remaining assets at a later point. Lastly, they pledge to pay jointly any obligations owed by their father at his death from the property that is still held in common.

The setting and contents of this inheritance division is rather unusual. First, it is issued at Babylon. This is, in fact, the only record known thus far that shows the sons of Aḫīqam traveling to Babylon; they normally do business in the province. The parties would have had to have gone far out of their way. Although it is not incongruous to assume that there might have been a dispute among them over their inheritance, one would expect them to be able to settle the matter either amicably or, with the help of some relatives and neighbors, closer to home. Furthermore, as members of both sets of brothers appear in later documents acting together, we need not presume that this division was triggered by serious quarrels among them. The whole process makes sense when we consider it as a secondary affair that happened when our protagonists were in Babylon for some other reason. Second, among the witnesses figure some individuals with Babylonian names and others with West Semitic or Judean names. We have to assume, therefore, that either the brothers went with an entourage of fellow Judeans to Babylon in order to settle their inheritance division (which seems unlikely given its modest value), or that some of the Judeans mentioned in this record were actually people local to Babylon. It does not seem impossible that a group of Judeans settled in Babylon and remained in contact with other Judeans from the provinces; they may also have done business together. Third, the objects of this transaction — slaves and vats — do not point so much to private inheritance divisions as they do to allocations of business shares among partners, as known from other archives.[36] Thus, Wunsch suggests that we consider this inheritance division as a by-product of some other legal dealing that led the brothers (or, at least, some of them) to Babylon, presumably to address the royal judges.[37] The key issue before the courts in this

---

[36] See, for example, the documents Strassmaier 1885: no. 13; Wunsch 2000: nos. 54 and 57; Strassmaier 1887: no. 244; and Contenau 1929: no. 160, all pertaining to the management and division of such a partnership from the Egibi archive. For details, see Wunsch 2000 vol. A: 100–05. When people conduct joint ventures and make profits, they tend to retire some of the business proceeds whenever they cannot invest them for further productive uses. In such cases, they buy, for example, houses, arable land, or slaves and sooner or later assign them to each of the partners when they balance accounts. Such records tell us that so-and-so many slaves or certain real estate was bought with capital of the *ḫarrānu* business, and that at this certain point these assets are divided

and personally assigned to the partners. As far as Aḫīqam's estate is concerned, one would expect him to have owned at least a house (not necessarily built on his own land, but with parts such as beams and doors that are valuable assets), and possibly some animals (sheep or shares in cows). No such assets are mentioned. Thus, it is likely that here only part of the inheritance is under discussion.

[37] One of the reasons people ventured to Babylon is to litigate lawsuits upon referral from local authorities. See BM 16996 (unpublished), issued in Nippur during the reign of Cyrus, a conditional verdict document in a private matter, which obliges two persons to litigate their case in Babylon. For further

case may have been the dissolution of a joint venture (what is known in Akkadian by the term *ḫarrānu*) between the heirs of the deceased Aḫīqam and his business partner. Once the business was disbanded, the brothers probably went on to divide immediately the proceeds that had been assigned as their father's share in the business capital, that is, the two slaves and the vats. Thus, this document reflects a secondary settlement between the brothers, involving lesser property than the main assets of the deceased.

IMMP 54 involves a slave sale transacted in the seventh year of Xerxes. The vendor is Iqīšaya, son of Barīk-il. We note that the seller has an Akkadian name but a West Semitic patronym, which indicates that his father had reached some level of acclimatization. The buyer is Šalammû, daughter of Ḥannan, and therefore most likely a Judean woman. According to the document, a slave woman and her baby are sold. Interestingly, the woman's name is Ana-muḫḫi-Nanaya-taklāk, a most proper Akkadian name, expressing reverence and trust to Nanaya, a goddess also popular in West Semitic names. The text reveals that her wrist was inscribed with the name of her former owner, Barīk-il, the seller's father. The son may have received her via inheritance or *donatio inter vivos* (a lifetime gift). She was sold for the price of three minas of silver, and the sale contract contains the usual guarantee clauses of Neo-Babylonian slave sale contracts.

Lastly, JWB 3 seemingly addresses a gift in favor of a daughter. Here, one Malēšu, son of Mī-kī-Yāma, is said to have voluntarily made out an official document and transferred as property his slave-woman Ḥuṭuatā and a half-share in a cow to his daughter Yāhû-ḫinni. The daughter has a Yahwistic name while the name of the slave woman appears to be non-Akkadian of unknown provenance and meaning. Furthermore, this record lists six witnesses with Yahwistic names.

This text is extremely unusual in that it has no date or place listed and, furthermore, the scribe is not mentioned. The operative section is based on the standard Neo-Babylonian formula for a property transfer, in this case from father to daughter. This is neither a dowry promise nor compensation for dowry items. Hence, we must assume that this text involves a property transfer that was meant as a bequest that would devolve to the daughter on her father's passing.

THE INSTITUTION OF SLAVERY AMONG THE JUDEANS IN EXILE

We must start this part of our discussion by stating two caveats. First, we have a limited number of texts. Second, all the texts were written by Babylonian scribes, who would understandably cast these records in traditional Neo-Babylonian forms. Thus, we cannot say anything absolutely definitive on the basis of these few Akkadian records. Nonetheless, certain aspects do begin to help us form a picture of slavery among the Judeans in exile, an area about which we previously knew quite little. What exactly do these texts, *in toto*, tell us about the institution of slavery in these communities?

First and most obviously, slavery was an extant institution in which the Judeans participated. The exiled Judeans pledged slaves in both regular and antichretic debt situations. Such slaves were fully transferable: they could be sold, transferred as part of an inheritance, or given by *inter vivos* gift. These slaves, therefore, are in the nature of chattel slaves because of their absolute transferability. Additionally, the Judeans in exile may have had Judean slaves,

---

on conditional verdict documents, see Wells 2004:
108–30; and Magdalene 2007: 78–88.

as well as foreign slaves, whose original names were maintained or changed to West-Semitc or Hebrew names.

We do not observe on the face of the texts any specially treated slaves. We note, instead, that whenever a slave with a Yahwistic name appears, no mention is made of either a time limit on slave service, as we find in Exodus 21:2 for Hebrew slaves owned by Hebrews, or the allowance of any slave to observe the Sabbath as in Deuteronomy 5:14. We note first, in the case of IMMP 45 two slaves, one with a Yahwistic name and another with a non-Hebrew name, are divided between two sets of brothers. If they were of different extraction and this indeed obliged their owners to a different treatment of them, one might argue that such implications were understood by the father and his sons and tacitly observed during the father's lifetime. The settlement between the brothers, however, does not indicate any such understanding, which should have been documented because it would have had important consequences for the status and value of both slaves. It is most unlikely that one set of sons would receive a Hebrew slave with unspoken limitations on his servitude and the other set a non-Hebrew slave with no such limitations. Hence, if the slaves with Yahwistic names are, indeed, of Judean descent, we must argue that the exilic community most probably adopted and applied Neo-Babylonian law regarding slaves and that they apparently did not seek in any manner to distinguish themselves in regard to the institution of slavery from the Babylonians. Only the less significant guarantee clauses were apparent exceptions, but these arose out of a practical necessity rather than a biblical injunction. Second, the Judeans were involved in various antichretic pledge arrangements, which the Hebrew Bible seems to disavow. Third, individuals in the Judean communities owned and transferred the ownership of slaves with Yahwistic, West Semitic, Akkadian, and partially Egyptian names. The fact that slaves of other ethnic groups, particular Akkadian slaves, were owned and transferred by persons with Yahwistic names indicates the integration of Judean individuals into the larger Babylonian society and their economic and political advancement therein. Fourth, these legal documents reflect typical contemporary Neo-Babylonian legal formulas and typology. We can therefore state that the Judeans actively used Babylonian legal forms and contracts in contact with outsiders and among themselves for business. Moreover, we also see that they even applied Babylonian legal forms and Babylonian private law to their own family affairs, or, at least, actively endorsed them by using Babylonian scribes to record the transfer of family property. Fifth, the Judeans apparently had full access to the legal system in that they could witness documents and bring suits, not only to settle their own status, as slaves were permitted, but also in regard to many other matters.

The usage of Neo-Babylonian legal formulas by Judeans and their standing to witness documents and to sue is especially important from a legal anthropological point of view. Legal anthropologists, who study the interaction of colonial and indigenous law in colonial situations, are keenly aware that a range of interaction may exist between colonial and indigenous legal systems. They also argue that, even where so-called home-rule is allowed to the indigenous population in the colonized peripheral regions, the indigenous legal system must make so many accommodations to the colonial law from the center of the empire that what is left of the indigenous system is often more fancy than fact. Hobsbawm and Ranger have character-ized what is typically left of the indigenous system under home-rule colonial systems, as the "invention of tradition"[38] and have made clear that, usually, a great rift is left between the law

---

[38] Hobsbawm and Ranger 1983; cf. Gocking 1994, where this is discussed this in the context of the British Gold Coast.

of the pre- and post-colonial society.[39] We can see this, for example, in British "home-rule" of South and Southeast Asia, where they allegedly enforced Islamic law, but tended to do so only in the area of family and personal-status law.[40] Commercial law, property law, criminal law, and the like were actually Western, a fact which left an indelible mark on these legal systems and created a form of legal neo-colonialism.[41]

Now the question becomes, How might this phenomenon apply to these ancient deported communities living at the center of the colonial power? Grätz has observed, for instance, that in the district of Herakleopolis in Lower Egypt during the Ptolemaic era, various ethnic groups lived in distinct communities, each with a distinct *politeuma*.[42] He defines these:

> This means a territorial association of *Ioudaioi* in Egypt[,] which had seemingly the rights of a partial autonomy, accomplished by an elite called *archontes*, within the realm of the Ptolemies. The members of such an association call themselves *politai* whereas the non-members are denoted as *allophyloi* (P. Polit. Iud. 1,17f.). The relationship of such an association is not only determined by the same ethnic origin but also by the above-mentioned partial legal sovereignty.[43]

He notes that these groups had especially strong rights to determine their own family law, which is often also true under colonial systems of so-called home-rule, as we just discussed. We do not, however, see this same phenomenon in the deported ethnic communities residing in Babylonia during either the Neo-Babylonian or Persian empires. The texts before us demonstrate, instead, that Neo-Babylonian law apparently structured even family and personal status law in the Judean communities. These groups do not seeem to posses legal sovereignty.

---

[39] Hobsbawm and Ranger 1983: 63.

[40] As Bin Hassan (2007: 289) states in regard to Malaysia: "One of the main policies of the British in the Malay Peninsula was non-interference in religious matters. However, this could not be said to be totally true, because there were many instances where Islamic practices, especially the implementation of Islamic laws, were severely curtailed through direct and indirect interference to the extent that only Islamic Personal Laws were allowed to be practiced." Bin Hassan (2007: 292) continues: "The constitution states, 'Islam is the religion of the Federation; but other religions may be practised in peace and harmony in any part of the Federation.' [Constitution of Malaysia, article 3.] However, they did not grant Malaysia independence so that it could become a religious state. The commission responsible for drafting the constitution stated in its report that, 'The observance of this principle shall not impose any disability on non-Muslim nationals professing and practising their own religions and shall not imply that the State is not a secular state.' [Federation of Malaya Constitutional Commission 1957: 73, paragraph 169]." See also Hussin 2007; cf. Mastura 1994.

[41] In examining this same phenomenon in British India and its aftermath, Kozlowski (1997: 223) reports: "As the *raj* gradually emerged as a distinct style of government, the British very quickly dropped any attempt to enforce the criminal punishments prescribed in some Islamic texts. In that, the British seem to have followed the practice of the Mughal state in which district police officials (*kotwals*), not *qazis*, handled all criminal offenses. Moreover, the *kotwals* did not render judgments in consonance with the physical punishments or rules of evidence contained in the manuals for *qazis* which [*sic*] were in circulation in India. By the middle years of the nineteenth century, the British had provided uniform codes for criminal law as well as for the law of evidence applicable throughout British India. Significantly, those legal reforms often occurred in India long before they did in Britain itself. Laws applicable to Muslims became restricted to the realm of 'personal law,' that is to say matters of inheritance and family relations. Those laws have remained uncodified in India, Pakistan and Bangladesh."

[42] Grätz 2009: 6–7.

[43] Grätz 2009: 7.

THE IMPLICATIONS FOR UNDERSTANDING BIBLICAL LAW

What we observe in this corpus is that some of the distinct features of biblical law when compared with Neo-Babylonian law seem not to have been in operation in the deported Judean communities in rural Babylonia. The phenomenon that exilic law is seemingly unrelated to biblical law is reminiscent of the legal materials of Elephantine and the Judean Dessert, where scholars have noted that certain critical biblical legal attributes are missing from the legal texts of those corpora. This fact raises some profound questions in regard to biblical law. For example, Knauf has described Elephantine Judaism as "pre-Biblical Judaism."[44] This may also be true of Babylonian Judaism. Greengus observes that there is much similarity between older Mesopotamian traditions regarding slavery and later rabbinic traditions, even though many of these provisions are missing from biblical law, positing that the solution to this connection lies in the "documentary trail."[45] He states: "The long occupation of Judea and all of Samaria by Assyria, beginning in the 8th century, and continuing with total Babylonian rule followed by that of Persia from the 6th through the 4th centuries B.C.E." gives us the answer,[46] although he does not speculate as to precisely why the biblical laws remain silent on these matters. It is possible, as we have stated previously, that the exilic community simply adopted Neo-Babylonian law. We tend toward agreeing with Greengus that connections exist among Mesopotamian, biblical, and rabbinic law in regard to slavery due to the cultural contacts that were made far more intense by colonial occupation and resettlement policies. Whether or not post-exilic biblical law follows, departs from, or remains silent on particular issues, it seems that the law was formed in all probability with Mesopotamian exemplars in mind. This leaves open the question as to what pre-exilic biblical or Israelite law might have contained. Careful study of this corpus will invite many more questions in regard to the development of biblical law and hopefully provide a few solutions.

WERE THE HEBREWS REALLY SLAVES IN BABYLONIA?

Because one key source of slaves is through raids and warfare in the ancient Near East, it is easy to believe that the Judeans might have been chattel slaves in Babylonia. Several texts within the Hebrew Bible assert, at least as a metaphor, that the people both at home and in exile were as chattel slaves (e.g., Jer. 25:14; 27:7, 9–10; 2 Chron. 36:20; cf. Isa. 49:7; Jer. 2:14). Bible passages describe the position of Judeans during the exile as bearing the heavy yoke of slavery (e.g., Isa. 47:6b; Lam. 1:3). Lamentations 5:5 and 13 indicate that the Judeans were yoked prisoners who received no rest, the young men were forced to grind corn, and they stumbled under heavy loads of wood. Jeremiah 27:7 states: "All the nations shall serve him and his son and his grandson, until the time of his own land comes; then many nations and great kings shall make him their slave." Moreover, Ezra states of the peoples' exile:

> O my God, I am too ashamed and embarrassed to lift my face to you, my God, for
> our iniquities have risen higher than our heads, and our guilt has mounted up to the
> heavens. From the days of our ancestors to this day we have been deep in guilt, and
> for our iniquities we, our kings, and our priests have been handed over to the kings of
> the lands, to the sword, to captivity, to plundering, and to utter shame, as is now the

---

[44] Knauf 2002: 187.

[45] Greengus 1997: 7.

[46] Greengus 1997: 7.

case. But now for a brief moment favor has been shown by the Lord our God, who has left us a remnant, and given us a stake in his holy place, in order that he may brighten our eyes and grant us a little sustenance in our slavery. For we are slaves; yet our God has not forsaken us in our slavery, but has extended to us his steadfast love before the kings of Persia, to give us new life to set up the house of our God, to repair its ruins, and to give us a wall in Judea and Jerusalem (Ezra 9:6–9).[47]

We ask whether Hebrew slavery, as a common exilic experience, is historically accurate or whether slavery is even fair to use as a metaphor for the exilic experience, based on the texts before us?

As early as 1992, Dandamaev argued in regard to Judean exiles in Babylonia:

> These captives, however, cannot be legally classified as [chattel] slaves at all since they were not included in the palace or temple households, but were settled in places set aside for them, particularly in the Nippur region. Initially, these people probably did not have the right to leave their place of residence. Referring to Yahweh's order, Jeremiah urged the prisoners that the captivity would be long, and he encourage them to build houses and lay out gardens, to marry and raise children (Jer. 29:4, 7, 28).[48]

Our findings are in accord. These texts indicate that the Judeans were integrated into the Neo-Babylonian legal, political, and economic systems. It appears that the Judean deportees and their descendants, while clearly not entirely free to determine where they would live, were obviously allowed at times to travel. The tablets discussed in this article, as well as the corpus as a whole, indicate that some groups of Judeans were settled in the area beyond Nippur toward the Tigris corridor on royal land in settlements of persons of distinct ethnic background and that deported families were given land subject to taxes and military and corvée duties, just as were ordinary Babylonians and non-Judean displaced ethnic groups. They do not exhibit that they themselves were anything like chattel slaves. According to records dealing with income from land that was cultivated by Judeans, they were holders of bow-fiefs[49] and were qualified as *šušānûs*,[50] a kind of personal status that precisely protected them from being sold as chattel slaves.[51] For example, IMMP 18 refers to a large amount of barley owed by Aḫīqam

---

[47] Because the terms for "slave" have diverse meanings in the various literary contexts of the Hebrew Bible (Dandamaev 1992: 62) and the context of its use in Ezra is ambiguous, different interpretations exist as to the meaning of "slaves" in Ezra 9:9. For example, Allen and Laniak (2003: 76) say that this refers to "political and economic bondage." Similarly, Blenkinsopp 1988: 183. Fensham (1982: 130) states of this: "Their situation in these countries is described as servitude. They were slaves of their overlord.... Only by living in their country and having the right to serve their lord properly were they free." Holmgren (1987: 69) indicates that this is an attempt by Ezra to relate the post-exilic return to Yehud with the Exodus story. Cf. Koch 1974: 184. We follow Holmgren in this regard.

[48] Dandamaev 1992: 63. He also notes: "The status of the rest was essentially the same as that of the local free population, as can be seen from the information contained in the documents of the Murashû archive."

[49] A kind of land holding in return for military service and taxes that is well-attested in the Murāšû archive but known to have already existed during Nebuchadnezzar's reign (Jursa 1998).

[50] The term *šušānu*, according to Stolper (1985: 82), designates proprietors of bow-lands who "held grants of income-producing property. They were bound to their holdings by restrictions on alienation, and by tax and service encumbrances. Their personal and professional services were controlled by the masters of the subordinate organizations to which they were attached."

[51] Guaranty clauses in slave sale contracts assert that the individual was neither of free status (*mār banî*) nor a temple dependent (*širku*), *šušānû* or royal slave (*arad šarri*).

to a representative of the royal administration who was ultimately answerable to the satrap of Transpotamia. This grain is said to be income from land "of the *šušānû*s of the Judeans," with Aḫīqam apparently acting on behalf of a group of settlers. Some Judeans climbed the administrative ladder even further, such as to headman of a local community. There are signs of increasing affluence and wealth in some families, and increasing social stratification appears among the Judean population over time. Some affluent individuals were able to rid themselves of some of their obligations to perform their corvée or military duty by hiring substitutes.[52] Judeans were capable of entering into legal relations for their own benefit, were able to witness legal documents, and had standing to sue within the legal system. Nothing in these documents reflects the three primary attributes of slave status for the exiled Judeans who had been allotted parcels of arable land: the slave's status as property, the totality of the power exercised over him, and his kinlessness.[53] These Judeans owned personal property themselves, including slaves whom they could pledge, sell, or devolve through gifts and inheritance. The Hebrew Bible itself acknowledges that some of the returnees to Yehud brought their chattel slaves with them (Ezra 2:64–65; Neh. 7:66–67). This property was not, then, in the nature of a slave's *peculium*.[54] It seems that the exiled Judeans were, in reality, able to integrate into the larger society and advance socially, economically, and politically to a fair degree.

CONCLUSION

Seven texts among the corpus of Neo-Babylonian documents relating to the Judean population of rural Babylonia include some reference to slavery. Nothing in these texts reflects the Pentateuchal laws concerning slavery; clearly, these exiles did not use biblical law precepts in regard to slavery. Thus, we cannot determine the status of the pre-exilic law of slavery in Israel on the basis of these texts. It is quite possible, however, that post-exilic biblical law was shaped, at least in part, by the exilic experience.

Further, the exiles in rural Babylonia seem to possess none of the normal attributes of those in chattel slavery. From our brief study of these texts, we have learned that these Judeans were treated much like Babylonians and other non-Judean deported communities. They were given land with the same expectation of taxes and service as common Babylonians. Many integrated well into Neo-Babylonian society, and some were able to prosper in rural Babylonia, becoming affluent farmers, businessmen, and local officials, who might own their own chattel slaves of diverse ethnic backgrounds. All, in fact, were assigned a status that afforded them protection from being sold into chattel slavery. In sum, they apparently used the social, economic, legal, and political systems in place to advance themselves in the situation in which they found themselves. Over four generations, these Judeans became much like those Babylonians who were not from the most privileged urban families.

---

[52] According to JWB 4, in the tenth year of Darius, a certain Zabudu, son of Iltammeš-ḫaza, "will do two months of service for the king in the land of Elam on behalf of Šalam-Yāma, son of Nubâ, where the colleagues of Šalam-Yāma (perform) the king's service in the land of Elam." He receives five shekels of silver in return, apart from travel provisions and equipment.

[53] See note 8 above.

[54] On the slave's *peculium* in the Neo-Babylonian period, see Dandamaev 1972; and Head 2009.

BIBLIOGRAPHY

Abraham, Kathleen

2005/06   "West Semitic and Judean Brides in Cuneiform Sources from the Sixth Century B.C.E.: New Evidence from a Marriage Contract from Al-Yahudu." *Archiv für Orientforschung* 51: 198–219.

2007   "An Inheritance Division among Judeans in Babylonia from the Early Persian Period." In *New Seals and Inscriptions, Hebrew, Idumean and Cuneiform*, edited by M. Lubetski, pp. 206–21. Hebrew Bible Monographs 8. Sheffield: Sheffield Phoenix Press.

Allen, Leslie C., and Timothy S. Laniak

2003   *Ezra, Nehemiah, Esther*. New International Biblical Commentary 9. Peabody: Hendrickson.

Baltzer, Klaus

1987   "Liberation from Debt Slavery after the Exile in Second Isaiah and Nehemiah." In *Ancient Israelite Religion: Essays in Honor of Frank Moore Cross*, edited by P. D. Miller, P. D. Hanson, and S. D. McBride, pp. 477–84. Philadelphia: Fortress Press.

Barstad, Hans M.

1997   *The Babylonian Captivity of the Book of Isaiah: "Exilic" Judah and the Provenance of Isaiah 40–55*. Serie B: Skrifter 102. Oslo: Novus: Instituttet for sammenlignende kulturforskning.

Bin Hassan, Muhammad Haniff

2007   "Explaining Islam's Special Position and the Politic of Islam in Malaysia." *Muslim World* 97: 287–316.

Blenkinsopp, Joseph

1988   *Ezra-Nehemiah: A Commentary*. Old Testament Library. Philadelphia: Westminster Press.

Carmichael, Calum M.

2000   "The Three Laws on the Release of Slaves (Exodus 21:2–11; Deuteronomy 15:12–18; Leviticus 25:39–46). *Zeitschrift für die alttestamentliche Wissenschaft* 112: 509–25.

Chavel, Simeon

1997   "'Let My People Go!' Emancipation, Revelation, and Scribal-Activity in Jeremiah 34.8–14." *Journal for the Study of the Old Testament* 76: 71–95.

Chilton, Bruce

1992   "'Debts." In *Anchor Bible Dictionary*, vol. 2, edited by D. N. Freedman, pp. 114–16. New York: Doubleday.

Chirichigno, Gregory

1993   *Debt-Slavery in Israel and the Ancient Near East*. Journal for the Study of the Old Testament, Supplement Series 141. Sheffield: Journal for the Study of the Old Testament Press.

Contenau, G.

1929   *Contrats Néo-Babyloniens*, Volume 2: *Achéménides et Séleucides*. Textes cunéiformes du Louvre 13. Paris: Paul Geuthner.

Coogan, Michael D.

1976a   *West Semitic Personal Names in the Murašû Documents*. Harvard Semitic Monographs 7. Missoula: Scholars Press.

1976b   "More Yahwistic Names in the Murašu Documents." *Journal for the Study of Judaism in Persian, Hellenistic and Roman Period* 7: 199–200.

Dandamaev, Muhammad A.
1972   "The Economic and Legal Character of the Slaves' peculium in the Neo-Babylonian
               and Achaemenid Periods." In *Gesellschaftsklassen im alten Zweistromland und in den
               angrenzenden Gebieten* (18. Rencontre Assyriologique Internationale, München, 29.
               Juni bis 3. Juli 1970), edited by D. O. Edzard, pp. 35–39. Bayerische Akademie der
               Wissenschaften. Philosophisch-Historische Klasse, Abhandlungen, n.F., 75. Munich:
               Bayerische Akademie der Wissenschaften.
1974   Рабство в Вавилонии VII–IV вв. до н.э. (626–331 гг.). Moscow: Nauka.
1984   *Slavery in Babylonia: From Nabopolassar to Alexander the Great (626–331 B.C.).*
               Revised edition. Edited by M. A. Powell and D. B. Weisberg, translated by V. A.
               Powell. DeKalb: Northern Illinois University Press.
1992   "Slavery." In *Anchor Bible Dictionary*, vol. 6, edited by D. N. Freedman, pp. 58–65.
               New York: Doubleday.

Donbaz, Veysel, and Matthew W. Stolper
1997   *Istanbul Murašû Texts*. Uitgaven van het Nederlands Historisch-Archaeologisch
               Instituut te Istanbul 79. Istanbul: Nederlands Historisch-Archaeologisch Instituut.

Driel, G. van
2002   *Elusive Silver: In Search of a Role for a Market in an Agrarian Environment; Aspects
               of Mesopotamia's Society.* Uitgaven van het Nederlands Historisch-Archaeologisch
               Instituut te Istanbul 95. Leiden: Nederlands Institutut voor het Nabije Oosten.

Driver, Godfrey Rolles, and John C. Miles
1956–60   *The Babylonian Laws.* 2 volumes. Reissued with revisions. Oxford: Clarendon Press
               (1st edition printed 1952–55).

Fensham, F. Charles
1982   *The Books of Ezra and Nehemiah.* New International Commentary on the Old
               Testament. Grand Rapids: Eerdmans.

Finley, Moses I.
1980   *Ancient Slavery and Modern Ideology.* New York: Viking.

Federation of Malaya Constitutional Commission
1957   *Report of the Federation of Malaya Constitutional Commission, 1957.* London:
               Colonial Office of Great Britian.

Frymer-Kensky, Tikva S.
2003   "Israel." In *A History of Ancient Near Eastern Law*, edited by R. Westbrook, vol. 2,
               pp. 975–1046. Handbuch der Orientalistik 72. Leiden: Brill.

Gocking, R.
1994   "Indirect Rule in the Gold Coast: Competition for Office and the Invention of
               Tradition." *Canadian Journal of African Studies / Revue Canadienne des Ètudes
               Africaines* 28: 421–46.

Grätz, Sebastian
2009   "The Question of 'Mixed Marriages': The Extrabiblical Evidence." Paper presented
               at the annual international meeting of the Society of Biblical Literature, Rome, Italy,
               July 2, 2009.

Greengus, Samuel
1997   "The Selling of Slaves: Laws Missing from the Hebrew Bible?" *Zeitschrift für
               Altorientalische und Biblische Rechtsgeschichte* 3: 1–11.

Harris, William V.
1999   "Demography, Geography and the Sources of Roman Slaves." *Journal of Roman
               Studies* 89: 62–75.

Head, Ronan
    2010   The Business Activities of Neo-Babylonian Private "Slaves" and the Problem of
                peculium. Ph.D. dissertation, Johns Hopkins University.

Hezser, Catherine
    2005   *Jewish Slavery in Antiquity.* Oxford: Oxford University Press.

Hiers, Richard H.
    2002   "Biblical Social Welfare Legislation: Protected Classes and Provisions for Persons
                in Need." *Journal of Law and Religion* 17: 49–96.

Hobsbawm, E. J., and T. O. Ranger
    1983   "Introduction: Inventing Traditions." In *The Invention of Tradition*, edited by E. J.
                Hobsbawm and T. O. Ranger, pp. 1–14. Cambridge: Cambridge University Press.

Holmgren, Fredrick Carlson
    1987   *Israel Alive Again: A Commentary on the Books of Ezra and Nehemiah.* International
                Theological Commentary. Grand Rapids: Eerdmans.

Hussin, I.
    2007   "The Pursuit of the Perak Regalia: Islam, Law, and the Politics of Authority in the
                Colonial State." *Law and Social Inquiry* 32: 759–88.

Jackson, Bernard S.
    1988   "Biblical Laws of Slavery: A Comparative Approach." In *Slavery and Other Forms of
                Unfree Labour*, edited by L. J. Archer, pp. 86–89. History Workshop Series. London:
                Routledge.

Joannès, François, and André Lemaire
    1999   "Trois tablettes cunéiformes à l'onomastique ouest-sémitique." *Transeuphratène* 17:
                17–34.

Jones, Alonzo Trévier
    2004   *The Empires of the Bible from the Confusion of Tongues to the Babylonian Captivity.*
                New York: TEACH Services.

Jursa, Michael
    1998   "Bogenland schon unter Nebukadnezar II." *Nouvelles assyriologiques brèves et uti-
                litaires* 1998: no. 124.

    2005   *Neo-Babylonian Legal and Administrative Documents: Typology, Contents and
                Archives.* Guides to the Mesopotamian Textual Record 1. Münster: Ugarit-Verlag.

    2008   "Nabû-šarrūssu-ukīn, rab ša-rēši, und 'Nebusarsekim' (Jer. 39:3)." *Nouvelles
                Assyriologiques Brèves et Utilitaires* 2008: 5.

    2009   "On Aspects of Taxation in Achaemenid Babylon: New Evidence from Borsippa."
                In *Organisation des pouvoirs et contacts culturels dans les pays de l'empire aché-
                ménide*, edited by P. Briant and M. Chauveau, pp. 237–69. Persika 14. Paris: De
                Boccard.

Kaufmann, Yehezkel
    1977   *History of the Religion of Israel*, Volume 4: *From the Babylonian Captivity to the
                End of Prophecy.* New York: KTAV.

Knauf, Ernst A.
    2002   "Elephantine und das vor-biblische Judentum." In *Religion und Religionskontakte im
                Zeitalter der Achämeniden*, edited by R. G. Kratz, pp. 179–88. Veröffentlichungen
                der Wissenschaftlichen Gesellschaft für Theologie 22. Gütersloh: Kaiser/Gütersloher.

Koch, Klaus
    1974   "Ezra and the Origins of Judaism." *Journal of Semitic Studies* 29: 173–97.

Kozlowski, Gregory C.
    1997   "Islamic Law in Contemporary South Asia." *Muslim World* 87: 221–34.

Levine, Baruch A.
    2004   "Tracing the Biblical Accounting Register: Terminology and the Signification of Quantity." In *Commerce and Monetary Systems in the Ancient World: Means of Transmission and Cultural Interaction* (Proceedings of the Fifth Annual Symposium of the Assyrian and Babylonian Intellectual Heritage Project, Held in Innsbruck, Austria, October 3rd–8th, 2002), edited by R. Rollinger and C. Ulf, pp. 420–43. Melammu Symposia 5. Stuttgart: Franz Steiner.

Levinson, Bernard M.
    2006   "The Manumission of Hermeneutics: The Slave Laws of the Pentateuch as a Challenge to Contemporary Pentateuchal Theory." In *Congress Volume Leiden 2004*, edited by A. Lemaire, pp. 281–324. Vetus Testamentum Supplements 109. Leiden: Brill.

Magdalene, F. Rachel
    2007   *On the Scales of Righteousness: Neo-Babylonian Trial Law and the Book of Job.* Brown Judaic Studies 348. Providence: Brown Judaic Studies.
    Forthcoming "Legal Science Then and Now: Theory and Method in the Work of Raymond Westbrook." *Maarav* 16/2.

Martin, Dale B.
    1993   "Slavery and the Ancient Jewish Family." In *The Jewish Family in Antiquity*, edited by S. J. D. Cohen, pp. 113–29. Brown Judaic Studies 289. Atlanta: Scholars Press.

Mastura, Michael O.
    1994   "Legal Pluralism in the Philippines." *Law and Society Review* 28: 461–75.

Matthews, Victor H.
    1994   "The Anthropology of Slavery in the Covenant Code." In *Theory and Method in Biblical and Cuneiform Law: Revision, Interpolation, and Development*, edited by B. M. Levinson, pp. 119–35. Journal for the Study of the Old Testament Supplement Series 181. Sheffield: Sheffield Academic.

Mendelsohn, Isaac
    1949   *Slavery in the Ancient Near East: A Comparative Study of Slavery in Babylonia, Assyria, Syria, and Palestine, from the Middle of the Third Millennium to the End of the First Millennium.* Oxford: Oxford University Press.

Menezes, Rui de
    1999   "Was There Slavery in Ancient Israel?" *Vidyajyoti Journal of Theological Reflection* 63: 799–811.

Mooney, D. Jeffrey
    2008   "Israel in Slavery and Slavery in Israel." *Southern Baptist Journal of Theology* 12: 64–80.

Nelson, Richard D.
    2002   *Deuteronomy: A Commentary.* Old Testament Library. Louisville: Westminster John Knox Press.

Oelsner, Joachim
    2001   "The Neo-Babylonian Period." In *Security for Debt in Ancient Near Eastern Law*, edited by R. Westbrook and R. L. Jasnow, pp. 289–305. Culture and History of the Ancient Near East 9, Leiden: Brill.

Oelsner, Joachim; Bruce Wells; and Cornelia Wunsch
    2003   "Neo-Babylonian Period." In *A History of Ancient Near Eastern Law*, edited by R. Westbrook, vol. 2, pp. 911–74. Handbuch der Orientalistik 72. Leiden: Brill.

Oppenheim, A. Leo
    1955   "'Siege-Documents' from Nippur." *Iraq* 17: 69–89.

Patterson, Orlando
  1982   *Slavery and Social Death: A Comparative Study.* Cambridge: Harvard University
                Press.

Paul, Shalom
  1970   *Studies in the Book of the Covenant in Light of Cuneiform and Biblical Laws.*
                Supplements to Vetus Testamentum 18. Leiden: Brill.

Pearce, Laurie E., and Cornelia Wunsch
  Forthcoming   *Into the Midst of Many People: Judaean and West Semitic Exiles in Mesopotamia.*
                Cornell University Studies in Assyriology and Sumerology 18. Bethesda: CDL Press.

Phillips, Anthony
  1984   "The Laws of Slavery: Exodus 21.2–11." *Journal for the Study for the Old Testament*
                30: 51–66.

Ploeg, J. P. M. van der
  1972   "Slavery in the Old Testament." In *Supplements to Vetus Testamentum* 22, pp. 72–87.
                Leiden: Brill.

Schenker, Adrian
  1998   "The Biblical Legislation on the Release of Slaves: The Road from Exodus to
                Leviticus." *Journal for the Study of the Old Testament* 78: 23–41.

Scheidel, Walter
  1977   "Quantifying the Sources of Slaves in the Roman Empire." *Journal of Roman Studies*
                87: 159–69.

Stolper, Matthew W.
  1985   *Entrepreneurs and Empire: The Murašû Archive, the Murašû Firm, and Persian Rule
                in Babylonia.* Uitgaven van het Nederlands Historisch-Archaeologisch Instituut te
                Istanbul 54. Istanbul: Nederlands Historisch-Archaeologisch Instituut.

  1992   "The Murašû Texts from Susa." *Revue d'assyriologie et d'archéologie orientale* 86:
                69–77.

  2001   "Fifth Century Nippur: Texts of the Murašûs and from Their Surroundings." *Journal
                of Cuneiform Studies* 53: 83–132.

Strassmaier, Johann N.
  1885   *Die babylonischen Inschriften im Museum zu Liverpool nebst andern aus der zeit von
                Nebukadnezzar bis Darius.* Actes du 6ᵉ Congrès International des Orientalistes, Part
                2, Section 1. Leiden: Brill.

  1887   *Inschriften von Nabonidus, König von Babylon (555–538 v. Chr.).* Babylonische Texte
                1–4. Leipzig; E. Pfeiffer.

Vanderhooft, David Stephen
  1999   *The Neo-Babylonian Empire and Babylon in the Latter Prophets.* Harvard Semitic
                Monographs 59. Atlanta: Scholars Press.

Van Seters, John
  1996   "The Law of the Hebrew Slave." *Zeitschrift für die alttestamentliche Wissenschaft*
                108: 534–46.

  2007   "Law of the Hebrew Slave: A Continuing Debate." *Zeitschrift für die alttestamentliche
                Wissenschaft* 119: 169–83.

Vasholz, Robert I.
  1991   "A Legal 'Brief' on Deuteronomy 23:15-16." *Presbyterion* 17: 127.

Waerzeggers, Caroline
  2003/04   "The Babylonian Revolts Against Xerxes and the 'End of Archives.'" *Archiv für
                Orientforschung* 50: 150–73.

2005   "The Dispersal History of the Borsippa Archive." In *Approaching the Babylonian Economy* (Proceedings of the START Project Symposium Held in Vienna, 1–3 July 2004), edited by H. D. Baker and M. Jursa, pp. 343–79. Alter Orient und Altes Testament 330. Münster: Ugarit-Verlag.

Wallis, Gerhard
1964   "Aus dem Leben eines jüdischen Sklaven in Babylon." In *... und fragten nach Jesus: Beträge aus Theologie, Kirche und Geschichte: Festschrift für Ernst Barnikol zum 70. Geburtstag*, pp. 14–20. Berlin: Evangelische Verlagsanstalt.

Weidner, Ernst F.
1939   "Jojachin, König von Juda, in babylonischen Keilschrifttexten." In *Mélanges syriens offerts à monsieur René Dussaud*, edited by the Académie des inscriptions & belles-lettres, vol. 2, pp. 923–35. Bibliothèque Archéologique et Historique 30. Paris: P. Geuthner.

Wells, Bruce
2004   *The Law of Testimony in the Pentateuchal Codes*. Beiträge zur Zeitschrift für altorientalische und biblische Rechtsgeschichte 4. Wiesbaden: Harrassowitz.

Westbrook, Raymond
1995   "Slave and Master in Ancient Near Eastern Law." *Chicago-Kent Law Review* 70: 1631–76.

1998   "The Female Slave." In *Gender and Law in the Hebrew Bible and the Ancient Near East*, edited by B. M. Levinson, V. H. Matthews, and T. S. Frymer-Kensky, pp. 214–38. Journal for the Study of the Old Testament Supplement Series 262. Sheffield: Sheffield Academic Press.

2003   "Introduction: The Character of Ancient Near Eastern Law." In *A History of Ancient Near Eastern Law*, edited by R. Westbrook, vol. 1, pp. 1–90. Handbuch der Orientalistik 72. Leiden: Brill.

Wunsch, Cornelia
2000   *Das Egibi-Archiv* I. *Die Felder und Gärten*. Cuneiform Monographs 20A/B. Groningen: Styx.

2001   "Debt, Interest, Pledge and Forfeiture in the Neo-Babylonian and Early Achaemenid Period: The Evidence from Private Archives." In *Debt and Economic Renewal in Antiquity*, edited by M. Hudson and M. Van De Mieroop, pp. 221–55. International Scholars Conference on Ancient Near Eastern Economies 3. Bethesda: CDL Press.

Forthcoming   *Judeans by the Waters of Babylon: New Historical Evidence in Cuneiform Sources from Rural Babylonia*. Babylonische Archive. Dresden: ISLET.

Zadok, Ran
1979   *The Jews in Babylonia during the Chaldean and Achaemenian Periods According to the Babylonian Sources*. Studies in the History of the Jewish People and the Land of Israel 3. Haifa: University of Haifa.

2002   *The Earliest Diaspora: Israelites and Judaens in Pre-Hellenistic Mesopotamia*. Publications of the Diaspora Research Institute. Tel Aviv: Diaspora Research Institute, Tel Aviv University.

Zaccagnini, Carlo
2003   "Nuzi." In *A History of Ancient Near Eastern Law*, edited by R. Westbrook, pp. 565–617. Handbuch der Orientalistik 72, vol. 1. Leiden: Brill.

9

HOUSEHOLD STRUCTURE AND POPULATION DYNAMICS IN THE MIDDLE BABYLONIAN PROVINCIAL "SLAVE" POPULATION

JONATHAN S. TENNEY, LOYOLA UNIVERSITY NEW ORLEANS AND UNIVERSITY OF COPENHAGEN*

INTRODUCTION

From 1470 until 1155 B.C., Babylonia was ruled by a dynasty of kings of Kassite ethnic descent.[1] The Kassite historical era, sometimes referred to as the Middle Babylonian period (a chronological division referring to the language of most of Babylonia's written records from this time), is characterized by stability and a respect for earlier traditions. The Kassites held on to the royal seat for over three centuries despite suffering multiple Elamite invasions and ruling opposite at least three aggressive Assyrian kings,[2] but lost control when the Elamites captured the final dynast and took him as a prisoner to their capital, Susa.

While the dynasty was in power, the Babylonian military, economy, and diplomatic apparatus seems to have been on par with contemporary nations like Egypt and Hatti, and the region was marked by cultural and intellectual growth. Members of the dynasty communicated freely with the rulers of other ancient Near Eastern nations about matters of state, diplomatic marriages, and the exchange of gifts. Babylonians traded luxury textiles, horses, chariots, and precious stones in the international economic networks of the Late Bronze Age, and for a time southern Mesopotamia operated on the gold standard (Edzard 1960; Brinkman 1972: 275–76).

Babylonian society had been ruralizing for centuries, and the trend toward smaller settlements accelerated under the Kassites' stable rule (Adams 1981: 138–39, 166–67, and 172–73; Brinkman 1984: 169–80). An associated population shift is evident in the province of Nippur, from where the majority of Middle Babylonian records have been recovered. The maintenance of irrigation infrastructure was of considerable concern in some regions, and correspondence generated by provincial officers often concern canals and ditch work (note the letters in Radau 1908). The same governors oversaw a large population of people[3] who were forced by the administrators of Nippur province in central Babylonia to work in weaving houses, kitchens, gardens, and pastures for the government, the temples, and private individuals.

---

* I would like to thank Laura Culbertson, the members of the seminar candidate selection committee, Gil Stein, and the Oriental Institute Publications Office for the invitation to this seminar and for editing the final work.

[1] The historical reconstruction presented in this introduction is based on two articles by J. A. Brinkman (1972 and 1974). Statements given in these first three paragraphs without direct citation should be attributed to these publications.

[2] Adad-nirari I (1305–1274 B.C.), Shalmaneser I (1273–1244 B.C.), and Tukulti-Ninurta I (1243–1207 B.C.).

[3] As many as 8,000 people.

FREE OR UNFREE

Although the degree of their unfreedom is never explicitly stated in any written source, the quantitative data from administrative records demonstrate that this population was under considerable stress and had a demographic profile similar to a recently established slave population (Tenney 2009: 65–81, 133–48, and 174–76). The types of social labels that assyriologists use to define segments of the Babylonian population, for example, *ardu/andu* "slave," are almost entirely lacking for these people because the source documents are administrative records meant for internal circulation among the Nippur governor's staff (expressions of legal and social status were understood and unnecessary) and are damaged in key areas (Tenney 2009: 53–54, 56). The word *amīlūtu* is a term that is sometimes applied to groups of workers and to groups of individuals being sold (Brinkman 1980: 21; Tenney 2009: 167), but it is not endemic in the source material.[4] The lack of a concrete and identifiable native Babylonian term for these people is noteworthy and makes it difficult to pin down their civil status.

Direct evidence that these laborers of Nippur province could be considered slaves consists of references to persons — both singly and in families — bought by the governor and his agents for (possible) integration into the public institutional work force (Petschow 1983), foreigners (Elamites, Assyrians, Kassites, and Lullubians) and people described as booty (*ḫubbutānu*) taken away[5] during the reigns of specific Kassite rulers, and workers bestowed on the governor of Nippur province by the king in Babylon (Tenney 2009: 157–62). References to people trying to escape the system are common, and the gender patterns for runaways are similar to patterns of flight of black slaves in the American South (Tenney 2009: 137–39).[6] Last, the state supplied members of the population with rations regardless of age (nursing babies to elderly adults), something one would not expect of wage or corvée laborers.

The administrators of the servile system also decided the place where at least some, if not all, workers would live. Thousands were combined into mobile work groups that were moved around Nippur province, while others seem to have been loaned or parceled out to free citizens.

All evidence demonstrates that this was a closed system — children born to servile parents also became members — with almost no chance of legitimate release. Statistically speaking, a worker had a better chance of dying during an escape attempt than being freed.

If freedom is imagined as a continuum with chattel slavery on one end and complete freedom of movement, work, and obligation on the other end, and, if one considers population profile, the scattered references to slavery, historical comparisons, and all the possible forms of human bondage (prison labor, thralldom, serfdom, leveé, etc.), it becomes clear that these workers certainly track toward the former end of the spectrum of freedom. They were not serfs tied to the land, but at least some of them had no choice in place of residence. There are no records of them being sold out of the system — which is one of the chief characteristics of chattel slaves — but in a province that might have been experiencing chronic labor shortages like Nippur, it may be that there was never any desire or need for the governor to sell off such a valuable resource.

As expected, forced laborers were permitted to live in family groups, and the family was co-opted by administrators as a means to organize and supply the work force. Household

---

[4] In the preceding historical period, this word (as *awīlūtum*) denoted the "status of a full citizen" (Brinkman 1980: 21).

[5] *Leqû*; perhaps representing a transfer of personnel within the kingdom, rather than the transport of people from a foreign region to Babylonia.

[6] The data are presented in table 9.2 of this article.

members were labeled by government administrators with terms that are ubiquitous in documents describing the free population of Babylonia (like *aššatu* "wife" and *kallatu* "daughter-in-law"),[7] which indicates that these families were recognized as having (or striving toward) similar patterns and institutions as free families.

HOUSEHOLD AND FAMILY

The source material on Middle Babylonian servile workers — for the most part bureaucratic records kept by the governor of Nippur province[8] — are useful in reconstructing population dynamics, including the size and structure of servile families and households. These administrative tablets were not written for this purpose and, like all premodern quantitative material, the data set has limitations. This paper considers the themes "slaves and the family" and "slaves and the state" in light of the Middle Babylonian servile population. It examines what is known about the households of these public servile laborers, how their households were organized, how their households compare with those of other premodern societies, and how the household and family functioned as a unit of social and administrative cohesion.

The word "family" is used here in its most generic sense and encompasses parents and children, siblings, and individuals with blood and marital relation (grandparents, aunts, uncles, cousins, etc.). Further discussion requires terms that distinguish between domestic units (household) and blood relation (conjugal family unit), as well as the many other types of arrangement subsumed under the English word "family." Below are terms and definitions borrowed from the field of historical demography (Laslett 1972: 28–30).

The conjugal family unit, also referred to as the nuclear family, is the most basic element of family organization. It includes a married couple, or a married couple with offspring, or a widowed person with offspring, or other types of unwed women with children. According to the assembled data, the average nuclear family was modest, consisting on average of 4.36 people and 2.8 children, figures that agree with what is known about other premodern populations with high mortality.[9] The records of the texts that provide the sex of all offspring show the presence of more male children than female children (1.57 sons per family versus 0.96 daughters per family), which could be because daughters married and left the family at an earlier age, and/or because males were favored over females in laborer imports.

A household is a domestic and residential unit made up of related individuals who share a residence or are considered by the recording party to share a residence. It may consist of one or more conjugal family units and their relatives.[10] Within the Middle Babylonian provincial corpus there are 121 households whose composition is fully preserved or can be reconstructed

---

[7] Daughter-in-law is an imprecise translation for *kallatu*. A *kallatu* is understood to be an unrelated female brought into a household upon the agreement that she will wed the household head or one of the other males in the household. It has also been argued that *kallatu*s are females in one household that are betrothed to males in another household but that have not yet moved to the home of their marriage partner (Donbaz and Yoffee 1986: 63).

[8] About 550 tablets written in the Middle Babylonian language between 1370 and 1186 B.C.

[9] Egyptian families during the Roman period averaged 4.3 persons (Bagnall and Frier 1994: 67–68) and the households of Tuscany in A.D. 1427 averaged 4.42 (Herlihy and Klapisch-Zuber 1985: 282). Further statistics on family size can be found in the study by Burch (1967: 353, 355, and 360).

[10] To clarify, this paper considers slave households within a slave population and not households with slaves within the entire population, which in some situations tend to have a different demographic profile (consider Harris 1999: 69 and Scheidel 2005: 72–73). Cf. footnote 18.

to the point of being statistically and analytically useful. Three basic household types can be observed among the population: the simple-family household, the extended-family household, and the multiple-family household. Pictorial representations of all three attested types of household are given in figure 9.1. Males are indicated with triangles, females with circles, the head of household with solid fill, and the entire household enclosed with a dotted rectangle. Older generations appear at the top of the diagram; younger generations are laid out in descending order below them. Horizontal lines connect mating partners (line below mates) and siblings (line above siblings).

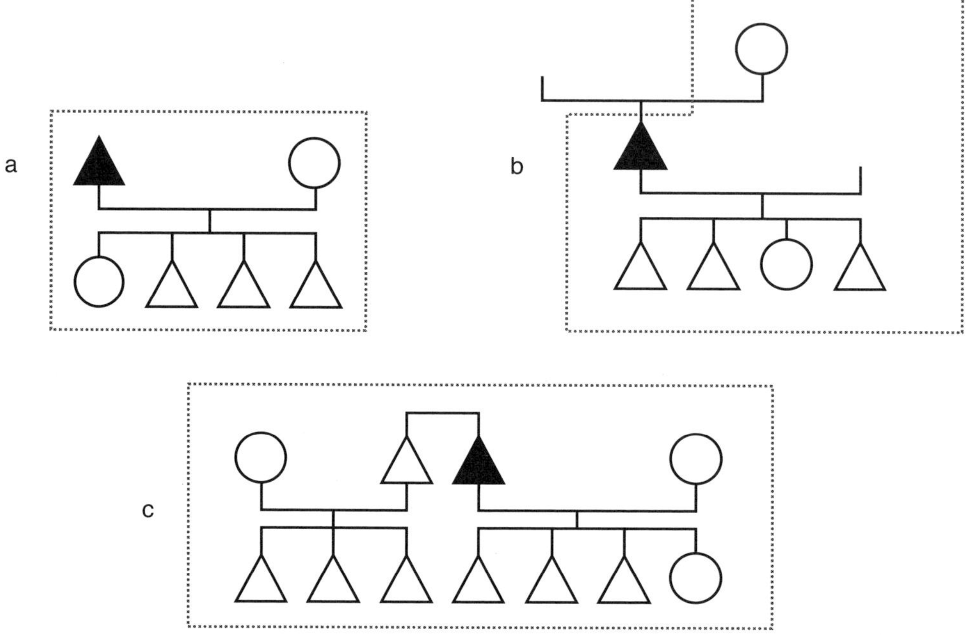

Figure 9.1. Sample diagrams of basic household types: (*a*) simple-family household, (*b*) extended-family household, and (*c*) multiple-family household

The simple-family household is a domestic group that consists of a conjugal family. It is the most common type of household, and accounts for 76 percent of all households for which household type can be identified. Moreover, the majority (61%) of simple-family households were headed by a woman. Evidence is presented below demonstrating that women played a considerable leadership role among servile families of all types.

The extended-family household comprises a conjugal family unit plus other family members. Most of the attested extended households in the population are extended laterally: if the head is male, then the laterally extended individuals are his brothers; if the head is female, then she usually has a sister living with her.

The multiple-family household is a domestic group that includes two or more conjugal family units that are connected by blood or marriage, but not all members need be part of a conjugal family unit. The majority of multiple-family households consist of siblings with their conjugal families or a formerly simple household that brings in the new bride of one of the sons.

In terms of frequency, the largest percentage of all households that can be fully identified are of the simple type (76%), followed by multiple families (17%), and extended families (7%).

A significant presence of female heads among single-family households has already been noted. When one examines conjugal family units, an even more basic unit of family organization, it seems that for 35 percent of them the husband is either deceased or not listed.[11] It is also noteworthy that these single-parent families averaged slightly more children, had a greater percentage of children in the youngest age group, and were more likely to have girls. The reasons why single mothers had more children is puzzling. On the one hand, if one removes childless families from the statistics (all of which still have the husband present), the average number of children for single mothers still exceeds that of married or widowed fathers. On the other hand, there are examples of a significant percentage of deaths in the families of single mothers.[12]

There are multiple reasons why such a high number of women were in charge of households and conjugal families, but one likely possibility is that these women were widows. The argument that adult men were more likely to die (from overwork, etc.) agrees with the information we have on workers listed as dead, and one calculation puts the ratio of dead husbands to dead wives at ten to one.

Moreover, in all clear attestations of a living grandparent, the surviving grandparent is the grandmother. Three-generation households are rare in early societies — especially when the members of the population have a short life expectancy (Levy 1965: 50; Burch 1967: 350) — but this does not really explain why married women would survive longer than married men.

The fact that there are more deaths recorded, both among males for the entire population and males who are married, and a high incidence of both widowed mothers and grandmothers, can be at least partly explained by the age at marriage of men and women at this time. Although an approximate age at marriage for females has yet to be concretely determined, previous research on this topic has concluded that husbands were usually older than their wives when they wed (Roth 1987: 736–37 and 746–47; Gehlken 2005: 102–03 and 107–08). This would mean that wives were more likely to outlive their husbands simply because they were younger. In addition, widows with little property may have found it more difficult to remarry, which may have put them and their children at a disadvantage. Such a social practice would go a long way in explaining the high incidence of female heads of household and single mothers. It certainly does not explain it away entirely, but it could have been a considerable factor in the patterns observed.

COMPARISONS

The data on servile households from Kassite Nippur can be compared with similar information from the two most significant studies of premodern populations in the ancient Mediterranean (Florence in the early fifteenth century A.D.[13] and Egypt in the middle of

---

[11] The female household head is a woman in charge of a household, while a single mother (for the purposes of this paper) is a female in charge of a conjugal family unit (Tenney 2009: 110 n. 87).

[12] As high as 75 percent of children dead (Ni. 1066+ 1069 rev. ii′ 12′–16′). However, there is no way to determine if these deaths happened at the same time, as some dead workers are kept on the rolls for over a year.

[13] The original source material is drawn from the Florentine Catasto of 1427, studied by Herlihy and Klapisch-Zuber (1985).

the second century A.D.[14]) and newly processed data from northern Iraq during the Neo-Assyrian period (800–614 B.C.).[15] These data indicate that the simple-family household was significantly more common among the servile population at Nippur than in the Mediterranean populations, but less so than is indicated in the Neo-Assyrian material (table 9.1). Scholars generally agree that the simple-family household (rather than the extended-family household or multiple-family household) has been the most common domestic arrangement in premodern societies, and this idea is backed up with solid demographic evidence from many other regions (Levy 1965: 41–42, 49–50; Burch 1967: 349, 353, 355, and 360).

Table 9.1. Percentages of attested households by type for the servile-worker population in Kassite Nippur compared with the servile population of Assyria in the Neo-Assyrian period and the general populations of Roman Egypt and medieval Tuscany

	Kassite Nippur	*Assyria*[16]	*Roman Middle Egypt*[17]	*Medieval Tuscany*
Simple-family Household	76.0%	94.6%	54.4%	65.2%
Extended-family Household	7.0%	4.3%	19.0%	12.6%
Multiple-family Household	17.0%	0.1%	26.6%	22.2%

However, the fact that nearly three-quarters of the households were simple is remarkable and may be an indication of the low status of the population, or perhaps the result of direct manipulation by administrators. The statistics from the two Mesopotamian populations are drawn from texts concerning servile populations, while those from Tuscany and Egypt involve census data from an entire population (free and unfree). Moreover, the Assyrian data are mostly compiled from legal records (purchases, court judgements) that probably deal with slaves intended to work in private households rather than large industrial or institutional systems (e.g., latifundia, Caribbean sugar plantations); these two types of slave populations have had historically different demographic profiles.[18] If such is the case, then these "households" in the Neo-Assyrian documents were actually conjugal family units that were not independent households, but rather members of a larger non-slave household. While many factors could

---

[14] The original source material is drawn from census records from three of the fifty nomes of Egypt. The the data were processed by Bagnall and Frier (1994).

[15] Galil 2007.

[16] Statistics for Assyria are drawn from table 21 in Galil 2007: 263. However, some categories of people were excluded from the statistics here (pledged people, Harran census, deportees, and royal grants) because the status of the people in the category is in doubt or is not comparable to the Nippur material, and/or the passages from which the data are drawn need further study.

[17] Statistics for Tuscany and Egypt are drawn from table 3.1 in Bagnall and Frier 1994: 60. Household types not attested (or undeterminable) in the Nippur material (i.e., solitary and no household types) were excluded from the statistics from medieval Tuscany and Roman Egypt.

[18] That is, some evidence suggests that the sex ratio of slave populations favored women when the proportion of slave to free is small and restricted to domestic spheres, and favored males when slaves made up a large percentage of the work force, for example, in institutional labor, mines, and large-scale agricultural estates (evidence presented and cautions raised in Harris 1999: 69–70).

have been at work, one could argue that servility influenced the average size of these Middle Babylonian households.[19]

FUNCTION AND STABILITY

The administrators in charge of the population utilized the household for the distribution of products, organization of labor,[20] and as a means of identifying individual workers through the use of a patronymic (which was standard Babylonian practice).[21] Robert Fogel, the Nobel Prize-winning economist from the University of Chicago, and Stanley Engerman pointed out that slave families in the American South, even though never legally recognized, functioned in the same way for plantation owners (Fogel and Engerman 1974: 127).

Families also stabilized the population by indirectly preventing runaways and enabling new births. Roughly 92 percent of escapees[22] whose sex can be identified are male, a statistic that is remarkably similar to the sex distribution in known escape attempts by slaves in the American South in the eighteenth century. In Virginia and North Carolina, runaways are estimated to have been 89 percent male, with male escapees accounting for 78–82 percent of the total number of runaway slaves in South Carolina.[23] The male to female ratio seen among Middle Babylonian escapees is much greater than the percentage of males within the entire attested Middle Babylonian adult worker population (59% male), so the 92 percent rate is not directly attributable to a corresponding number of males in the general population. Instead, the evidence suggests that the presence or absence of a conjugal family was significant in whether or not a worker decided to flee.

Table 9.2. Percentage of male runaways from selected laboring populations[24]

Public Servile Population, Nippur	92% male
Black Slaves, Virginia and North Carolina	89% male
Black Slaves, South Carolina	78–82% male

Over 99 percent of runaway males are not listed as having a spouse or offspring and so were presumably single adults or children.[25] There is only a single clear instance of a male head of household or father of a conjugal family unit who runs away leaving his family. As many as eight but no more than thirteen escaped males come from work groups who also list an escaped female as a member; and it is possible, although not stated in the text, that these

---

[19] As compared to the general populations from societies outside Mesopotamia, not as compared to the entire Babylonian population (whose population statistics, e.g., size, sex ratio, are unknown for any ancient historical period).

[20] For example, very young children worked alongside their mothers, especially in weaving and textile production (Tenney 2009: 129).

[21] Escapees were usually listed with a patronymic, deceased workers rarely were, even though the purpose of recording whether a worker was dead or escaped

was the same, that is, to state that workers were not available for work and did not need to be fed.

[22] Escapees are identified in the text with the designation ZAḪ₂ (= *ḫalāqu*) (Brinkman 1982: 5–6; Tenney 2009: 135–37).

[23] See Windley 1974: 65; Mullen 1972: 89 and 103; Littlefield 1981: 144; and Morgan 1983: 100 (table 12).

[24] Morgan 1983: 100 (table 12).

[25] The statistics and references for this and the next paragraph are set out in detail in Tenney 2009: 140–42.

escaped males and females formed romantic pairs. In total, the data suggest that somewhere between 6 and 10 percent of the male escapees had a female partner and that, in all but one case, the pair escaped together.

Females were less likely to run, and, if they did, they probably did so in the company of a male and brought their children along with them. At least 57 percent, but probably more, of female runaways may have escaped with a male partner.[26] The evidence also suggests that the very youngest boys listed as escaped did so as part of a group containing at least one adult female, presumably the boy's mother; and there is a single instance of single mother and her daughter who escaped together. Only one woman is known to have abandoned her children.

It seems that responsibilities to the immediate family were strongly considered by workers who were contemplating an escape attempt. Males were considerably more likely to escape than females; and, although the evidence is not ideal, it seems that the high rate among male escapees could be attributed to the men being young and unattached to an immediate family. Conversely, women were less likely to escape because of familial ties; and when they did run, would do so with a man and/or bring their children along with them.

The Nippur government tracked absent workers and pursued escapees. The reasons why the government went to such lengths to return runaways rather than recruit new workers from within Babylonia raises questions about the viability (and legal status) of the population. Again, a partial answer can be found in population dynamics. One indirect means of establishing the living conditions of forced laborers can be found in a common demographic measure, the sex ratio. Sex ratio is a statistic that represents sex composition and is defined as the ratio of males to females in the population. It is normally expressed as the number of males per 100 females, usually reduced to just a single number, that is, a ratio of 103:100 is usually expressed as 103 (Newell 1988: 27). A number greater than 100 indicates that there are more males than females in the survey; a number less than 100 means that the population has more females than males. The normal, accepted sex ratio at birth is 105 (more boys are always born, but are less likely to survive infancy); and, because in most of the modern, developed world the mortality rate for men is higher than for women, it tends to drift toward 100 as the population ages.

In the Middle Babylonian servile population, the sex ratio was abnormally skewed toward males (137) which is a similar situation to that of slaves in the American South in the eighteenth century (125–130),[27] but very different than slaves in Rome (200–233),[28] or slaves in Babylonia from the seventh to fourth centuries B.C. (259).[29]

The male-oriented population influenced the long-term viability of the entire work force. Nippur administrators kept records that summarized additions (births, returned escapees) and losses (deaths, runaways). These records, combined with a raw count of individual workers listed as an addition or loss in non-summary rosters, suggest that the population experienced 20 percent more losses than additions (Tenney 2009: 147–48, esp. n. 125).

---

[26] Many times, the female escapee appears immediately adjacent to a male escapee on the roster in which the group is listed.

[27] Evidence from Maryland and South Carolina suggests that the ratio was much higher in the seventeenth century, when the slave population was being established (Menard 1975: 33, 38–39; 1995: 286).

[28] These ratios were factored from Roman epitaphs, hardly ideal source material (Harris 1999: 69).

[29] Ratio calculated from numbers given in Dandamaev 1984: 218.

Table 9.3. Sex ratios of selected premodern populations, rounded off and organized by ratio

Roman Egypt (general population)	110
Medieval Tuscany (general population)	110
American plantations, eighteenth century A.D. (slave population)	125–130
Nippur, fourteenth–thirteenth centuries B.C. (servile population)	137
Post-Republican Rome (slave population)	200 or 233
Babylonia, seventh–fourth centuries B.C. (slave population)[30]	259

This crude evidence hints that the work force lost more members through death or flight than were added by births (internal reproduction) or by the return of fugitives. This is also a characteristic shared by large slave populations being used by governments, institutions, or industrial, cash-crop-oriented plantations. The only historical example of an internally viable slave population was blacks toiling in the plantations of the American South. In the first century of black slave labor in the United States and its British colonial forbears, males far outnumbered females and the sex ratio was skewed in a way that was very similar to the data available on Middle Babylonian public workers. Gradually, the birth and survival rates among these black slaves led to a balanced natural population and to an increase in population size. In contrast, slave populations in the Caribbean, Central and South America, and the agricultural estates (plantations) of Roman Italy had a severely male-dominated population and these operations required fresh workers (2–5% decrease per annum). In fact, even though 94 percent of slaves shipped to the Americas from Africa went to the sugar plantations of the Caribbean and Central and South America, by the year 1825 36 percent of the black slave population of the New World lived in the United States, making the young nation the largest slaveholding region in the West (Fogel and Engerman 1974: 14, 25–29).

CONCLUSION

There was a large, unfree population living in Nippur and its environs in the fourteenth and thirteenth centuries B.C., controlled by the governor of Nippur province. Their population statistics and other characteristics share some similarities with populations in the Mediterranean and Near East, but are also evocative of large-scale slave populations, that is, they were not just slaves living in private households. However, it is not clear whether they were chattel slaves.

The servile family stabilized the population in at least two ways. It limited the amount of decrease the population would experience through flight and death and facilitated new births. It was also used by administrative authorities to accomplish a variety of bureaucratic necessities, such as food supply and work assignment. By doing so, bureaucrats tacitly recognized the value of the family as an important and unifying institution. The native terminology used in administrative documents suggests that the population followed traditional Mesopotamian marriage and household norms despite their disadvantaged status, but were perhaps less

---

[30] The attested sex ratio for privately owned slaves is 236.1, while the ratio for institutional (temple) slaves is 533.3 (statistics drawn from Dandamaev 1984: 218).

successful in their efforts. This serves as further proof that the family is the oldest, most resilient unit of human organization.

ABBREVIATION

Ni.   Tablets excavated at Nippur, in the collections of the Archaeological Museum of Istanbul

BIBLIOGRAPHY

Adams, Robert McC.
1981   *Heartland of Cities: Surveys of Ancient Settlement and Land Use on the Central Floodplain of the Euphrates.* Chicago: University of Chicago Press.

Bagnall, Roger S., and Bruce W. Frier
1994   *The Demography of Roman Egypt.* Cambridge Studies in Population, Economy, and Society in Past Time 23. Cambridge: Cambridge University Press.

Brinkman, John. A.
1972   "Foreign Relations of Babylonia from 1600 to 625 B.C." *American Journal of Archaeology* 76: 271–81.

1974   "The Monarchy in the Time of the Kassite Dynasty." In *Le palais et la royauté (Archéologie et Civilisation)*, edited by P. Garelli, pp. 395–408. 19ᵉ Rencontre Assyriologique Internationale. Paris: Paul Geuthner.

1980   "Forced Laborers in the Middle Babylonian Period." *Journal of Cuneiform Studies* 32: 17–22.

1982   "Sex, Age, and Physical Condition Designations for Servile Laborers in the Middle Babylonian Period." In *Zikir šumim: Assyriological Studies Presented to F. R. Kraus*, edited by G. van Driel, Th. J. H. Krispijn, M. Stol, and K. R. Veenhof, pp. 1–8. Studia Francisci Scholten memoriae dicata 5. Leiden: Nederlands Instituut voor het Nabije Oosten.

1984   "Settlement Surveys and Documentary Evidence: Regional Variation and Secular Trend in Mesopotamian Demography." *Journal of Near Eastern Studies* 43: 169–80.

Burch, Thomas K.
1967   "The Size and Structure of Families: A Comparative Analysis of Census Data." *American Sociological Review* 32: 347–63.

1972   "Some Demographic Determinants of Average Household Size: An Analytic Approach." In *Household and Family in Past Time: Comparative Studies in the Size and Structure of the Domestic Group over the Last Three Centuries in England, France, Serbia, Japan and Colonial North America, with further Materials from Western Europe*, edited by P. Laslett with assistance by R. Wall, pp. 91–124. Cambridge: Cambridge University Press.

Clay, Albert T.
1906a   *Documents from the Temple Archives of Nippur Dated in the Reigns of Cassite Rulers (Complete Dates).* The Babylonian Expedition of the University of Pennsylvania, Series A: Cuneiform Texts 14. Philadelphia: Department of Archaeology, University of Pennsylvania.

1906b   *Documents from the Temple Archives of Nippur Dated in the Reigns of Cassite Rulers (Incomplete Dates).* The Babylonian Expedition of the University of Pennsylvania,

Series A: Cuneiform Texts 15. Philadelphia: Department of Archaeology, University of Pennsylvania.

1912   *Documents from the Temple Archives of Nippur Dated in the Reigns of Cassite Rulers.* University of Pennsylvania, Publications of the Babylonian Section 2/2. Philadelphia: University Museum.

Coale, Ansley J.

1971   "Age Patterns of Marriage." *Population Studies* 25: 193–214.

Coale, Ansley J., editor

1964   *Aspects of the Analysis of Family Structure.* Princeton: Princeton University Press.

Donbaz, Veysel, and Norman Yoffee

1986   *Old Babylonian Texts from Kish Conserved in the Istanbul Archaeological Museums.* Bibliotheca Mesopotamica 17. Malibu: Undena Publications.

Edzard, Dietz Otto

1960   "Die Beziehungen Babyloniens und Ägyptens in der mittelbabylonischen Zeit und das Gold." *Journal of the Economic and Social History of the Orient* 3: 38–55.

Fallers, Lloyd

1965   "The Range in Variations in Actual Family Size: A Critique of Marion J. Levy Jr.'s Argument." In *Aspects of the Analysis of Family Structure*, edited by A. J. Coale, pp. 70–82. Princeton: Princeton University Press.

Fogel, Robert William, and Stanley L. Engerman

1974   *Time on the Cross: The Economics of American Negro Slavery.* 2 volumes. Boston: Little, Brown & Co.

Gehlken, Erlend

2005   "Childhood and Youth, Work and Old Age in Babylonia — A Statistical Analysis." In *Approaching the Babylonian Economy: Proceedings of the START Project Symposium Held in Vienna, 1–3 July 2004*, edited by H. D. Baker and M. Jursa, pp. 89–120. Alter Orient und Altes Testament 330. Münster: Ugarit-Verlag.

Gibson, McGuire

1992   "Patterns of Occupation at Nippur." In *Nippur at the Centennial: Papers Read at the 35ᵉ Rencontre Assyriologique Internationale, Philadelphia, 1988*, edited by M. deJ. Ellis, pp. 33–54. Occasional Publications of the Samuel Noah Kramer Fund 14. Philadelphia: University Museum.

Harris, William V.

1999   "Demography, Geography and the Sources of Roman Slaves." *The Journal of Roman Studies* 89: 62–75.

Herlihy, David, and Christiane Klapisch-Zuber

1985   *Tuscans and Their Families: A Study of the Florentine Catasto of 1427.* Yale Series in Economic History. New Haven: Yale University Press.

Laslett, Peter

1972   "Introduction: The History of the Family." In *Household and Family in Past Time: Comparative Studies in the Size and Structure of the Domestic Group over the Last Three Centuries in England, France, Serbia, Japan and Colonial North America, with further Materials from Western Europe*, edited by P. Laslett with assistance by R. Wall, pp. 1–89. Cambridge: Cambridge University Press.

Levy, Marion J.

1965   "Aspects of the Analysis of Family Structure." In *Aspects of the Analysis of Family Structure*, edited by A. J. Coale, pp. 1–63. Princeton: Princeton University Press.

Littlefield, Daniel C.
  1981   *Rice and Slaves: Ethnicity and the Slave Trade in Colonial South Carolina.* Baton
              Rouge: Louisiana State University Press.

Menard, Russell R.
  1975   "The Maryland Slave Population, 1658–1730: A Demographic Profile of Blacks in
              Four Counties." *The William and Mary Quarterly*, third series, 32: 29–54.
  1995   "Slave Demography in the Lowcountry, 1670–1740: From Frontier Society to
              Plantation Regime." *The South Carolina Historical Magazine* 96: 280–303.

Morgan, Philip D.
  1983   "Black Society in the Lowcountry, 1760–1810." In *Slavery and Freedom in the Age of
              the American Revolution*, edited by I. Berlin and R. Hoffman, 83–142. Charlottesville:
              University Press of Virginia.

Mullen, Gerald W.
  1972   *Flight and Rebellion: Slave Resistance in Eighteenth-Century Virginia.* Oxford:
              Oxford University Press.

Newell, Colin
  1988   *Methods and Models in Demography.* New York: Guilford Press.

Petschow, Herbert P. H.
  1983   "Die Sklavenkaufverträge des *šandabakku* Enlil-kidinnī von Nippur." *Orientalia* 52:
              143–55.

Radau, Hugo
  1908   *Letters to Cassite Kings from the Temple Archives of Nippur.* The Babylonian
              Expedition of the University of Pennsylvania, Series A: Cuneiform Texts 17, Part 1.
              Philadelphia: Department of Archaeology, University of Pennsylvania.

Roth, Martha T.
  1987   "Age at Marriage and the Household: A Study of Neo-Babylonian and Neo-Assyrian
              Forms." *Comparative Studies in Society and History* 29: 715–47.

Scheidel, Walter
  1996   *Measuring Sex, Age and Death in the Roman Empire: Explorations in Ancient
              Demography.* Journal of Roman Archaeology Supplemental Series 21. Ann Arbor:
              Journal of Roman Archaeology.
  2005   "Human Mobility in Roman Italy, II: The Slave Population." *The Journal of Roman
              Studies* 95: 64–79.

Tenney, Jonathan S.
  2009   Life at the Bottom of Babylonian Society: Servile Laborers at Nippur in the 14th and
              13th Centuries B.C. Ph.D. dissertation, University of Chicago.

Windley, Lathan Algera
  1974   Profile of Runaway Slaves in Virginia and South Carolina from 1730 through 1787.
              Ph.D dissertation, University of Iowa.

SECTION FOUR:
RESPONSE

10

SLAVES AND HOUSEHOLDS IN THE NEAR EAST: A RESPONSE

INDRANI CHATTERJEE, RUTGERS UNIVERSITY

The temporal depth of West Asian histories — from the third millennium B.C. to the late eighteenth century A.D. — is rarely available in any one conference on either slavery or the household. This temporal depth alone offers the greatest potential for what, following Dipesh Chakrabarty, we may call "provincializing Europe." After all, there was no "Europe" in the third millennium B.C. Nor, if the debates about the interpretation of cuneiform are taken seriously, was "English" or even logocentrism available as a uniform mode of expression. These early histories thus allow us to shrink both Europe and English into "vernacularisms" devised at a later period, even though today they appear as the currency in which all intellectual exchanges occur.

This recognition is liberating. It reminds us that the very terms in which we speak here today — slavery, family, household — are coinages of a later period. These terms contain the ghosts of debates that occurred from the later seventeenth century onward about the nature of individual humanity, labor, and dignity. Using these words requires caution, since they are inhabited by ghosts of intellectual ancestors — the many historians, political theorists, feminist activists — who have all at one point or another used them as shorthand. But these historians, political theorists, and others lived in a particular political economy. When they said "slave," they meant a particular kind of laborer easily identifiable to them.

These meanings have been used so often, and with such force in print media of the eighteenth to twentieth centuries, that the meanings have become commonplace, almost as the default standard for gauging other systems of long ago. Therefore, usages, languages, forms specific to a West Asian or Near Eastern past, appear to be amenable to those meanings of both "slavery" and "household" that may not inhere in terms and languages used in that past. Kleber's paper reminds us of that most forcibly, in her insistence that we use the term *širku* just as we use the word "helot" today. So, as an experiment in trying to hear the papers in terms outside of the over-heated meanings of "forced labor," "deracination," or "rightlessness," let me try to summarize the themes that emerged in terms of other vocabulary.

The first term we encounter is "corporations," pertaining to extremely young "herds of humans" (Englund 2009), sometimes gathered through war or forced deportation as suggested by Magdalene (Judeans in Babylonia), and formed as corporate units or the *amīlūtu* (Tenney), military regiments (Gordon or Toledano), or troops of singers (Gordon). After having been established in collectives of some kind to work at subsistence or at wealth-generating activities, they appear in the records as "dispersed" in ones and twos as gifts, inheritances, mortgage-credit operations. Corporate responsibility for all alike appears as the norm, whether it was that of the kin of a merchant who had died in debt or it was that of shepherds. Under those conditions, particular individuals were put into circulation, including both kinsmen and non-kinsmen of the debtor and the deceased.

One factor deserving of greater emphasis is urbanism, given that Mesopotamian history refers to the world of urbanism, the very location of the earliest cities, themselves ports in the region proximate to multiple seas; thus some idea of whether or not this circulation or transfers of individuals was linked to an early history of cosmopolitanism warrants note. Mesopotamia was, after all, the earliest crossroad of cultural formations for which we have evidence. Were "outsiders" or deportees (such as the Judeans) important to the Babylonians because they had some special crafts or skills the Babylonians wanted? Such as canal irrigated agriculture, or navigation, in the development of "new" crafts? Were these "outsiders" purveyors of new cultures, such as linguistic ones, or the world of manners suggested in Toledano's piece?

What was being circulated was corpus, that is, bodies, or, in keeping with the pre-Cartesian logic that I am trying to retain, the body-mind continuum. This body-mind continuum is implicitly suggested in Seri's work, which refers to wombs of females hired or taken in permanent liaisons, and by the cases of the singing throats and musical fingers that underwent hours of grueling practice to become treasures for their holders. Both the assignments of some bodies to such work and the aspects of rigorous training that would make some workers more valuable than others are referred to in Toledano's and others' papers in terms of commitments. It is only by keeping the body-mind together can one understand that the cultivation of the interiorized state — that some papers are referring to as "affection," "trust," "tenderness," or "bonds" — also expresses a physical aspect of such cultivation, whether one calls it military or any other kind of training.

Together, these papers allow us to re-imagine entire pasts from outside the categories of Enlightenment thought, outside categories of rights, freedom, property, markets. In other words, they allow us to re-imagine the multiple processes involved in the transformation of (1) the unschooled prisoner of war/the barbarian "foreigner" into the socialized "citizen," and (2) the unschooled infant into fully mind-body disciplined adult. Indeed, one need not invoke the s-word and yet may still find the papers in question intelligible. As a result, I suggest that these contributions offer a genuinely momentous opportunity for the re-imagining and re-investigation of slavery itself as the sum of these transformative processes, perhaps never completed in one generation, but over many.

The gains of this re-imagination are many. For the present, it humbles every historian who stumbles upon one or the other fragment from the long-drawn-out and perhaps multi-generational processes that each of us finds in any archive. For the future, I believe that it will help us to historicize the "domus/domestic," both as a workplace and as a place of cultural production. Let us use the word "establishment"; when it is specialized, we can call it a residence or house; when it is personalized, we can call it an entourage. The word allows for perspective and scale: the single-mother-and-child unit who have to take in washing to survive are in a workplace which from the employer's or merchant's perspective seems "home" of the single-female worker. Yet, it also allows us to investigate the widowed or unmarried female as potentially the employer of another bought-up unskilled child, who in turn initiates a process of transformation. It is in this sense that the future of gender history appears to be a bright one.

Gender does not have to be investigated only in terms of relationships of men and women, but as relational shifts between dedicated and undedicated females (as in Seri's paper) in terms of systems of commitment and attachment and the maintenance and revisions thereof. I suggest this kind of usage would also unravel a couple of knots in several papers here — partly in the cases in which the "slave-family" is imagined as discrete from the non-slave family, or where household and slavery are somehow applicable to different segments of the same population. Partly, studies of slavery seldom also study marriage systems in the same society and time, neglecting to translate one form into another. Yet, if we think of "marriage" as a form of commitment, then the real issue is not one of whether or not slaves get married, but one of whose is the higher commitment — was the *nadītu*-woman's obligation to her deity or her father's transferred slave to her? By repositioning the terms of both discussions, future scholarship would interrogate the meanings of "production" and "reproduction" as universally valid categories that organize the scholarship on women and slavery in our times. Where is the frontier that separates the two? When one aged female trained singer buys or adopts another infant female and begins to "educate" her in a skill, is the establishment a "brothel" or a home? Moreover, is the aged female "producing," or is she "reproducing?" In terms of methodological consequences, the elder female's strategy of kin-acquisition should expand our discourses on family and kinship to include the polyvalent play of power and profit. "Slavery" and "family" do not need to be counterposed formations, nor should "the slave-family" be frozen in time and cut off from the "non-slave family," but rather these terms should be located within a moving frontier of contests, collusions, and control over the meanings of both "slavery and family."

This is precisely what we do find in the evidence that these papers provide about disputes about the standing of particular individuals (Culbertson), or their escape/non-fulfillment of contracts, that is, their criminality (Neumann). Synthesizing some of the particular histories presented in this collection of papers, we can read the period between the third millennium B.C. and the eighteenth century as a moving frontier of such meanings — a frontier that sedentarized only when complete control over the strategies and meanings of kinship was assured to the handful of people we conveniently call the State.

Disputes themselves require consideration of many layers: disputes among slaves and masters, between masters and mistresses about transfers of slaves, and another layer of disputes in our generations — between historians, philologists, translators. Again, there is no separation between disputatious scholars and disputatious slaves and ex-slaves. The latter were not alone in seeking redefinitions; scholars are as well. We too must struggle to liberate ourselves from the clutches of our intellectual ancestors and find alternative alliances in order to find new meanings for our work. It is in just that recognition that one can read these contributions, not as an autonomous or "free" individual, but as one who has found new allegiances and transferred her loyalties to the study of a different time and place.

BIBLIOGRAPHY

Englund, Robert
　　2009　　　　"The Smell of the Cage." *Cuneiform Digital Library Journal* 2009: 4.